PRAISE FOR *KaBOOM!*

"The story of Darell and KaBOOM! demonstrates that true leadership and innovation comes from not only celebrating successes, but also embracing and learning from failures. Through his tireless dedication and willingness to continually rethink traditional approaches to creating social change, Darell's reflections provide powerful insights into what it takes to become a trailblazer not just in the nonprofit sector, but in any sector."

—*Jean Case, CEO, The Case Foundation*

"Darell Hammond has led an extraordinary life and made extraordinary contributions to the lives of countless others. Part memoir, part manifesto, *KaBOOM!* is a passionate story of play's transformative power to deepen the quality of children's lives and strengthen the bonds of families and communities. A searching and practical journey through triumphs and disappointments, *KaBOOM!* will inspire and enlighten you with the boundless possibilities of imagination, creativity, and play."

—*Sir Ken Robinson,* New York Times *bestselling author,*
The Element: How Finding Your Passion Changes Everything

"Business entrepreneurs build economic prosperity in a society. Social entrepreneurs build communities and knit social fabric. Darell Hammond is an unusual combination of both. His story is both instructional and heart-warming."

—*Ram Charan, bestselling author,* What the CEO Wants You to Know

"No one speaks with more passion and authenticity than Darell Hammond when it comes to the needs of our children. In *KaBOOM!,* Darell Hammond shares important insight into the personal experiences and influences that led him to found one of the nation's most innovative nonprofits. Through his thoughtful exploration of how KaBOOM! became the successful organization it is today, Hammond inspires us all to take action in our own communities. He reminds us that there is no task more important than fighting for those most voiceless and vulnerable in our country—our children."

—*Bill Shore, Founder and Executive Director, Share Our Strength*

"Improving the quality of life in our communities is an important part of the NBA's mission, and working with Darell Hammond and the KaBOOM! team has enabled us to enrich children's lives across the country. In *KaBOOM!,* Darell demonstrates the extraordinary change that is possible with innovation and teamwork."

—*David Stern, NBA Commissioner*

"Darell Hammond is a quintessential social entrepreneur who has overcome personal challenges and built a dynamic organization that is bringing play to hard-hit communities across the country. At a time when play has been marginalized, Hammond's inspiring and pragmatic story shows how we can make our society a happier and healthier place for all children."

—*David Bornstein, author of* How to Change the World

"Darell Hammond's journey is as inspirational as it is illuminating. His passion for play and his organizational success makes for a book that is invaluable to anyone devoted to youth or community development."

—*Geoffrey Canada, President and CEO, Harlem Children's Zone*

"If you want to understand the heart of a great entrepreneur, you should read this book. Darell Hammond is one of America's best social entrepreneurs; he's bringing play and community back. In *KaBOOM!* he shares openly and humorously the life underlying his work."

—*Bill Drayton, Founder, Ashoka: Innovators for the Public and Ashoka's Youth Venture*

"*KaBOOM!* is extremely timely and full of hope and optimism. Darell's ability to see possibility in normal human enterprise is as deep as it is global in its implications for how to build a better world. I recommend this inspirational book without hesitation."

—*Bill Strickland, President and CEO, Manchester Bidwell Corporation*

KABOOM!

A MOVEMENT TO SAVE PLAY

DARELL HAMMOND, Founder and CEO of KaBOOM!
Foreword by STUART L. BROWN, MD, Founder of the National Institute of Play

RODALE.

© 2011 by Darell Hammond
Trade hardcover published in April 2011.
Trade paperback published in September 2012.

Rodale books may be purchased for business or promotional use or for special sales.
For information, please write to:
Special Markets Department, Rodale Inc., 733 Third Avenue, New York, NY 10017
Printed in the United States of America

Rodale Inc. makes every effort to use acid-free ♾, recycled paper ♻.

Book design by Christina Gaugler

Library of Congress Cataloging-in-Publication Data

Hammond, Darell.
    KaBOOM! : how one man built a movement to save play / Darell Hammond.
        p.   cm.
    ISBN 978-1-60529-075-1 hardcover
    ISBN 978-1-60961-924-4 paperback
    1. Playgrounds.   2. Play.   3. Hammond, Darell.   4. KaBOOM! (Organization)
    5. Community development.   6. Social change.   I. Title.
    GV423.H26   2011
    790.068—dc22   2011003853

Distributed to the trade by Macmillan
2   4   6   8   10   9   7   5   3   1   paperback

We inspire and enable people to improve their lives and the world around them

This book is dedicated to all who work to ensure every child has the time and the places to play. Play is the best natural resource in a creative economy.

Contents

FOREWORD

Before I read this book, I was already steeped in thinking about how the elegant trial and error of our evolutionary heritage has resulted in our unquestionable biological need for play. I had also recognized and researched the dire, across-the-board consequences for us all when play is not honored or prioritized. Playground, kid-organized play has diminished radically, making me fearful for our future, but Darell's leadership and KaBOOM!'s pioneering, playground-building record that has brought play to so many were already close to my heart.

But as I turned page after page, Darell's candid, deeply human, and profoundly inspirational life story moved me unexpectedly. I realized that Darell's life trajectory embodied a powerful, contemporary version of *The Hero's Journey*, the story of "entering the forest where there is no path," experiencing demons (one's own and those encountered in the forest), with the hero surviving to bring a boon back to society. It is these historically memorable, heroic life stories that have been the catalyst for many positive past cultural changes. They stir something that reflects major unmet societal needs, needs that are challenged and met by the heroic quest.

Our need for community heroism to salve our many societal needs is now *the* priority of our culture, and the KaBOOM! story bridges from individual to collective heroism, reflecting the movement away from the aggrandizement of the individual and toward an embrace of the community.

To reach readers at this level, I realized, meant that the Darell-KaBOOM! story, like all truly memorable prosocial narratives, was serving as a contagious model motivator for service to others. And though I suspect this reflection on his writing would make the very practical Darell uncomfortable, nonetheless it is very important to see that this book reaches and stirs a very broad audience. Darell Hammond's life has demonstrated that one very ordinary, non-privileged person has the power to fundamentally organize and connect us to our survival-based reliance on play and community.

Stuart L. Brown, MD
Founder and President
The National Institute for Play

INTRODUCTION

We all know communities like the Palms, an apartment complex in northwest Orlando, Florida—if we don't live there, we read about them every day in the newspapers. Back in 1985 a police officer investigating a burglary at the complex was shot in the shoulder by a 19-year-old resident. (The officer survived; the kid was charged with attempted murder.) In 1996 two teenagers shot and killed a man after an argument. In 2006 and 2007 Orlando police officers were called to the complex nearly 3,000 times for violent crimes and were called another 2,000 times in the first half of 2008 alone.

Then, on a hot afternoon in July 2008, the community was essentially brought to its knees. During an argument over some stolen property, a man with an assault rifle started shooting in a crowded apartment and killed three people, including two kids, one 18-year-old and another who was just 16. Police later said that residents were lucky more people weren't hurt or killed. The complex had a playground—decrepit, outdated, long ago stripped of swings—right outside that apartment, and some of the more than 600 kids who live at the complex were playing on it at the time of the shooting.

In the weeks following, the residents decided that they'd had enough. The Orlando Police Department stationed a permanent patrol in the complex. The management company brought in its own security team along with surveillance cameras for all the common areas. Residents formed a tenant association. A few people who lived nearby created a nonprofit, called Hopes and Dreams, specifically to help the women who lived in this community. The name of the complex was even changed—instead of the Palms, it would now be known as Windsor Cove.

These efforts stemmed the worst of the violence. Windsor Cove started becoming safer. But many moms who lived there were still afraid to let their kids play outside; they wanted a stronger and more connected community. This became a common denominator of fury among the women. One of them, a single mom of three named Yolanda Robinson, put it this way when she wrote to me: "You have people shooting and you have to think—well, if I send my kids outside today they just might get shot." Another mom wrote that she hadn't let her kids outside by themselves in *three years*. Imagine—all that time when these women were afraid to let their kids go outside to play.

This may be an extreme example, but those two basic issues—not enough play and not enough community involvement—dog hundreds of communities around this country. They cross all economic, social, racial, and educational groups. Parents instinctively know that play is important, and they want the best for their kids. But somehow, something terrible is happening in this country. Think of it as a play deficit, and, as with a budget deficit, the problems it foments compound over time. In the past two decades, kids have lost between 9 and 12 hours of free play each week. Two-thirds of American kids get less than 1 hour of physical activity a day (which is what the Centers for Disease Control and Prevention, or CDC, recommends as a minimum). One in four kids get no free-play time for physical activities at all. Zero.

Instead of being outside playing, kids between 8 and 18 spend more than 7 hours a day with electronic media. A child is six times more likely to play a video game on a typical day than ride a bike, according to surveys by the Kaiser Family Foundation and the CDC. (In some countries it's worse. A kid in South Korea died—yes, *died*—at an Internet café after playing video games for 50 hours straight. He stopped only for a few bathroom breaks and collapsed of heart failure due to exhaustion.)

Almost every one of these problems worsens as the income levels decrease. Kids who grow up in lower income environments play less, watch more TV, have fewer recreational outlets, and play on equipment that's more dangerous.

These are the problems that I've spent most of my life working to solve—creating more playgrounds for kids and helping foster stronger communities. The organization I cofounded, KaBOOM!, builds playgrounds in neighborhoods around the country. This work was inspired in part by the way I was raised. I grew up in a group home outside of Chicago, supported by a group of people who'd never met most of the kids who lived there. That facility had 1,200 acres, including a lake, multiple playgrounds, ball fields, and hundreds and hundreds of trees for us to climb. Our situation was different from that of a lot of kids, but it was a healthy and productive environment, where I had plenty of opportunities to play and explore.

I was fortunate to have ended up there, and my experience there influenced the unique model by which KaBOOM! operates. We don't just swoop in with a set of plans and a truckload of equipment and say, "Here, this is your playground." Instead, we're a kind of matchmaker. We work with corporations that want to set up volunteer projects for their employees, and we connect that money, muscle, and generous spirit to communities, primarily youth-serving nonprofits like charter schools, Boys and Girls Clubs, housing entities, homeless facilities, and domestic-abuse shelters—any organization that's in need of a playground and might not have the financial resources to make this happen otherwise.

The process involves a few months of planning, in which local people step forward as leaders and learn to tap into the resources around them. A lot of the people who end up leading our projects have been told for years that their neighborhoods have nothing. In fact, these neighborhoods typically have incredible resources. We work with these groups to identify all the assets they have, and we give them the tools and coach them to tap those resources to get needed products and support for the playground, which in turn helps strengthen ties within the community.

When it comes time to design the actual equipment, we get the local kids involved. After all, who knows what they want in a playground more than the children who are going to be playing on it? In effect, the kids become the architects, letting their voices be heard on a subject they care deeply about.

The whole experience culminates with what we call a "Build Day," in which a few hundred volunteers descend on a construction site and turn it from an empty lot to a gleaming new playground in about 6 hours. One single, magical day in which all that hard work by people on the ground in their local community comes together. That kind of transformation creates a "wow" impact, and it shows people the power of possibility. At the end of the build, you see kids pointing at a slide or a climber and declaring, "That's what I drew! This is my playground!" The people who live in these neighborhoods, the ones who do the heavy lifting to make each project happen, come away with a sense of ownership over what they accomplished. We call it the KaBOOMer-ang principle, our law of incredible returns: *Whatever you put into KaBOOM!—whether it's your time, advice, money, or sweat equity—always comes back to you in the form of changed lives, stronger communities, and brighter futures. KaBOOM!. It starts with a playground.*

And make no mistake: Playgrounds are crucial to the lives of kids and communities. In one housing complex, kids had put several old mattresses on the ground, stacking them up below a fire escape, and were jumping onto them from the second floor. This was simply a case of kids doing what comes natural—being creative and building a place to play when one doesn't exist. At another site in Washington, DC, two kids were playing in an alley, climbed into an abandoned car, and got locked inside during the heat of the summer, where they suffocated and died. These kids had no other alternative—safe—place to play, so they were playing in that car.

Could a playground really help allay these kinds of tragedies and solve this kind of deep-rooted community despair? I know that it can. I've seen it happen more than 2,000 times. That's the number of playgrounds KaBOOM! has built in our 15-year history.

I'm incredibly proud of those numbers, but the true beauty of these projects is what happens after the playgrounds are finished. People have come together to build this very tangible project, one that improves the lives of children and families in the neighborhood, and recognize their ability and power to do so much more. Through the planning process, they learn organizing skills and identify local assets, which they can then apply to other neighborhood projects after we're gone. Maybe the next thing they do is create a graffiti cleanup team or a Neighborhood Watch or an after-school program. Or maybe they want to convert a nearby lot in their neighborhood into a community garden. If we've done our job at KaBOOM!, we leave communities with the confidence and tools to enable them to create the change they want to see in their community.

In the past few years, we've worked to diversify our approach at KaBOOM!, so we could do more to support play and help create strong communities. In addition to the 2,000 playgrounds we've built, we've influenced, inspired, and supported thousands of towns to build playgrounds themselves, with guidance from us but without any direct support from KaBOOM!. We've also taken on a larger advocacy role, pushing municipal governments to make play more of a priority in their towns. We've highlighted people doing great work for the cause and connected those people with others like them around the country, so the base of knowledge gets stronger and people don't have to reinvent the wheel. And we've gotten behind some really innovative play designs, to keep pushing the edge of what's possible for kids. KaBOOM! can serve as a central hub for this knowledge, but we can't accomplish much without the eager participation of people on the ground in towns and communities across the country.

When we heard from the moms of Windsor Cove, we knew we could play a role in helping them turn their neighborhood around.

These moms wanted to take back control of their neighborhood. They wanted their kids to live in an environment devoid of fear, where they'd be able to run and play and be free. For that to happen, the moms also recognized that the people who live at Windsor Cove would need to become more of a community—one that would look out for each other and serve as a network of support. They wanted a new playground, and they wanted a stronger community. I was lucky enough to be in a position to help.

They e-mailed us in early 2010, and because they were so passionate about trying to turn their community around, the KaBOOM! employees who worked with them grew excited about the project, and I began to hear about it around the office. The more I heard, the more impressed I became with these extraordinary women.

The community at Windsor Cove is virtually all single moms who get assistance from the Department of Housing and Urban Development or state and local agencies, or some combination of the three. They're up against a lot of tough odds. On the application for a KaBOOM! playground, we ask for the average annual income of community residents, and for the Windsor Cove community, that number was "$4,000 to $5,000." That might appear to be a typo, but it isn't. Think about that for a moment—in the richest country in the history of the world, there are women trying to raise a family on $12 a day . . . $12 a day.

Even with those odds, you'd be foolish to bet against moms like Yolanda Robinson when it comes to taking on a project that can give their kids a great place to play. When they were applying to KaBOOM!, they met at Yolanda's apartment—she had a PC with an Internet connection, and she had computer experience. Many of the moms who worked to plan this project don't have computers, and a few had never used e-mail. Yolanda helped some of her neighbors to set up e-mail accounts to more easily correspond with us. Their venture into the online world alone is what we call an "achievable win"—the many individual successes along the way that keep the group motivated and increase their confidence with each step.

There were a lot of achievable wins throughout the planning process for the Windsor Cove playground. Volunteers on the food committee persuaded three local supermarkets to donate 4,000 bottles of water (a KaBOOM! record!) in addition to providing breakfast and lunch for 230 hungry volunteers. The local Rotary Club offered to come out to grill and serve the lunch. Local kids in the community came up with a plan for a popsicle station, where they distributed donated popsicles to help the volunteers stay cool while they were working hard.

There's always an obstacle, and overcoming it is part of the experience. When the planning committee encountered one, they got creative. There's a small convenience store next door to the Windsor Cove property, which is popular with residents. The food team asked the owner for donations several times, and each time they were turned away. The residents figured they should only support businesses that were supporting them, so they decided to boycott this store. A member of the planning team shared this with a friend who happened to know the owner of that store. The woman admitted she was losing business from Windsor Cove residents and came around. She ended up donating cases of water and hot dogs. Even more importantly, she volunteered to come out and help during the day the playground would be built.

All of their hard work paid off. On July 29, 2010, almost 2 years to the day after the triple-murder that first galvanized them to take action, the residents of Windsor Cove came together to build a beautiful new playground for their kids and a gathering place for everyone. In addition to two spiral slides, it also had a play dozer in the middle for kids to climb into and lots and lots of swings. Volunteers built a sandbox, four benches, two shade structures, and five picnic tables, complete with game tops for checkers and chess. They planted eight trees that had been donated by another local nonprofit, and they installed an accessible pathway.

At the end of the day, Yolanda and the entire planning committee, mostly moms from Windsor Cove, stood together in front of the transformed site and cut the ribbon. They were already working to plan their next project—laying sod to create a grassy area adjacent to the playground area. The shop owner who had originally refused to participate asked for a laminated copy of the playground design, so she could put it up in her store!

To some extent, even though the playground is up, the hard work doesn't end. The real test of this community and the KaBOOM! approach will be whether the site gets maintained. The community spirit that made this a reality needs to be sustained. Yolanda Robinson, and moms like her, are part of the KaBOOM! family now. They are the reason I love what I do.

After 15 years at KaBOOM!, you'd think I'd become inured to the effects of stories like this, but really, it never happens. It's special every time. People say that I should be proud of the things I've accomplished at KaBOOM!, and I am. But to be honest, our organization is really just the middleman; the communities that we work with and the funders who make the work possible are the ones who deserve the credit and the glory.

[1]

Looking Out
for Other People

A lot of mental health professionals talk about "breaking the cycle"—that is, trying to prevent people who grow up in an unhealthy environment from repeating the same problems as adults and teaching those same behaviors to their kids. For me, this idea has an extremely powerful meaning.

My father was one of 16 children. Today the word would be "dysfunctional," but back then the family was probably just called "bad." The state of Nebraska certainly thought so: It took all 16 children from their parents—my grandparents—who were declared unfit. (At the time there were only 15 of them, but my father's mother was pregnant with the 16th.) When my grandparents were later given a chance to get their kids back, they said no.

The state did what it could to keep the siblings together, but with a family that big, it was impossible. Four or five of the older boys were too old for an orphanage and got sent to a reform school instead. My father was raised by foster parents and later joined the Marines, where he served for 9 years. But the cycle would continue. Many of his brothers and sisters went on to have huge families: seven children, 13 children. One of my uncles had 11 kids from three different marriages.

There were eight of us. I was born in 1971, the second youngest. At that time we were living in Jerome, Idaho, a tiny town in the southern part of the state, but my family had moved around a lot back then, and most of my older siblings had been born somewhere else. We moved so often, partly so that my father could find work, but from what I understand, I think it was also to escape growing debts. The family lived in a few places in northern California and then moved on to Idaho. We ended up in Jerome because my father got a job as a ranch hand there around 1970. He had long worked with horses. A mustang kick once broke his right leg in two places below the knee.

Not long after we got to Jerome, he found a job as a long-haul trucker, a job that would take him away from us for days at a time. In October 1972, when I was 19 months old and my younger sister was a newborn, my father said he was going to unload a truck, and he never came back.

My mom was left trying to raise eight children by herself. She worked multiple jobs—one at a senior center, another with the Girl Scouts—but the bills began to pile up. According to what my older siblings tell me, we became the town charity. On holidays, my mother often had to work, so we were left on our own for Thanksgiving and Christmas. A lot of nights, our dinner was sandwiches of butter and sugar on white bread. The older kids started skipping school, ostensibly to take care of the younger ones, but they sometimes ended up getting into trouble, and their frequent absences eventually got the attention of social workers. The struggle became too much for my mother, and the county threatened to take us from her and split up the family. They talked about putting us in foster care—the cycle repeating. Instead, we all wound up at an institution called Mooseheart, 43 miles due west of Chicago and, at the time, surrounded by farmland.

Mooseheart is a storied place. It was founded in 1913 by Moose International, the fraternal organization that dates back to the late 1800s. Moose is similar to the Elks Lodge—the story goes that the founder wanted a mascot that was bigger than an elk, so he opted for a moose. Today the organization still has more than a million members, mostly in the United States, Canada, and Great Britain. The Moose members still provide virtually all of the funding for Mooseheart along with a similar facility outside of Jacksonville, Florida, for senior citizens. About $28 of each member's annual dues is allocated to fund the two facilities; they represent the main charities that Moose supports. And at a time when school districts across the country are cutting their budgets, eliminating sports teams, laying off teachers, and getting rid of music and art programs, Moose members are still giving their all to Mooseheart, which hasn't had to take any of these steps.

During most of the 20th century, Mooseheart was seen as a kind of insurance policy for members of the fraternity. If something happened to you, your children could go there and be taken care of. They'd be raised in a safe environment, and they'd get an education. At its height, during the Depression, Mooseheart housed more than 1,200 kids, but by the time I showed up the attendance was more like 300; it's down to about 250 today.

The campus looks more like a college than an orphanage or group home, with about 1,200 acres of lush lawns, a lake, and residence halls that look more like private homes (a significant upgrade from the barracks-style living arrangements of my early days at Mooseheart, where at times we had 24 boys sleeping in a single room). For decades the facility operated its own post office and fire department and even generated its own electricity. It also maintained a farm and dairy, where a lot of the food for the kids was grown and raised, though in recent years remote slices of the land have been sold off, including the farm, to help cover operating costs.

More than 11,000 kids have come through Mooseheart in its nearly 100 years of operation. During the first 60 or 70 years, the institution accepted children only if their parents were members of Moose International. Eventually that policy was relaxed to allow more distant family, as long as they had some relation to a member. (In my case it was an uncle, our mother's brother.) And in 1994, membership in the fraternity stopped being a requirement at all. Families now apply, and if a child's need is deemed legitimate, if he or she can abide by the rules and guidelines of the facility, and if there is space, they're in.

▲ ■ ●

My earliest memory is the 1,600-mile flight from Idaho to Chicago. I was 4 years old, and I spent the flight curled up on the floor to try and escape the cigarette smoke that hung heavy in the air. I hate that smell to this day.

When my family landed at O'Hare, people from the Mooseheart staff picked us up in two station wagons for the hour-long drive west to the campus, near Aurora, Illinois. Once we got there, my siblings and I spent a few weeks living together in a single dorm building, called Arizona Hall, where we learned the rules of the place and got all our vaccinations. After that we were split up by age and sent to different "houses," which is what the residence halls are called. That term is pretty accurate— they're much more like houses than dorms. Most are named for the state Moose association and chapter that raised the money to build and maintain them. I initially lived in what they called Baby Village. The houses are organized by age and gender, so you move a lot, typically every year when you're younger and every 2 years once you're older. That arrangement meant that I never lived with any of my brothers or sisters during my 14 years at Mooseheart.

When people find out I grew up in a place like this, they always assume I'm an orphan. It's a reasonable assumption, but it isn't accurate in my case. All eight of us arrived escorted by our mom. A great element of Mooseheart back then was that mothers were allowed to live on the campus if they wanted to remain close to their children, and our mom did. She stayed there until my younger sister, the last Hammond kid, graduated from Mooseheart High School nearly 15 years later.

Some might imagine an orphanage to be miserable, like something out of a Charles Dickens novel. But I'm very lucky to have been raised at Mooseheart. Our upbringing certainly was unusual and probably more disciplined than most, largely due to the complex logistics of raising a few hundred children together. The limits and strict rules of Mooseheart were good for me, and I imagine good for most of us who were raised there. The boys' and girls' campuses were completely separated, for example. I remember not being allowed to walk on the grass around the buildings—even as children we had to walk on pathways. We had few belongings, basically one box of stuff, something like a foot locker, which made the annual moves quick and painless. Whistles blew when we had to be someplace, and you needed written permission to move from one building to another at certain times, like during school hours, after dark, or whenever you were supposed to be somewhere specific, whether it was church or mealtime.

Our family vacations were a little unusual. Mooseheart has a 300-acre lake on the property, complete with a cabin on its shore. Once or twice a year, especially when I was young, my mom reserved the cabin for us, and my brothers and sisters and I would all go spend the night, lined up on the floor in sleeping bags. My mom always made fried dough for us, like the elephant ears you get at state fairs. I couldn't get enough of it, slathered in peanut butter. The cabin also had a working fireplace; my brother Pat and I were Boy Scouts, and we would build the biggest, hottest, most raging fire we could. In the middle of winter, the cabin would be 90 degrees inside. As I got older, these trips became less frequent, partly because my brothers and sisters had all graduated and moved away. In hindsight I realize they weren't much like a typical family vacation. We would only go for a single night, not even 24 hours, and we were less than a mile from the residences, close enough that we always walked both ways. But they're good memories and really the only time I recall my entire family being together in the 15 years I lived at Mooseheart.

On the whole we were happy. We didn't know any different—we thought all kids lived this way. Our food was good. A central kitchen delivered three meals a day to each house. The house parents, who served as live-in chaperones for each residence hall, rarely cooked, and that was probably for the best; many were young and often not given much training. Our laundry was done for us in an industrial facility on campus. Every student got a code that had to be marked on all clothes so they could be sorted out. Mine was H-322, and my brother Pat's was H-321—the *H* stood for Hammond. After he outgrew some of his clothes, I got his hand-me-downs.

We had a beautiful, huge campus as our playground. There were lots of trees (climbing trees was a favorite pastime for me—I once built a horizontal ladder that connected two trees to each other), the lake, a set of swings and two playgrounds, a sandbox, several basketball courts, and athletic fields in different places throughout the campus. You could always find pockets of kids somewhere to play with and pickup games to start or join.

We attended a school on campus, though I didn't love academics. I worked hard and actually wound up graduating as valedictorian of my class in 1989. That probably sounds impressive until you realize we only had about 25 students.

To be honest, I learned more about life from the football field, where the other kids and I could vent our frustrations by knocking the hell out of each other. One drill we used to run was called Walking Tackle, in which we practiced our form by tackling a ballcarrier who wasn't allowed to run. It was brutal—and fun.

I was named all-conference my sophomore, junior, and senior years, and all-state as a junior and senior. But it was the freshman season that taught me the most. We were undefeated that season, and I got to play a lot, largely because the upper classes had so few students. The coaches needed every kid who was willing to suit up, and we had to play in any position where the team had a gap. I was just happy to get onto the field and would have done anything the coaches asked.

The state of Illinois had rules that a player's number had to correspond to his position. (Linebackers were in the 50s, offensive linemen in the 70s, and so on.) As a freshman and sophomore, I played guard, tackle, fullback, and linebacker, so I often had to change jerseys, even on the sidelines during the game. We were a small team from a small school, going up against kids who were almost always better natural athletes than we were. So if we were going to achieve anything on the field, we all had to do what was best for the team, not simply what we wanted to do. Still hanging in the Mooseheart field house is a collage of photos from that season, with a bunch of uniform numbers next to my name corresponding to all the different positions I played—something I'm still proud of.

A lot of the values I learned on the football field are encapsulated in a set of expressions that we use around the office called Boomerisms. (We refer to employees at KaBOOM! as "Boomers.") These expressions used to be called Darell-isms, because they were things that I'd say again and again, in meetings or during individual conversations with employees. And over time they became part of our culture and our organizational DNA. They reflect where we've come from and how high we aim. And several of them date back to my childhood at Mooseheart.

One of them is "Practice doesn't make perfect. Perfect practice makes perfect." This comes directly from my football coach at Mooseheart. He felt that players would sometimes go through the motions during the week and think they could get into a game and perform at a higher level. So he ended practice every day by making us run four perfect plays in a row. All the coaches were there, watching everything we did—all our footwork and technique—and if we didn't do all four consecutive plays perfectly, we started over at the first one. Sometimes it was just an excuse to make us run wind sprints. But that lesson really sunk in—the idea that you don't need more practice, you need *better* practice, and you need to train to exceed expectations over and over again. It's not your all-time best performance that matters, it's how you perform consistently, day in and day out.

▲ ■ ●

At Mooseheart I learned the importance of looking out for other people. After all, that's what the facility was doing for us. There were some grim family stories among the kids there. Many were literally orphans, and some had been physically removed from their parents' care. There were some who tended to feel sorry for themselves, others who refused to be the victim, and others who became the protectors. My guess is this isn't all that different from most groups of people, where those dynamics probably come into play. It did feel sometimes that the numbers of kids at Mooseheart who were in the "feel sorry for me" group was bigger than it should have been. To be honest, that used to annoy me . . . and still does. A few of the people I know from Mooseheart feel sorry for themselves to this day. They believe they were dealt a bad hand and just cannot get over it. A lot of other kids at Mooseheart learned that you could get through life by doing the minimum requirements and nothing more. Some learned that if you remained in the middle of the pack, you were basically invisible and could get by pretty uneventfully (absolutely not appealing to me). Others became overachievers and worked to prove that they would outperform any limitations you might put on them.

Aside from being passionate about football, I had a knack for defending other kids, and I picked up the nickname "The Lawyer." I honestly don't know if I did it because I was compelled to help them or if it was simply the challenge of facing an authority figure. But I had a willingness to go to the administration whenever I thought someone wasn't being treated fairly or if I perceived that something that was happening wasn't fair. The school's senior administrators were housed in a large daunting building on campus near the main gate, and it had an ominous reputation. It was filled with authority figures—older, powerful people, and some kids felt like we were at Mooseheart because of the goodwill of others, so we shouldn't make too many waves. But I somehow had the audacity and courage to knock on their doors and argue our case. I don't think I won a lot of those arguments, but I always got a fair hearing, and I learned to speak up when someone needed it. In addition to learning to handle myself in front of people with authority, I learned that those people almost always cared and wanted to do what was best for us.

Sometimes I argued simply to improve our physical environment (sort of funny, considering what I do now). During my high school years, I lived in Pennsylvania Hall, which is a scaled-down replica of the exterior of the famed and historic Independence Hall in Philadelphia and is maintained by the Pennsylvania Moose Association. The bedrooms were on the second floor, but because the building was aging and hadn't been properly maintained, the showers on that floor had been closed down for years, probably a decade—gathering dust and mold. Whenever we wanted to take a shower, we had to walk down two floors, past the living room and dining room to the bathrooms down in the basement, where there was a group shower (like in a locker room) next to the boiler and furnace that heated the house.

One night, with involvement from some higher level staff, we invited the head of membership, a powerful figure within the Moose organization, to a spaghetti dinner at the house, offering him a tour. On the second floor we told him where we showered. "We have to go all the way down to the basement," we told him. "But you have showers right here," he said. When we pointed out that they didn't work, he took a look and was horrified. The school took immediate steps to fix the problem. We were moved into a temporary home while Pennsylvania Hall was renovated and upgraded, and in rapid succession the other residence halls at Mooseheart were modernized as well. It demonstrated to me that the people who could impact change sometimes just needed to know that changes were required.

Through experiences like those, I became close to one of the senior people from the Moose, named Bill Airey, who today is the director general of the organization (akin to a CEO) and still goes to work every day at Mooseheart, where he's been since 1982. Mr. Airey started looking out for me and became a kind of surrogate father—which is why I could never refer to him as "Bill," even today. To me, he's Mr. Airey or Pops. When he ventured out on his travels to local Moose lodges around the country, he started bringing me along. I like to joke that I somehow had become the "tin cup," the Mooseheart kid who could put a face on the institution for members of the fraternity who had supported it all these years but had never seen it.

I learned to talk to a roomful of people and to convince them of the worthiness of a cause—a skill that would come in extremely handy when I was talking to corporations about getting involved with KaBOOM!. In addition to learning how to give a halfway decent speech, my experience with Mr. Airey got me off the campus, and at the time, that was extremely important to me. I was craving the freedom. Even though I was in high school at that point, the campus was still pretty restricted. Students were typically allowed to leave just four times a year.

When I started going off-campus and showed that I was responsible enough to be trusted, Mooseheart administrators began to ease the rules for me. By respecting those relaxed rules, I earned greater trust, and I believe that the rules were eased a bit for the rest of the students. I was lucky enough to earn a trip to England with Mr. Airey and three other students, and another trip to Russia right after I graduated. Eventually, Mr. Airey started to bring me and a few other members of the football team for pizza at his family's home 6 miles away. Soon I became a long-term resident at the home of Bill and Jean Airey along with seven other students that summer. The Aireys were very good people to open their home up so generously.

▲ ■ ●

People might look quickly at my background at Mooseheart and at my father's desertion of the family, and feel inclined to feel sorry for me, which is why for a long time, I just didn't talk about it. To be honest, it isn't that I'm so proud that I don't want people to pity me; rather it's because my situation really doesn't warrant pity. People may also assume that I must have launched a nonprofit and devoted my life to service because of my experience at Mooseheart: I was helped as a child, so I went on to help other children.

That explanation makes sense on a superficial level, but I'm not sure it's true. Mooseheart's motto, carved in stone near the front gate, is "Enter to learn, leave to serve," and throughout its history, some people have left there to do impressive things in their careers. Many joined the armed forces, and during World War II, a Mooseheart alum earned the Congressional Medal of Honor for single-handedly killing four German soldiers and capturing another 12 during a battle in France. Other graduates have become doctors and teachers, and some have had successful careers in business.

Very few Mooseheart students have worked in the nonprofit field, and, as I said, some Mooseheart alums continue to feel sorry for themselves. I would say that even a couple of my siblings have, for the most part, led somewhat dissolute lives. Only three of the eight of us have graduated college—and, to be fair, I'm not one of them. My older sister Kitty was the first of us to obtain a bachelor's degree, and that put her on a pedestal to the rest of us. My mom was a role model for working hard and caring a lot about our well-being; she just couldn't raise eight kids on her own.

I don't like to think about what my life would have been like without Mooseheart. I also don't think it's the sole reason I ended up devoting myself to service and children's causes. It's a significant factor but not the only one. In fact, the biggest lessons I learned there were not taught through some organized component of the school, but rather by what I *didn't* see. We were seldom pushed to go beyond our limits. The school was set up to take children who were in bad situations and make those situations less bad. It was like the expression "When you're in a hole, stop digging." I don't know that there was a driving force pushing us to get ourselves out of the hole. To a certain extent, getting by without attention was a positive proposition: As long as we were mediocre and behaved well enough, we could get through the place without any problems. Somewhere, somehow I became averse to mediocrity. It became something I did not want to see in myself or in those around me.

▲ ■ ●

I don't talk much about Mooseheart to the staff at KaBOOM!, but a lot of my values were shaped by my time there, and I try to make those part of the organization's culture. Among other things, those values are a way of thinking about challenges and obstacles, and they hold that you have to push beyond such limits if you really want to transform yourself. The limits could be the diminished expectations of others or even those that you hold for yourself—it doesn't really matter. Regardless of what you do for a living, you'll never reach your full potential until you realize how artificial limits can be. Growth comes from making yourself a little uncomfortable and spurring yourself beyond what you've always done in the past. Especially when it's done in service to others.

The current administration at Mooseheart is starting to change these standards. They're providing better training for the house parents and emphasizing their responsibility as role models. That added support and training is certainly a good thing. I think about going back to work at Mooseheart at some point in my career. The place is special, not just for me but also for generations of people who grew up there and for the members of the fraternity who supported it. I think Mooseheart is really good at what it does. I also think it is continuing to get better, in part by maintaining the discipline and holding higher standards of performance and behavior while sharing ideas and experiences with the kids of what they can do with their lives—and giving them the compliment of higher expectations.

[2]

Half-Full
Not Half-Empty

When I graduated high school, I was ready to leave Mooseheart, but I wasn't ready for the world yet. I was socially immature and used to living in a place with very rigid rules; though they felt confining at the time, they were also a source of comfort. After growing up in such a safe and predictable environment, it was disorienting to be so free, where everything depended on the choices you made, good or bad.

This showed up in a hundred small and large ways. I had gotten my driver's license, but I almost never drove (students weren't allowed to drive on campus). So although I had lived in the area my whole life, I didn't know my way around. People would mention a road that was a mile or two from the gate, and I'd ask, "Where's that?"

In 1989, just after graduating from high school and moving from Mooseheart, I spent $800 on a 1972 VW Beetle, bright orange, with 200,000 miles on it, against the advice of everyone who knew me. It had a stick shift, so I had to teach myself how to drive it, lurching around empty parking lots.

My sister Dawn, a source of great counsel to me at many points of my life, told me I needed insurance. I found an agent. He was very persuasive and saw a kid wet behind the ears walk in his door: He sold me everything he had. I paid more for insurance than I had for the car. I didn't know any better. I attributed it to not having someone to show me the ropes.

Three weeks after we graduated, a classmate got arrested for drunk driving. With no parents to bail him out, he spent a week in jail. Four months after graduation, I learned that another classmate was pregnant. We could barely take care of ourselves, so of course she wasn't prepared to take care of a baby—what 18-year-old is? That child later ended up at Mooseheart and graduated 19 years after his mom.

Even as valedictorian, none of the universities where I'd applied—schools like the University of Michigan and Northern Illinois—accepted me, so I moved in with the Aireys and attended local Waubonsee Community College, in Sugar Grove, Illinois. I was there for 2 years, but I wasn't handling my newfound freedom well, and I didn't take the academics seriously. The classes were huge, 70 or 80 people, and I felt anonymous, with no connection to the school. I was shocked at how much books cost—one was almost a hundred dollars—so in some cases, I just didn't buy them. The teaching assistants would take attendance in some classes, and if you got there a few minutes early, you could get marked down as present, then duck out to go to the bathroom and just never come back. I did that more than a few times.

Mooseheart gives a college scholarship to students who need it—something a lot of kids there (including me) didn't fully appreciate or take full advantage of. You have to maintain a certain grade level to keep it. At the time, the requirement was a 3.0, and my first semester of community college I got a 2.5, which was generous on the part of the Waubonsee faculty. The Moose fraternity scholarship fund put me on probation, and the second semester I brought in a lower grade point average—2.0. I was making very poor decisions and not taking my education or the opportunities I had seriously.

That was it. A week or so later a letter arrived at the Aireys' house, a white envelope with the Moose logo on it, and the single-page letter inside announced that my scholarship had been revoked. No drama, no lecturing tone, just a simple message: "You no longer meet the requirements." It was a tough lesson to learn, that I'd blown this fantastic opportunity, and I'm not sure I fully understood the consequences of it back then. In 2 years I accumulated just 20 credits, which some students can get in a single semester.

Ripon College became my next missed opportunity. Ripon is a small liberal arts school in Wisconsin, halfway between Milwaukee and Madison. One of my football coaches at Mooseheart had attended college there. It's fairly prestigious and also very expensive—tuition and other expenses back then were about $20,000 a year. So I loaded up on student loans and showed up at Ripon in the fall of 1991. Because I'd built up so few credits, I went in as a freshman.

Ripon was a fantastic experience—small classes, accessible professors. I'd never been in a place with such an atmosphere of curiosity. I took some education classes, thinking that maybe I'd become a teacher. I also loved a class on ornithology taught by the president of the school—it fueled an appreciation for birds that I have to this day. I became a kicker for the football team.

Most of the people I knew at Ripon came from more conventional backgrounds, with traditional families that came to visit them all the time (the vast majority of students were in-state). When one of my roommates needed gas money, $20 showed up in the mail. He didn't live far away, and his mom continued to do his laundry for him while he was in college—she showed up on weekends with a hamper of neatly folded clothes.

My situation was a lot different. I remember feeling that I was on my own, without much of a support structure, and that whatever happened, good or bad, would be up to me. I had to find my own way back and forth from the Aireys to the school, and during some vacations and long weekends I often stayed in the dorms. I was also conscious of not talking about my background. I never concocted a story or lied, but I deliberately tried to avoid revealing too much about my situation. I was different—that was all. I never felt sorry for myself, and I really don't recall feeling isolated or lonely.

Like most college kids, I never had enough money, so I worked whenever I could. On longer breaks, when I could find a ride for the 4-hour drive home, I bartended at the local Moose lodge in Batavia, Illinois, near the gates of Mooseheart. My brother was a regular bartender there, and I would fill in whenever he couldn't make his shift. It was strictly for tips, but the regulars who came into the bar knew we had graduated from Mooseheart and were always generous.

One of those regulars was Dale Valentine. He owned a rivet factory nearby, and he said if I ever wanted to make some real money, I should come and work for him. At 5:30 every afternoon, you could find him at the Moose lodge in Batavia, having a scotch and then a beer chaser before heading home. The job he was offering came with union wages, $18 an hour, and I jumped at it.

My first summer home from Ripon, I worked the 3 p.m. to 2 a.m. shift in the shipping and receiving department at the Fox Valley Rivet Factory, 5 or 6 days a week. The factory was loud and hot, and the plant's machinery required so much lubrication that the air itself felt greasy. You wore the same clothes each day, and the factory would wash them for you. You didn't want those grease-soaked rags in with your normal clothes. I learned to drive a forklift, hauling rivets from one end of the place to the other, where they were sorted, sent out to be plated in different metals, and categorized in giant bins. We had to sort them for customers and get them ready to be shipped. Within a half hour or so of starting a shift, your hands would be black. At break time, the "roach coach"—the catering truck—rolled in, and we all lined up for our sodas and sandwiches.

It was hard, grungy work—especially compared to some of my friends' glamorous summer jobs, like lifeguarding or being a camp counselor—but the money was good, and I took every shift I could. The job also turned out to be motivating in a more unexpected way. When I talked to some of the full-timers there, I realized that it wasn't for me long-term. I was thinking about my future, about what I wanted to do with my life, and these were grizzled men whose future was in the factory. I began to figure out what I didn't want.

Dale Valentine played a role in my life at Ripon as well. He owned a vacation home on Green Lake, which was up in Wisconsin, about 20 miles from the college. He paid me to take care of the home—turning the water on in springtime and sealing it up after the season was over. It was right on the lake, and he had two boats, one of which was a pontoon. On sunny fall days, my Ripon friends and I would take the pontoon out and cruise around the lake with a keg of beer tied to the back. Dale always knew we had used it, but he trusted me and he liked that the boat was being used rather than just sitting at the dock getting dusty.

As inspiring as I found the academic setting at Ripon, classes there were tough. I threw myself into the social component of learning, almost to the exclusion of doing the actual work. I had always hated reading—I frequently had to read things five or six times just to comprehend them—and as the books got more difficult and the assignments grew longer, I learned to adapt by talking to people. For an assignment on Edgar Allen Poe, I'd ask people, "What did you think of it? Why'd you think that? How did you draw those conclusions?" Eventually I stopped buying the books altogether, just like at the community college.

Writing assignments didn't go much better. Mine were atrocious. One night, during a class trip to a Milwaukee Brewers game, my English professor said, "I don't mean to pry, and no one's going to hold anything against you, but I think you have some kind of learning disability." She said she looked at my lack of comprehension in things I read, and how hard I struggled to get through a piece of writing, and the way I often mixed up words and transposed letters. "It's classic," she said.

Initially I was in denial—the professor and I had butted heads before that, and I dropped out of her class not once but twice—but her diagnosis was confirmed through a formal test at Oshkosh University. Then I started using the diagnosis as a crutch. *I can't do that reading. I'm dyslexic.* This has continued to impact my life, even today. I'm an atrocious speller, and around the KaBOOM! office I use a thick felt-tip pen to scribble notes on documents in nearly illegible handwriting, so the mistakes are less obvious. Back then, as my grades suffered and the debt piled up—$42,000 over 2 years, an amount that I wouldn't end up paying off until my mid-30s—I realized that I wasn't going to make it to graduation at Ripon. Instead, I'd have to figure something else out.

Around this time a tragedy in my family shook me to my core and pulled any foundation out from under me. For my 21st birthday, two friends and I traveled to a remote cabin in Wisconsin for a weekend of ice fishing, where we got snowed in. At one point, we heard some snowmobiles approaching. They turned out to be the state police. They were coming to tell me that my sister Kitty had been killed.

Kitty was four years older than me, and she had been the first of my siblings to graduate from college. She was shy but incredibly empathetic, the kind of person friends trusted for advice. I had always looked up to Kitty and respected her—all my brothers and sisters did. After graduating from the University of Oklahoma, she married a man who physically abused her. She had the strength to leave the situation and divorced him. Kitty then joined the Air Force, entering as a second lieutenant because of her college degree. She met another Air Force officer, and they married soon afterward. He'd been married previously, and he and his former wife were in an ugly fight over custody of the kids. That caused problems in Kitty's marriage to him. No one ever figured out what triggered the fatal fight, but police and investigators told us that she killed her husband and then turned the gun on herself.

Everyone in my family, including me, resisted this version of events. We all thought there must have been some other explanation, some missing piece of evidence that would point to a third person—maybe a burglar (though there were no signs of a break-in) or the ex-wife. We were all in denial. We all want to believe the best of the people we love.

Kitty had a college education, she was an officer in the Air Force. She could not have murdered her husband, and she never would have killed herself. But the evidence and the police investigation were clear.

Over time I was able to face the harsh truth. But not all of us have reconciled to this: My mother and some of my siblings still deny what happened. I struggle with this even today. It doesn't feel plausible that Kitty killed her husband, and it scares me.

The experience would have a profound effect on me, at a time in my life when I was still trying to figure out who I was. At her funeral, I listened to Kitty's friends tell me how much she had meant to them, how much they always felt they could confide in her. What an awful waste this had been. Two lives ended—Kitty, with so much promise, and Mark, a father—and all those people grieving around them, and for what? It spurred in me a ferocious desire to shake the family I was born into. I remember a thought forming inside me that seems harsh in hindsight, and I am not proud to admit, but was true nonetheless: *I don't want to be like some of them.*

I didn't yet have a direction for my life or an answer to the question of who I was, but Kitty's death clearly told me who I didn't want to be. I didn't want that kind of dysfunction and violence in my life. Something else was out there, but I had to find it. I believe that we all have the opportunity to shape our own destiny, and I would put that theory to the test.

Without college and without strong family roots, I would have to build up a life and a set of values and beliefs almost from scratch.

▲ ■ ●

During the spring of 1993, I took part in an Urban Studies Fellowship run by Northwestern University and the Associated Colleges of the Midwest (which included Ripon). Some people I knew at the school had done the fellowship and raved about it. It aims to help young people understand social policy from the ground level. You live in Chicago public housing and work as an intern at a nonprofit. There are some lectures and some reading, though not a lot. The fellowship fell into the category of real-world learning. No textbooks—just discussion and observation and experience and a lot of hard work. Everything I heard about it sounded like a better fit for me than my previous experiences in college.

I was lucky enough to get paired with Dr. Jody Kretzmann, who is a legend in community-organizing circles. Along with a colleague, Jody founded the Asset-Based Community Development (ABCD) Institute at Northwestern University. That philosophy of "asset-based" organizing is built on the premise that we need to focus on the things a community *has* rather than the things it lacks. Like Windsor Cove in Orlando, many communities are constantly told they have nothing— no decent schools, no jobs, no reputable businesses, no tax base. In fact these places have things that they can leverage to improve their situation, especially if they work together to identify that social capital and connect all their diverse strengths and assets.

Like what? Like a neighborhood association. Or a block watch. Or a minister who can deliver a few hundred people from his church to a volunteer project, as long as it's something they believe in. Or a few residents with construction skills, and a hardware store willing to loan tools for a local project. Or another resident who works at a local radio station that can help promote an event. Or . . . you get the picture. Asset-based development is a very authentic, very grassroots kind of process. The wins come much slower, but they're also far more significant and lasting.

Here's an example: One of the harder-hit neighborhoods in Cincinnati is called Over-the-Rhine. A local congregation there, New Prospect Baptist Church, has run a soup kitchen in its basement for years and years. Every night it feeds dinner to 300 people, making it the biggest such facility in the city. About a decade ago, the church volunteers who served the meals realized that they were seeing the same people each night. Those people were being fed, but nothing was really changing in their lives.

So the pastor and some senior people in the church sat down and talked to 250 of the homeless people. Really talked. And instead of the usual dynamic that happens in this situation—the person with resources looks across the table at the person on the other side and says, "Tell me how bad your situation is"—the church flipped the dynamic around and asked the homeless people what they were good at. What were their skills, their gifts, their dreams? Or rather, what were their assets?

About 40 people, mostly men, said that they were good at construction. The pastor organized those people into a construction co-op that started rehabbing the abandoned and decrepit properties around the neighborhood. Another group of people said they were good musicians. They started performing each night in a jazz combo. Yet another group said they were good cooks. Twenty of them, in fact. So those people were invited behind the counter. They could still eat, of course, but they started working as well.

And in another twist, the volunteers started coming out from behind the counter—they could still work, but they started eating meals with the homeless people as well. It was no longer donors and recipients with a big thick line between the two but a *community*, where people started actually getting to know each other and working together. This approach didn't end hunger or homelessness in the neighborhood, of course. But it gave people in the community a chance to organize around their strengths—their assets—instead of being beaten down by constant reminders of everything that was missing from their community.

Early in her career, Michelle Obama was an adjutant faculty member of the ABCD Institute and worked with Jody Kretzmann. She recently gave a speech in which she talked about the central role that Asset-Based Community Development plays in her philosophy of service and how it can erase the line between donors and recipients: "[T]he approach acknowledges that every single one of us breathing in this community, in this planet, those of us serving and those of us who are being served, that we're both half-full and half-empty. We all have skills and talents that make us good friends, family members, workers, and leaders, and we also have needs and shortcomings that come along with those strengths.

We can't do well serving these communities, I learned . . . if we believe that we, the givers, are the ones that are half-full, and that everybody we're serving is half-empty."

▲ ■ ●

For the record, I lied to get into the Urban Studies program. It was restricted to upperclassmen with a certain number of credits, though after I was accepted, I told Jody about this, and he said I could stay. He liked that I was resourceful enough to get myself in. (Jody's very entrepreneurial.)

I had never lived in a city before, and after the predictability and stability of Mooseheart—along with a population of students and faculty that was virtually homogenous—Chicago was eye-opening. I lived in a 40-story public-housing building in uptown Chicago that was like a miniature United Nations. People of just about every nationality lived there, and at mealtimes you could tell where they were from by the smells drifting outside their doors. My contribution was less exotic—I remember frequent trips to Aldi, the local supermarket, where I would buy the cheapest hamburger meat I could find along with buns and Velveeta. That was my dinner four or five nights each week. This was my first time ever cooking for myself, and I wasn't particularly adventurous.

The building was nonstop chaos, and the cinder-block-and-concrete construction meant that every sound echoed. It had three elevators, though often none of them worked; a lot of people on the higher floors rarely left their apartments. Think about that: 40 floors and no working elevator. Our situation wasn't as bad—we were on the 14th floor and we were young, so we could reasonably, and slowly, get up and down.

Residents were awake at all hours, blaring stereos, yelling, heading out to late shifts. That winter we got a ton of snow in Chicago, and drivers used to spin their tires trying to get in and out of parking spots— a high-pitched whizzing noise I could clearly hear in my bedroom 14 stories up. When the weather turned warm, that sound was replaced by car alarms.

One morning at about 5 a.m. my roommates and I were awakened by yelling and pounding in the hallway—the police had come to arrest a man across the hall for domestic violence. He refused to come out, and the cops spent a long time, more than an hour, convincing him that it would be much easier for everyone involved if he would just open the door. Once he finally did, they still had to march him down all 14 flights of stairs—the elevators weren't working.

Another time I saw a family of three generations—grandmother, mom, and a couple of young kids—who'd been evicted. All their belongings were lined up on the curb outside, everything they owned in the world, and the grandmother was sobbing into her hands. After growing up at Mooseheart, where everything was safe and stable and nurturing, this was the first time I had ever seen that kind of chaos, the unpredictability and daily crises that happen to people who live so close to the margins of society. I realized how tough the world is and, frankly, how cruel it can be. I can still see that grandmother sobbing into her hands; I imagine the fear and helplessness she felt. I still wonder what became of that family.

The coursework of the program only reinforced these lessons. The program was broken into four sections, and one of them was an elective. I chose race relations, which was taught by Salim Muwakkil, a fairly radical African American hell-raiser. He was an editor at *In These Times*, a left-leaning magazine that points out the imbalances—racial, financial, educational, and otherwise—in American society.

Many of Salim's lectures consisted of him bringing in his friends to tell us their personal stories of injustice. Like Delbert Tibbs, who was convicted in Florida in 1974 for a rape and murder he never committed. The prosecutor who put him away later admitted, years after the trial, that Tibbs was completely innocent, even though he ended up serving 8 years in prison. It was so striking to me—up until then, I had nursed the naïve belief that the law was the law and that everything was always done for the right reason. Those lectures just imploded my sense of justice and what was fair.

The service component of the program was an internship with the Chicago Park District, where I worked for Helen Doria, who later became a founding board member of KaBOOM!. Helen's a firebrand who knows anybody and everybody in Chicago politics. She had worked for the mayor's office, doing community relations projects, so she had strong contacts in every corner of the city. At the time, the Park District was being cleaned up after a wave of corruption, so there was plenty of work to do.

My first day on the job, I wore neat, pressed khakis and a polo shirt. My work history to that point had consisted of: bartender, rec center manager, camp counselor at Mooseheart, forklift driver at the rivet factory, and the front desk at the Ripon library (part of my work-study while a student there). I was nervous about showing up on time and was new to Chicago mass transit, so I left about 2 hours early, for a bus trip that took less than 15 minutes. The Park District offices back then were part of the Soldier Field complex, across the street from the Field Museum. Helen took me around the building to meet everyone, and I remember that she never once used the word *intern*. It was always just, "This is Darell"—her way of showing me some respect before I even deserved it. Her department was small, six people working out of an office and an adjacent conference room with the door between them taken down. It was informal and hectic, and they were so busy that they threw me into the middle of things right away.

That day, the office was in the middle of a squabble with the Chicago Bears. The Park District managed Soldier Field, the Bears leased it, and the dispute was over the quality of the grass. So I ended up going next door to the stadium with the marketing director, Kim Rudd (who later became an employee at KaBOOM! and today serves on the board of directors), where we scooped up shovels of the dirt and put them in tiny vials. It was partly to raise money and partly a marketing gimmick. That was my task for the first day on the job: fill hundreds and hundreds of vials with genuine Soldier Field dirt, while Kim stuck tiny labels on them.

My time at the Park District was full of days like that. I was only an intern, but Helen gave me as much responsibility as I could handle. Because of all the corruption and turmoil, morale had been bad there, but there was an attitude that we were going to transform the place, so we needed to pull up our bootstraps and get this job done and have some fun doing it.

I learned some important things during my time there. One key learning is that titles are meaningless. All people, regardless of what their business card says (or whether they even have business cards), should get treated with decency and courtesy, and you can usually learn more about an organization by talking to the administrative professionals than you can from its top executives. What's more, those administrative individuals are the ones who keep the place humming, and they deserve respect, which they don't always get from visitors or outsiders.

Though I'd been shy up to then, I made a point of going around the building and meeting everyone I could, to learn as much as possible about how the operation worked. Some people didn't always love the fact that an intern kept coming in to pester them, and a handful of those people weren't shy about letting me know. To me, that represented a challenge—I had to win them over.

The director of the Park District had an assistant, a woman named Stephanie, who had worked there for decades, outlasted several directors, and was only a year or so from retiring. Stephanie was short and wore a sundress most days, which did not make her any less intimidating, and everyone on staff both loved and feared her (but mostly feared). She was a get-it-done person, and she liked things a certain way—one of her ironclad rules was that she didn't want to waste time and she wanted information up front. Official business required a phone call or a memo (this was before e-mail). You didn't just drop by her desk.

Perhaps initially out of naïveté, I didn't follow the protocol. I was trying to deliver results quickly and felt that everything had urgency.

Even today I'm a big believer in face-to-face, desk-side conversations. In my first few days at the Park District, Stephanie sharply admonished me multiple times because I came into the reception area of the director's office with simple questions for her or messages from my department that probably could have been written up in a memo. Yet even though I never adhered to the advance-memo protocol, I ultimately did achieve a relationship with Stephanie. I liked her and respected her, and I think she would have admitted the same about me.

Helen tells a story about when we were all working late one night. It was a Friday, about 9:30 p.m., and everyone was still in the office. The head of the Park District walked past, poked his head in the door, and said, "Wow, look at these hard workers. Even the intern's here. How are you, Darell?" Helen looked at me, dumbstruck. "He knows your name?" she asked. About 10 minutes later, Stephanie came by on her way out. She gestured to me from the door, and when I walked over, she handed me a plate of homemade cookies. Helen nearly fell off her chair. "She's *baking* for you?" she asked. I grinned and happily passed the cookies around.

▲ ■ ●

Another key thing I learned was pivotal in the founding of KaBOOM!. Chicago has 77 neighborhoods, many of them ethnically specific, and for a long time the city would sponsor a block party in each neighborhood. In earlier years the city government used to contract with a single set of vendors and have them do all 77 events. That was easier to set up, but the events sometimes flopped. The band that a Puerto Rican neighborhood loved might not be such a hit in the Greek neighborhood just a few streets over.

Helen's idea was that each neighborhood should plan its own block party—with its own food, vendors, services, music, the works. That way each group could pick the most culturally relevant stuff and make the day a truly local celebration. Initially people balked, both within the city government and in many neighborhoods. Why? In large part because it was new and untested, but also because it meant a lot more work for everyone involved. Instead of one set of vendors, the Park District now had to handle 77. And local neighborhoods would now have to play a bigger role in planning and overseeing the events. The true success of the event would now be pushed down to the local level, and if it failed, the planners would no longer be able to blame "the man" down at the central office.

I went to a bunch of the planning meetings with Helen, and they were far more contentious than we had anticipated. I couldn't believe how much yelling people could do over a simple block party. But Helen listened to each of these groups and then calmed them down. "It's your park, your neighborhood, and your day," she said. "We'll support you and get you the resources you need, but ultimately you're running the show."

In some cases the city's support came down to the wire. In one Russian neighborhood in the western part of the city, several of the restaurants that locals loved weren't licensed to work with the city. In the past the city had served Polish food in this neighborhood. So we had to scramble around and get the places licensed to work with the city in just a few days.

But in the end, the new approach turned out to be wildly popular, justifying all the extra effort. More people came to the block parties, in many cases coming with multiple generations—grandkids and grandparents together—and they stayed longer. Helen and I managed to make it to a bunch of them, including the Russian festival, where I saw the food from the place we rushed to get licensed. It was sumptuously displayed: blinis, plates heaped with cabbage and potatoes, cold vegetable soup, dumplings called *pelmini*.

This struck me as such a pivotal concept—that community events like this are almost always better when they're planned and executed *by* local people, instead of *for* local people. An organization looking to foster this sense of community has to motivate people at the outset by giving them something joyful to organize around, and then push decisions to the community members themselves. You can give people tools and resources and ideas, and step out of the way and let the community do the work. In exchange, they get an event that's more relevant to them and much more meaningful and personal. And best of all, it's their win.

[3]

The Process Is as
Important as the Product

When the Urban Studies Fellowship ended in the spring of
1994, I knew I wasn't going back to Ripon or any other school. After
all my experiences in Chicago, the idea of sitting in a classroom held
almost no appeal. The service world was calling me. More practically,
I was already deep in debt from school and needed money. I had volunteered at a few places during my time in Chicago, and I knew that
City Year, the Boston-based volunteer group, was about to open an
office there.

Founded in 1988 by a pair of roommates at Harvard Law School,
City Year was built around the simple and revolutionary idea that
young people ages 17 to 24 could devote a year of their lives to fulltime service work. In the nearly 25 years since then, the organization
has expanded around the world, but in 1994, it was still small and
just starting to venture out of its base in Boston. That year it opened
new offices in five cities in the Midwest, including Chicago, and in
July 1994 I was one of the first local people hired for that office.

We briefly shared office space with a nonprofit called Public Allies,
run by Michelle Robinson (now known as Michelle Obama). Her
organization was matching AmeriCorps volunteers to more than 30
local groups in Chicago that needed volunteer help, and it was here that
she applied the teachings of Dr. Kretzmann and the ABCD Institute in

a significant way. Public Allies was already up and running when the City Year office opened, so we looked to it as a kind of institutional model. And we needed one.

During those first few months, we were building the organization's infrastructure in the city, lining up potential volunteers and projects. Everyone in the office was idealistic and entrepreneurial, and we worked long days. It was an exciting time in the national service community. President Clinton had brought a wave of enthusiasm that year by launching the AmeriCorps program, which formalized and expanded the federal government's domestic service programs. In the midst of this atmosphere, City Year was a great place to be.

A woman named Liz Thompson was the first executive director of the Chicago office, and I learned a lot about management from her. She always praised people on the staff in public, and whenever any of us did anything wrong, she coached us in private. Liz could be absolutely direct and honest, and she wasn't afraid to have tough conversations, but she always gave us the courtesy of holding those behind closed doors, which is a really good rule of thumb for treating employees. In that and a lot of other ways, Liz taught me that the respect between a boss and a staff runs both ways—it has to be mutual.

In the fall of that year, I was asked to go to Columbus, Ohio, and plan a service project for City Year's first national conference. The organization still holds these events, in which City Year volunteers from around the country gather at the end of their 1-year term, and the events are still called by the same name—Cyzygy. It's a twist on the Greek word *syzygy*, which means an alignment of celestial bodies.

In addition to seminars and recaps of how the year of service went, City Year likes to hold a massive service project. In its early days, when all of the volunteers were in Boston, it would stage serve-a-thons, in which a bunch of people, including corporate teams, college students, and other volunteers, would come to Boston Commons for a kickoff ceremony and then fan out across the city on the "T," Boston's mass-transit system. City Year's leaders initially wanted something similar for the Columbus event, but I did some research and realized it might be hard to pull off. The public transportation system wasn't as good, and there were other logistical challenges.

I had another idea. In my freshman year at Ripon, as a favor to a friend's mother, I had helped some people build a playground in Evanston, Illinois.

The playground was built through Leathers and Associates, an architectural firm in Ithaca, New York. Leathers and another company, Learning Structures in Portsmouth, New Hampshire, both specialize in designing playgrounds from scratch. They don't use prefabricated components but rather create them individually, from things like railroad ties and lumber and discarded tires. During construction, they get local people in the community to help. In that way, they were precursors to the community-building component of KaBOOM!, though they applied it more or less exclusively to middle- and high-income neighborhoods.

In the Hollywood version of this story, the day we built the playground in Evanston would represent a major turning point in my life— the day when I knew for sure that I would spend the rest of my life building playgrounds. But the reality is that it wasn't like that. I was still young and naïve and rootless, and the experience didn't resonate in that way for me. It represented a road trip and some free beer, and it was a fun couple of days.

That said, my Urban Studies experience and my playground-building experience inspired me to think that something similar could work for City Year, and I presented it as an option to the organization's top management. Instead of a bunch of smaller programs, what about focusing on one big one? More specifically, what if we built a playground?

▲ ■ ●

The project in Columbus actually turned out to be two playgrounds, one at Indianola Middle School and another in a housing project called

Emerald Glen. I moved to the city in January 1994, to an apartment on North High Street, and spent the next 6 months prepping for the projects. It was a hectic process from the very first day. City Year had never run a project like this, and the organization had its hands full trying to oversee new operations in five cities, so I had to solve most of the problems I came across on my own. I had never taken on anything with this kind of scope (each playground, prior to in-kind donations, was valued at about $150,000), so I was susceptible to ideas from other people. Probably too susceptible.

One big issue was that a bunch of different organizations were all involved in the planning, and each one had its own agenda. In addition to City Year, I worked closely with Ohio State University, particularly its community outreach program, Campus Partners. That group had been given a nice amount of money from the university for projects like these, and it was actually paying for one of the two playgrounds. This meant that Campus Partners wanted a big say in how the project was executed. There is no question that partnerships are incredibly important, but there has to be one clear leader or decision maker. This project was beginning to have too many people who thought they should fill that role.

We also used different playground contractors for the two sites, which is really regrettable in hindsight—it meant two different designs, two sets of hardware, two sets of shipping instructions and inventories and everything else. And City Year had its own sponsor for the project, a large bank, which offered a senior person to help me during the planning phase.

The man from the bank—I'll call him Joe—was a particular challenge. He had worked at the bank for years and now had the sole responsibility of coordinating its volunteer programs. He also had an outsized ego. He had clashed with Campus Partners in the past, and they flat-out told me, "If he's involved in this, we don't want to touch it."

He started overruling my decisions right away, often behind my back. For example, the middle school wanted a large outdoor wooden stage in addition to the playground. There was a natural grassy slope, where kids could sit for outdoor classes, assemblies, and the like. We had plans for the stage drawn up and approved, and we put in a massive lumber order for it. Without telling me, Joe canceled the order. I didn't find out until the day the lumber was supposed to arrive. I had been waiting for the truck for an hour or so, standing in the schoolyard and checking my watch, as I had a lot of other things that needed to be done. When I found out the order was canceled, I confronted Joe. He said, "They don't need a stage." I immediately put in a new order for everything we'd need, but time had been wasted and the delay would put the project in jeopardy. Executing these projects successfully meant working quickly; there was almost no wiggle room in the schedule.

There was more. The wooden components of the playground called for a type of hardware called a lag bolt. It gets sunk into the wood to fasten pieces together and doesn't stick out the other end. That's important because anything that sticks out becomes a safety hazard for kids—they can run into it or snag their clothing on it. Joe had built big projects in the past (though never a playground), and he took one look at the inventory list and lined out all the lag bolts. In their place, he put an equal number of standard nuts and bolts—the ones that get used in most other projects but that create an unsafe condition on a playground.

A week or so before construction was to start, the contractors showed up to inventory everything, and we realized that the proper bolts had not been ordered. I immediately realized that Joe had done it to me again. No lag bolts—zero—and thousands of bolts that we could not use. A lot of people were looking at me and wondering how I had let this happen. Even *I* was wondering why I had let this happen. For the contractors, it was their worst nightmare come true—they weren't used to coordinating with outside organizations like this. Instead, they were typically commissioned directly from neighborhood residents (almost exclusively in middle- and upper-income areas), who would write them a check, sign off on the design, and then show up with a dozen or so people to swing hammers during construction. I got the distinct sense that the contractors enjoyed watching us fumble along—as if it proved that what we were trying to do wouldn't work.

We placed a rush order for the lag bolts, but again, the damage had been done, and it was beginning to impact my credibility. These were massive projects, requiring equipment that arrived in truckloads, so it wasn't possible to just run down to the hardware store to pick up a few things we needed. After that second incident, I never saw Joe again. He went AWOL—no explanation or apology—but I couldn't worry about it. I had too many other fires to put out.

Yet another crisis was brewing. It turned out that a local architect wanted to be involved but had not been chosen for the project. He was upset and taking issue with the decision. He actually went to the neighborhood association and to the city council and asked that they deny us the necessary construction permits. We found out on a Friday afternoon and were told that the council was meeting to give us an official verdict on Monday morning. That architect—one person!—could have killed the entire project.

So the small planning committee and I spent that entire weekend knocking on doors in the neighborhood. The message we gave residents went something like this: "Do you think there is a need for a playground at Indianola Middle School? Would you sign a petition and could you show up on Monday to the city council meeting?" We shared that there were some people who were saying it wasn't needed and the playground might not happen if we didn't get the community to the meeting telling them otherwise. We asked, "Can you come to the council meeting on Monday and tell them what you think?" About a hundred people showed up and expressed themselves, loudly. The council clearly heard from the community and was not about to say no to them.

So much of my experience in Columbus was like that. We wound up doing everything three times—once the way I thought it should happen, once the way someone else thought it should happen, and then the final way, which I hoped was the right way. But in the end, over the course of two long weekends in June 1995, after 6 months of 18-hour days and a lot of mad scrambles at the end, the playgrounds ultimately got built. The stage at the middle school even went up (about a week behind schedule).

From an external perspective, the project was a success. It was a cool experience for all the City Year volunteers, and it came in on-budget. Yet after all the headaches and struggles, I realized that these projects weren't just about the end result. If your only goal was to put up a playground, the manufacturers could do that a lot faster without a few hundred volunteers getting in their way. But that simply wouldn't be very meaningful to that specific community or the people who lived in it. If we operated that way, and if installers did all the work, and if the playground magically went up, it would not have nearly the same impact. The process is as important as the product.

In that way, the experience only reinforced the things I'd learned from the Chicago Park District and its attempt to change the planning for local block parties. It wasn't just about the event. The planning and organizing—all the advance work, as well as the things that happened during the comparatively short construction period—were just as crucial as the end result. And the more that local people could be involved in that work, the more they'd feel like the playground was truly *theirs* and not an outright gift that had been handed to them from well-meaning outsiders. The process would truly change things in the neighborhood. I began to identify and apply some of the asset-based philosophy in my own work that Jody Kretzmann taught me about.

The process is as important as the product. This would become a foundational concept at KaBOOM!, but at the time, it was just a rough concept in my head. I knew there was nothing like it for any service-related project, especially playgrounds. And as the City Year project wrapped up, I started thinking a lot about how that might work—how a third-party organization could work with playground contractors or manufacturers and a local community, coordinating things and getting all the needed elements lined up so that the process would happen smoothly and the people in that community could turn to each other at the end of construction and say, *We built this. Not Darell, not the manufacturer—us.*

I came away from Columbus knowing that if I got another chance at building a playground, I was going to do things differently. As luck would have it, I didn't have to wait too long.

[4]

A 7-Year-Old's Grin

After the project in Columbus, Ohio, ended, I was back to needing a job. I could have returned to Chicago—Liz Thompson had asked me to come back to City Year as a team leader—but that didn't feel like progress to me, and I had a lot of ideas bumping around in my head. I had also heard from another national service group called Youth Service America (YSA), which was based in Washington, DC. They were looking for someone to plan a big volunteer service event, similar to City Year's Cyzygy conference. In the summer of 1995, YSA hired me as a contractor, and I moved to Washington to plan another playground construction project for them.

As soon as I was in Washington, I met Dawn Hutchison, who I knew through John Sarvey, a City Year colleague who had been in Columbus with me working on the Cyzygy Conference. Dawn also happened to be working with YSA, and she had an extra room in her apartment, so I moved in. Dawn struck me immediately in her contrasts. She is petite in stature and huge in personality. Her brain works quickly and she talks even faster; she is one of those people who never meets a stranger and is comfortable in any situation. She was coordinating other aspects of the conference, but she started helping me on the playground planning as well.

We decided on the site, Livingston Manor—a housing project in the southeastern part of DC—in a somewhat circular way. The housing partner at Emerald Glen in Columbus connected me to her counterpart in Washington, who was running Jubilee Enterprise. Jubilee is a non-profit that develops affordable housing for people in the city. At the time, Jubilee owned Livingston Manor, and some of the tenants there were trying to start a resident council. The management at Jubilee thought that the playground would be a great goal to help the council get organized.

We didn't have anyone else lined up, but we required Jubilee to go through an application process just the same. In fact, we didn't even have an application at that point, but I created one just for them. In all my correspondence with the resident council, I wrote, "We're evaluating your application against all the others that came in." We wanted the residents to think that the process was competitive, so they would put their best foot forward. I was already starting to realize that if you give something away, you run the risk that people will simply sit back and accept it without really appreciating it. There would be a greater value in underscoring the investment of time and resources. As we have learned over time, that investment creates a much deeper level of ownership and pride in the outcome, which contributes not only to the sustainability of the physical space but to a transformative experience within the community itself.

Livingston Manor consisted of two-story, dark red brick apartment buildings that resembled military barracks. Four buildings were clustered around a common courtyard, each with about six apartments. The playground would serve the entire complex. One of the first things I did at Livingston Manor was check out the site, which was an empty lot next to one of the clusters of apartments. I went there to measure the space, take some photographs, and get a better understanding of the grade (slope) where we would be building. Soon after I arrived, a 7-year-old named Ashley Brodie came bounding out to talk to me. She had bright eyes and skinny legs, and her hair was up in two pigtails. I had to chuckle when she grinned, revealing a big gap in her front teeth. Over the next few months, I would see that smile a lot.

At first Ashley wondered why I was in her neighborhood. Then she said, "Have you come to build the playground?" I was stunned and not quite ready to reveal to the community that we were selecting them for this project. I said, "A playground, what a good idea!" She ran back inside and emerged with two pages pulled from her refrigerator—crayon drawings she'd made of the playground she'd been dreaming about. For months and months, she'd stared out at the lot through the torn screens in her bedroom window, thinking about the playground she'd build. So when she saw me, she already had her plan in place. "There has to be a slide," she told me. "And lots of swings, and monkey bars!"

Livingston Manor was a tough, tough place for a kid to grow up. The littered lot where the playground would go was a magnet for drugs and violence. A dumpster nearby had been tagged, "Moe R.I.P." in memory of a resident who'd been shot in the throat. Ashley was one of six children living with a single mother and the mother's boyfriend, all in a small, two-bedroom corner apartment that looked directly out onto the lot.

During the early planning for the project, another grim story broke in Washington, DC. It happened in a neighborhood in Anacostia, just a few miles from where Ashley lived. The *Washington Post* story was headlined, "No Place to Play." A 4-year-old girl named Iesha and her 2-year-old brother, Clendon, who lived at the Stoddert Terrace housing complex, climbed into a Pontiac on a hot, humid day to play and got locked inside. Summers in Washington are brutally hot, and the two children suffocated. The story in the *Post* talked about how there was no playground in close proximity to Stoddert Terrace.

Imagine—two children dead because there was no playground nearby. After the tragedy, no one did anything except blame someone else. It was an example of the cycle of poverty and dysfunction repeating, where kids get punished because of grim conditions in the place where they happen to be born. Suddenly, the stakes seemed a little higher, and our project gained a new sense of urgency.

We asked Ashley and her friends to help us design the playground, establishing a key part of the process that's still used at every playground that KaBOOM! builds today. The local kids tell us what they want. They draw it for us. We incorporate their dreams—and those of their parents—in putting together the finished product. That means every playground is different. Each one reflects the wishes of the local community, which gives them a sense of ownership and pride in it.

Today we call the event a Design Day, and that first one was chaotic. An architect named Kit Clews was there. Kit owned Learning Structures, the playground manufacturer in Portsmouth, New Hampshire (and one of the two that I'd worked with in Columbus). Kit's a great guy who does excellent work—he's quiet and thoughtful, and we put him in an apartment at Livingston Manor that was doubling as a community center, with 50 or 60 kids all shouting directions at him. He was completely overwhelmed. I remember at dinner that night, and he said, "It's the right thing to do, building this playground. I'm just not sure I'm up to it." But in the end, he was—he designed an incredible 80-foot jungle gym shaped like a pirate ship, which we called the Tire-tanic. It had a tree house, a 24-foot slide that could fit six people at once, swings, and even a dinosaur made of tires.

To build it, we needed roughly 100 volunteers and about $40,000 for construction materials and supplies, both of which would be tough to line up in this community filled with single moms who had little money and even less spare time. A lot of people told us we'd never hit our goal, and to be honest, sometimes I thought they were right. But we couldn't quit. So many nonprofits promise the moon to communities like this and never deliver. Ashley was always there to remind me what we were working for.

Even though she was only 7, she had no problem going door-to-door with the apartment complex's community manager to slip fliers under residents' doors—a rare bit of good news in a place where most times, the papers being slid under doors were reminders to pay the rent on time. (In her family's hallway, all the other families had been evicted except hers.) She also walked around to neighborhood restaurants and stores to put donation canisters on the counters. One difficult day when we were particularly frustrated, she showed up with $9.97 in pennies that she'd collected over the previous week. We pressed ahead.

Then some other pieces started to come together. The local lumber yard offered to donate a tractor-trailer full of wood plus enough mulch to cover the site (which is important because it provides a cushioned surface for when kids fall). A paint store gave us brushes along with cans and cans of white paint. A local pizza place agreed to donate 325 pies to feed the volunteers over multiple days, and Ben & Jerry's donated ice cream bars. We scoured the East Coast for tires—which had to be older ones; you can't use steel-belted tires on a playground because of the risk that an exposed piece of steel might cut a child. One of Dawn's friends hired a U-Haul with her own money and drove from Washington, DC, down to Nashville and then up to Carlisle, Pennsylvania, collecting tires from two sources she'd lined up. Before long the empty lot was heaped high with supplies.

▲ ■ ●

Construction started on October 18, 1995. The process took 4 days, and it rained the first 3 we were there. Even after my stint in Columbus, I had almost no experience in that kind of construction. So even though we'd been planning it for months, we ran into some problems—like a sinkhole. While we were building, a giant hole opened up on the site, and I fell in water up to my chest. I also got sick from working so hard in the rain, but there was no way I could stop. (The following week, chest x-rays confirmed that I had developed pneumonia.) Despite the rain, on each of the first 3 days we got about 100 volunteers.

And, of course, Ashley was there the whole time, a constant reminder of who we were working for. The first morning, she was up at 6 and got permission from her mother to stay home from school to help out. Ashley bounded out and asked a volunteer coordinator, "What do I do? What do I do?" We gave her some small projects, and from then on she showed up every day, usually before her mom was even awake. She struggled with a shovel that was taller than she was. Someone gave her a pair of work gloves that swallowed her hands to her elbows, something she showed off to everyone who walked by. She even appeared the morning after her mom's boyfriend had been carted away by the police (he'd been drinking and had gotten into a fight). Sometimes while she worked, she came up with a strategy for how she would play: "First thing, I go on the swings. Second thing, the sliding board. Third, I run around. Fourth, I play on the monkey bars. Fifth thing, play on the tires."

A few of those days, we were there until 10 or 11 at night, working in front of the headlights of our cars. Sometimes we were trying to make up ground so we'd be ready the following morning, and other times we were fixing mistakes. The volunteers wore donated ponchos, and some of our tools disappeared under them. We were just naïve to think that might not happen.

Little by little, as if through sheer will, the playground went up. On the fourth and final day, we had close to 500 volunteers, including hundreds from YSA's conference participants. Some local residents of the housing complex served sandwiches and orange slices to workers; others opened their homes to let people use the bathroom. Ashley's mom got involved, helping shovel woodchips into a wheelbarrow. And by that afternoon, we were finally done.

The finished product included 500 tires, nine steering wheels, and 8,500 feet of lumber. The kids were overjoyed—they were bouncing up and down, laughing and giggling. We tried to keep them off the playground, because we'd painted eyes and ears on the tires, and the paint hadn't dried yet. But after all the buildup, it was impossible. The kids were too excited, and they swarmed all over it. Dawn remembers seeing a girl laughing ecstatically, with paint everywhere, even on her teeth. One of the volunteers had put up posters that said "Ashley Brodie for Mayor, 2020."

Dawn and I sat on a bench, thoroughly exhausted but even more inspired, and we realized we had built something bigger than just a playground. The next day, we watched families come from Maryland. They had seen the playground on the news. That was so powerful to us—that a suburban family would come in and let their kids play on this playground in a neighborhood they wouldn't have even driven through a week before.

The Livingston Manor playground got covered in a few other places besides the local television news, like the *Washington Post* and a magazine called *Who Cares*, which covered social causes. Some major corporations noticed all the coverage. Discover card was holding a conference in San Antonio in a few months, and they asked if we would be willing to go down there and help their employees build a playground as a team-building exercise. They wanted me to fly to their headquarters just north of Chicago to give a presentation on how it worked, but I was sick with pneumonia and couldn't travel. Instead, I FedEx'd a carousel of slides and narrated it for them via a conference call, trying not to cough too much into the phone. They liked it, and we had our second project in the works.

▲ ■ ●

It was around this point that we incorporated as KaBOOM!. Dawn came up with the name. We were walking around our neighborhood in the Adams Morgan district of Washington. We had all these grand ideas—opening retail stores, manufacturing our own playground equipment. (Even at that stage, we had big dreams.) We were talking about how to describe this. Dawn said, "You have people and ideas, and this flurry of activity, and then KaBOOM!. There's a playground. That was it." I loved it. The word was a perfect expression of the power of our aspiration and the explosive possibility of hope and opportunity. The name itself was something of a risk, in that it didn't say the kind of work we did or what we were about—the way, for example, that "Habitat for Humanity" did—but we loved it.

I came up with the logo while sketching on a napkin on the flight to San Antonio. I drew the burst and filled it in with the letters that spelled "KaBOOM!" with the exclamation point at the end. Later, a community-activist friend who'd designed things for a few organizations helped to stylize it. The distinctive orange-and-purple color scheme was based on that of FedEx—we had some of their envelopes sitting out on a table and liked that combination, though we tweaked the colors a bit. Also, we needed something that was only two colors, as a third costs more when you print things, and we had no money.

Even then we were extremely cautious about the iconography and imagery of our brand. We wanted everything to look professional and sharp. In most cases it didn't cost more money; it cost time. For presentations, we used to glue pieces of orange and purple construction paper together and use an X-Acto knife to cut out a corner, so it would look like fancier paper that had been printed in two colors.

I remember traveling around to office supply stores right after the back-to-school season ended—this was before online shopping really took off—so I could buy all the unsold purple folders in bulk. They were two for a dime, and for a while we had boxes and boxes of them stored in the office to use throughout the year.

Throughout this period, we had the key support of two pillars in the community—Sid and Bernice Drazin, who owned a local institution called Comet Deli and Liquors a few doors down from our apartment. Adams Morgan is now a hip part of Washington, filled with shops and restaurants, but in the mid-1990s there were almost no places to eat, especially during the day. So we spent a lot of time at Comet, and it gradually became our de facto office.

Sid was an amazing character. He served in the navy during World War II, and later worked for the Washington Senators. He owned a print shop and another liquor store in the city before opening Comet, which became a main social hub in town. At any time of day, you could find what Sid called his "Kitchen Cabinet"—locals, regulars, business owners, plus a few oddballs to keep things interesting. It was a community. Sid had nine chairs around three tables in the middle of the store. If he had one more, he would have been required to have a restroom open to the public. Those nine chairs were almost always full. On somewhat frequent occasions, three more chairs would appear from a back room and just as quickly disappear.

I still have some of our marketing materials from back then (in distinctive purple folders), and they list our corporate address as 1841 Columbia Road, Suite 701, which is funny in that there was no suite— that was the apartment where I lived. But we really ran KaBOOM! out of Comet. When we had no money, Sid let us eat at the deli on a seemingly bottomless tab that he never let us pay. During a few stretches when times were really tight, we had what we called BLD days, when we ate breakfast, lunch, and dinner at Comet. If we needed something faxed, we used the machine at the Video King next door, and they charged us two bucks a page. It didn't open until noon, so occasionally someone would call in the morning and ask if we'd received a fax yet, and we'd say, "Let me call you back around 12:15."

Sid also helped me with advice and introductions to key players around Washington—he knew everyone—and when we needed food for an event, we only had to ask and he'd send over a platter. (The catch was that we couldn't tell anyone we'd gotten it from him.) I don't think I can quite convey how important Sid was to me, and Bernice, the two of them. Sid loved smoking cigars in his family rec room in the basement of their house and watching football, and I loved sitting there with him. They were my de facto family.

He died on March 15, 2005, just a few days after he and Bernice celebrated their 55th wedding anniversary. The *Washington Post* ran an article about his life and his contribution to the city. The deli closed later that year, and Bernice died not long after that. They were incredible mentors and even better friends to me, and I can't say enough about what they meant for KaBOOM!.

▲ ■ ●

After the Livingston Manor project, Youth Service America offered me another contract for a playground or two as part of their annual National Youth Service Day the following April. But there were other opportunities that were developing. I was able to meet with some community affairs representatives for The Home Depot, which was just starting to get big. The company had been involved in the Livingston Manor build by loaning some power tools and providing Home Depot Associates—its term for employees—as volunteers. (It also used the opportunity to demonstrate some Black & Decker tools.) The local store manager was happy with what he'd seen. The community affairs people from the company told me they could help us more directly if we ventured out on our own. They even got their corporate counsel to file our incorporation paperwork, pro bono.

Discover hired us to do the playground project in San Antonio (the one I narrated via conference call when I had pneumonia), and by the time that project happened in February 1996, we were officially known as KaBOOM!. We were a 501(c)3—a registered nonprofit. We were legit. I went to a mall in San Antonio a few days before construction and had hats embroidered and business cards made up with our name and a drawing of some tools on them, so we'd look professional.

The community organization behind that project was incredibly strong. There was a group of older people, mostly retired, who wanted to do something that would directly benefit the children in their neighborhood. A former schoolteacher in the community, Wray Hood, oversaw the planning. Mrs. Hood was 72 at the time, and her grandkids were already too old for a playground, but she knew that this was something that could revitalize her community. She was also a church elder and incredibly respected in the community. I noticed that Mrs. Hood never came to meetings alone—she always brought her constituency, and they spoke with one voice. It was a lesson to me in social clout, and how reaching the right people in a neighborhood could give you some credibility with others.

The neighborhood was called Coliseum Oaks, a formerly middle-class part of town that had begun to experience hard times. Businesses had closed down and moved out of the neighborhood, and there was a growing number of abandoned buildings. Coliseum Oaks literally had the proverbial set of railroad tracks that divided the poor side of the community from the wealthy side. Mrs. Hood had this vision about building something that was so beautiful it would reverse the perception of those two areas and make people from the rich side want to come to where the poor people lived. And she accomplished that.

Mrs. Hood worked in conjunction with a local police officer, Gerald Tyler, who was trying to single-handedly change the relationship between police officers and people in the neighborhood by putting a face on the police force. He used to tell me he was tired of arresting people without knowing their names. If nothing else came of the community build process, he wanted to know their names and he wanted them to know his. He wanted a connection to the community he was serving.

That was another 5-day build—this was before we realized the magic of the done-in-a-day philosophy—and we had some more bad weather, including rain and an ice storm, almost unheard of for San Antonio. But we started developing the philosophy that only lightning or some other unsafe situation would stop the project. Merely wet and uncomfortable? You kept working. By the time we were at a site, many wheels had already been set in motion, and we couldn't simply tell a hundred or so community volunteers, plus another hundred corporate employees who may not even live in the area, that they all had to go home and come back tomorrow.

We had a couple of long, wet, cold days during the project, and it struck me that no one ever complained or asked to leave early. People bundled up and kept going.

[5]

"We've Got a Problem"

I've been lucky enough to have some great mentors over the years. One of the most important is Marian Wright Edelman. She founded the Children's Defense Fund, and, like Mr. Airey at Mooseheart, she was one of the central figures in my development. Mrs. Edelman was the first true advocate for children's rights in the United States, and, astonishingly, her organization only goes back about 40 years—she created the Children's Defense Fund in 1973, 2 years after I was born.

That just shows the low status that children had throughout much of American history. Animals actually had legal protection in this country before children did, and the first case of child abuse didn't get prosecuted until 1874. It was taken up by a lawyer for the American Society for the Prevention of Cruelty to Animals. The concept of offering legal protection to children was so novel that no one did that type of work.

The lawyer who prosecuted the case made this a central part of his argument. He carried the victim—an 11-year-old girl whose stepmother had beaten her daily with a leather whip and cut her face with scissors—into the courtroom in a horse blanket to underscore the difference between the rights of animals and the rights of children. The stepmother was ultimately convicted and sentenced to a year of hard labor, and the case spurred the creation of the New York Society for

the Prevention of Cruelty to Children, the first child protective
agency in the world and the direct predecessor of organizations like
Mrs. Edelman's.

She was one of the people who showed me the true conditions that
a lot of kids live in across the United States. People say that we put
our children first in this country, but if you look at how decisions get
made, it's pretty clear that they're far down on the list. In fact, some
of the statistics on childhood welfare make it hard to believe that we
could be living in the richest and most powerful country in the history of the world.

Every 19 seconds a child is arrested in this country, according to
the Children's Defense Fund. Every 35 seconds a child is confirmed as
abused or neglected. Every 18 minutes a child dies before his or her
first birthday. Every 6 hours a child is killed because of abuse or
neglect. Nine million children (or roughly one of every nine in the
United States) have no health insurance.

By early 1997 I had come to know Mrs. Edelman's son, Jonah, who I
met through a mutual friend. Jonah was living with his parents at their
home in the Cleveland Park neighborhood of DC, and he invited me
over. We sat on the porch for a couple of hours, and then his mother and
father came out and joined us. Mrs. Edelman first struck me as being the
"every mom," which is funny to me now that I understand the legend she
is. In this first meeting, she was warm and open, her hair was pulled back
loosely, and she was wearing large, oversized glasses. She spoke with a lilt-
ing rhythm that captivated my attention. Whether in a private conversation or on a stage, Mrs. Edelman is as commanding as anyone I have ever
met. But this was the first time meeting her, and I had not yet heard her
speak passionately to others about her cause—children. Tonight she was
simply Jonah's mom.

Mrs. Edelman and her husband, Peter, had lived in this home for
years, and I was struck by a couple of things. First, the house was
filled with photos of family. Even though Mrs. Edelman has pictures

of herself with every recent president and many heads of state and celebrated personalities, those pictures are not the ones that line the walls of her home.

The second thing that impressed me was the sense of their family's connection within their own neighborhood. As we all sat on the porch visiting, a neighbor came home from a trip to the Eastern Shore of Maryland. There was a flurry of neighborly conversation as they spoke across their porches. Pretty soon a bushel of Maryland crabs was passed over the fence, and the Edelmans were encouraged to take as many as they liked. Other neighbors were also out, and the bushel of crabs was passed along from family to family. I was struck by the deep sense of home and the friendships they all shared.

We were a young organization that had been operating out of an apartment and a liquor store/deli. Mrs. Edelman generously offered to donate office space. Our first real office! This was huge for us. It was probably one of the most important stamps of approval; her support by way of the office space demonstrated support to our cause and mission. We had actual employees, though we weren't yet paying them actual salaries. Four of us—Dawn and I along with two friends, Ted Adams and Ian Fisk—hunkered down in a space the size of a closet, where we shared a cafeteria table as a joint desk. Ted jokingly put masking tape down in a rectangle on the table to mark off "his" section. (Ted's first date with his soon-to-be-wife was at the Livingston Manor project.)

In addition to the office space, Mrs. Edelman also provided us another opportunity to build a playground. She had organized a massive march on Washington that spring that was named Stand for Children, to bring attention to children's needs and rights. The day before the march, we coordinated a playground build in Washington, DC, officially our second as KaBOOM!. It was around this time Mrs. Edelman took me to the White House for a meeting with President Clinton on service initiatives, where KaBOOM! was one of a handful of nonprofits at the table. She and I met beforehand, and when I showed up in slacks and a sports coat, a kid in my early 20s, she said, "Darell, you need to get yourself a suit." She still teases me about this.

We were starting to gain momentum, and each playground we built further convinced us of the soundness of the idea: to pair corporate money and volunteers with a community in need, and then rally everyone around the tangible goal of building a playground.

This public-private partnership model distinguished us from many other nonprofits at the time. The corporations weren't funding their work with KaBOOM! through traditional ways—via community-outreach departments or company-sponsored foundations—but instead through individual department budgets. We were getting funded through HR, corporate communications, marketing and sales departments, and departments that were organizing conferences and meetings, all places that had not traditionally dealt with nonprofits. And the funding was sustainable. Honestly, it was brilliant.

The key was to ensure top-quality service to the funders. We had to be certain we would pull off what we committed to pull off. If a build was set for September 4, we had to come through and build on September 4—no matter what. This also meant some trade-offs, and for a while in the late 1990s and early 2000s, we started to swing too far toward the team-building aspects of our work for the corporations and started to lose a bit of focus on the community-building aspect of our mission. Fortunately, we have righted this, and we carefully walk a fine line between our mission and our financial model.

The next step was to change the schedule so that an entire playground could be built in a single day, start to finish. Up until this point, our projects had involved 4 or 5 days of actual construction, and they involved literally moving to a specific city to do all the planning and organizing. I had moved to Columbus for 6 months to set up the City Year projects, and I spent 6 weeks in San Antonio leading up to that playground, but I knew that we couldn't keep operating that way—it limited the number of projects we could take on. It was expensive—it cost us a lot of time and a lot more money—and with construction spanning several days, the volunteers who showed up on day one were not necessarily the volunteers who could be there on day four. So the people who helped earlier in the project were not there to witness the final shovel of mulch, the final wheelbarrow of concrete, or the final twist of the Allen key. We realized that the volunteer experience would be that much more transformative and magical if the volunteers could be there from beginning to end, showing up in the morning and seeing the empty lot transformed into the finished product by the end of the day.

The playground manufacturers told us this wasn't possible. There were a small number of companies using volunteers to build playgrounds, but no one was building them in a single day, and no one could envision how it could work. There was just no way, the manufacturers kept telling me. No way. There was too much to do.

If you haven't figured it out by now, when someone says no to me, I tend to dig in and figure out how to make it a yes. The people we hire today have that same quality—we call it "can-do, will-do."

We decided to reverse-engineer the process—if we absolutely had to finish in a day, how would we change things? We knew that it would have to be well thought out, well planned, and extremely well organized. We needed to create a project-manager system, in which a single KaBOOM! employee would have primary responsibility for a given playground (or playgrounds).

That person would travel to the site twice. The first trip would be for a single day to do the Design Day (important for lots of reasons, not the least of which was building trust and relationships), meet with kids, meet with parents and adults from the community and representatives from the funding partner, form a planning committee, draw the exact site with all the correct measurements, and begin to think through any site conditions that would need to be managed (low power lines that might keep a truck from getting through, fences, trees, sewers, etc.). Then, after 8 to 10 weeks of weekly meetings with the planning committee via telephone/conference calls, that person would return to the site for the construction. But the project manager would not remain there in the interim.

This would allow the bandwidth for each project manager to work on multiple playgrounds at once, and it would keep a lot of the planning and organizing work where it should be—at the local level, with community residents, local leadership, and funding partner representatives who have formed the planning committee. We would have the whole process mapped out, and we would coach the committee (long distance) through every step of the "road map." We would motivate and be a resource, and if they hit challenges, we'd step in and help more directly. We would be building the community from the inside out, instead of from the outside in, which is the more traditional manner of community-building. (This actually set us up for a lot of criticism from some of the hard-core community-builders. But I think if they get the opportunity to fully witness our process, they begin to get it.)

We'd be back there for 2 days of hard work prior to each build, with 20 or so volunteers, to dig the 30-odd holes (2½ feet deep and 18–24 inches wide), oversee deliveries, unload and label everything while inventorying it (key to ensure nothing's missing), organize, prep for side projects, and make sure everything was ready for the single day when the 200-plus volunteers arrived.

Finishing playgrounds in a single day would let volunteers see the fruits of their labor right away, and we thought that if they saw the site transformed before their eyes, from an empty lot to a finished playground, the sense of accomplishment would be that much deeper. And if they had an excellent volunteer experience, that would light a spark and they would be more likely to volunteer in general. Inspiring the Build Day volunteers to continue to volunteer would promote civic engagement—a win-win situation. The last thing we wanted was for a volunteer to have a bad experience and possibly never volunteer again. It was important that the experience be not just a good one, but a great one.

We decided a couple of things: We wanted the KaBOOM! experience to be exceptional and exceptionally well organized. Each build would need a good number of leaders (we now call them build captains), and each leader would have a team of volunteers and have a specific responsibility. We wanted the volunteers to understand the impact they were having. The two partners—funder and community—should feel connected to each other, so we knew it would be important that they work side by side. We also knew that we wanted the kids to be a part of the day. There had to be plenty of tools so everyone had something to do at all times (a volunteer without a job or a tool in hand is a bored volunteer and a missed opportunity).

We recognized that having a product at the end of the day—the completely finished playground and the transformed site—would set us apart from many other volunteer experiences out there. It wouldn't necessarily make us better—but it would set us apart. Tutoring, providing services to seniors, working with kids in a hospital, delivering meals, painting and refurbishing a home, cleaning up a park—all of these services are incredibly important and very rewarding. But we understood that a single day of service would be more powerful if it resulted in a *thing* being built, an object that you can point to and touch and even climb on.

This was significant in the service movement, and this would become our signature, our trademark—and it's important for any organization to have something that sets it apart. KaBOOM! projects would be done in a day by volunteers who in turn could stand proudly and say, "I did that!" and then come back to visit and tell their friends about it. They could return with their kids and watch their own children or others playing on what they built 10 or even 15 years later. The result is just so tangible and occurs in a relatively short period of time—less than 12 weeks after the first meeting for the project. And for the community that is a part of building their own playground, it can be extremely empowering.

This was something I learned on the first anniversary of the Stand for Children march. We commemorated the event by building five playgrounds in a single day in the DC metro area. After construction wrapped up on one of the sites, something really amazing happened, which luckily got recorded on video. Two older women were dancing and laughing next to the colorful new playground they had just helped build. One of the women shouts to the other, "What are we going to do next?" That was key for me—not what is KaBOOM! going to do next or what is some external organization going to do, but "What are *we* going to do next!?" That's the power of the idea.

▲ ■ ●

KaBOOM! might have continued doing playground projects like this, one at a time, but new challenges lay ahead. Kimberly-Clark, the giant paper and lumber corporation and the maker of products like Huggies and Kleenex, was celebrating its 125th anniversary and wanted to include some kind of service component in the celebration. Cone Communications, a marketing and public relations firm in Boston, was working with Kimberly-Clark to identify specific options, and Habitat for Humanity was already a strong candidate. Fortunately for us, a few people at Cone saw the story about KaBOOM! and the Livingston Manor project in *Who Cares* magazine and decided to include us as well.

We made a presentation, arranged by Cone, to some Kimberly-Clark executives to explain how we work, and they agreed to offer it up to their local offices—the towns across the United States where lumber mills and other production facilities are located. Each office would get a menu of options for service projects, and they could choose to build a playground if they wanted, or a house with Habitat, or something else. Kimberly-Clark figured we'd maybe get 10, and they were nervous about our ability to pull that many off. We were, too.

We now had a potential big-budget project, and we had a lot of work to do to prepare to take it on, but we didn't have any money yet and we needed to start lining up staff. That led to some strange and difficult conversations with potential employees in which we said, "Would you work for us? We can't pay you yet, but we think we'll be able to pretty soon." I was young, just 24, and the organization had only existed for about a year. The whole venture felt incredibly fragile, as if a single wrong move could bring everything crashing down around us.

When the forms started being faxed in from Kimberly-Clark's mill towns, we were so excited. Then we got to 10, and we thought, wow, that's a lot. Then we got to 17 and started thinking, uh-oh.

When the faxes finally stopped coming, we had 37 confirmed sites that wanted a playground. Thirty-seven in 1 year—we couldn't believe it. Each of the projects we'd done so far had required 2 or 3 months of planning, and we'd done fewer than 10 total in our entire history.

Kimberly-Clark sent a check for $575,000, as a first payment on a total budget of $2.7 million. This was the first real check we had received that was made out to KaBOOM!. With the Discover playground in San Antonio, it was handled more as a services contract where Discover covered the expenses and paid us as consultants. This check was big time, and it meant we needed to establish a KaBOOM! account.

Dawn and I took it to the local bank where we both had personal accounts and asked to deposit it, and they looked at us like we were crazy. The check needed to go into a KaBOOM! account. We needed our articles of incorporation and bylaws, a tax ID number, and we had to set up signature cards (which meant we needed to decide who would have signing authority, etc.). We had no idea that opening a new business account was so complicated and that you couldn't just walk in and hand over a check for that amount. We shared the dilemma with Sid, and he had a temporary solution. We stored the check in the old World War II battleship safe at Comet Deli for 5 days while bankers came to our new offices and met with us. That's how we knew we had finally started to make it. The bankers came to us.

We realized that we'd have to hire a lot more employees than we'd originally thought. We brought people in to meet—friends of friends, anyone we knew—and in a lot of cases, our primary criteria was that we wanted someone who could do the job and, frankly, who wouldn't embarrass us. There wasn't much evaluating of specific talents or personality types—or even a very serious interview process. We do it very differently today. There is no doubt that our employees are our most important asset. Boomers are passionate, creative, and hardworking. Today we strive to attract, identify, and hire a talented team; back then I would sit down with the person, talk for a few minutes, and if I got a good feeling, we'd give them the nod.

We brought in a dozen people in a very short time, expanding fourfold in a matter of months, with almost no policies or procedures. We realized we'd need some kind of employee handbook, and after having been at City Year, I knew they had a good handbook. Michael Brown, the cofounder of City Year, gave us an electronic copy of theirs, and through the miracle of word-processing software, we went through and changed every mention of City Year to KaBOOM!. (An employee realized this 3 or 4 years later, one of the few people who actually read the document all the way through, when he spotted a reference to City Year with an extra space—the word processor find-and-replace function hadn't caught that one.)

Today we have an employee handbook/style guide that I am terribly proud of. It's called FUNdamentals, and it was created in-house by our marketing and communications teams. It was a benchmark for success to me when we sent it to Michael Brown years ago, and he confirmed to me that it was probably the best example of an organizational handbook he had seen. We've come 180 degrees from our early fly-by-the-seat-of-your-pants days when we rushed and copied things in a haphazard way.

For example, on one of the earliest days, once all the new hires were in place, one of them asked Dawn, "You guys have staff meetings, right?" And she said, "Staff meetings? Right. Of course we do." The idea had never occurred to us.

Reality set in pretty fast, and the stress of the project started to mount. We had sold a big idea, and the challenge of being able to execute that idea was nearly overwhelming. Even with project managers assigned to specific playgrounds, the venture would still require a tremendous amount of travel and training. There were a lot of different groups and constituencies involved right away—hundreds of employees at Kimberly-Clark in sites across the country along with local volunteers in each of those communities.

I remember being on a flight to Dallas to meet with Tina Barry, the executive who oversaw the Kimberly-Clark foundation. We knew that she had legitimate concerns about our ability to pull this whole thing off. On that flight, I had an epiphany. Instead of sending people around to each individual community, what if we brought everyone from all 37 communities together in one room? That would be much more efficient. We could have a central training session for the projects rather than traveling around the country and teaching people how to build playgrounds site by site.

A team at KaBOOM! spent a few weeks putting together a booklet called "The Getting Started Kit," followed by a more detailed project manual. I felt like people were going to be looking for any excuse to tell us no, so we sweated every last detail of our presentation. We had a few hundred of the manuals printed, but when the bound versions came back, we thought they looked sloppy. Some of the text wasn't positioned correctly on the pages, and the ink looked faded in spots. When you're young and running a new organization, you need to do everything possible to put forward a professional front (actually, I believe this is true regardless of your age or the organization's age . . . but it was an indispensable truth in our situation). The project manual had to be high quality and professional in appearance, so we leased a state-of-the-art color copier and ran it around the clock for 6 days straight, making sure every document we handed out would look absolutely perfect.

The event was called the Playground Institute. We held it in

Appleton, Wisconsin, and when the day arrived the state was hit by a major snowstorm. That didn't hold us back, though. All the mill managers managed to make it in, along with community representatives of the neighborhoods where each playground would go up. These were the people who would serve as construction leaders on their individual projects, about 150 people total. Jody Kretzmann, who had taught me so much about community development through his ABCD Institute, came to speak. We were honored to get him.

We had persuaded four playground manufacturers to each ship $15,000 worth of components, which we piled up inside the cafeteria to be assembled by Kimberly-Clark employees and community members from each recipient neighborhood. We had built our earlier playgrounds from scratch, out of lumber, but we had never assembled prefabricated plastic and metal components before. (We made this change in large part because wooden playgrounds need a lot of heavy maintenance from the communities to keep them safe. In the communities in which we were working, the playgrounds were getting a lot of use by a large number of kids, and the wooden structures were not holding up well. Metal and plastic playgrounds are simply more durable.) Each one was like a garage-size piece of Ikea furniture, with directions at varying levels of complexity.

One of the manufacturers sent equipment with missing pieces. They didn't seem to be taking what we were doing seriously and were setting themselves apart from the other three vendors. It was starting to become clear that customer service and relationships meant a lot in this industry. We knew we couldn't risk something like this for an actual build, so they lost a big opportunity; none of the 37 playgrounds we built would be purchased through this manufacturer.

The experience also made us realize how much we didn't know about playgrounds. People asked us tough, technical questions about surfacing and whether the holes needed to be drilled to different depths in different areas because of frost lines. Frankly, we didn't have all the answers, and we realized we would have to get smarter in a hurry. In that regard, the experience helped turn us into playground experts much faster than if we had built 37 playgrounds one at a time.

▲ ■ ●

While these plans were moving forward, we moved into a bigger office at 2213 M Street in Washington—a long skinny space that we shared with the American Task Force for Lebanon (an advocacy group that amounted to two likable guys named George and Deeb). We devoted the wall of a tiny narrow hallway to two 8-by-10-foot whiteboards, which we marked up with a massive grid to check off the various steps for each Kimberly-Clark playground.

The system helped us share information—everyone on the staff could see where everything stood rather than people keeping individual files in their desks. In some cases we reordered the sequence of planning steps and standardized the process based on things we were learning. There was one catch, though: Because of the cramped geometry of the floor plan, you couldn't stand far enough from the whiteboard to take in all of it at once. Instead, you had to move along it, like you were climbing around a giant spreadsheet.

▲ ■ ●

Even though we were getting better at the logistics, we were facing other problems in the office, specifically with people. Some of the problems would have come up at any organization growing this rapidly, but to be honest, a lot of them were my own fault. I'd had fantastic mentors for some things in my life, but I didn't know how to manage employees. Several people we'd hired in that mad rush were older than me, and others had much more nonprofit experience and different skills—like accounting—that at the time I didn't fully understand and didn't know how to evaluate. To complicate matters, I was traveling nonstop, but I still wanted to do everything and control everything. So

I made every management mistake in the book, stuff that really makes me cringe when I think back on it. In fact, I think I invented some management mistakes as well.

One basic guideline is that you should always praise people in public and reprimand them in private. That's what Liz Thompson did with us back at the Chicago office of City Year, and even though it struck me at the time as a really effective way to build loyalty among a staff, as soon as I became a manager I promptly forgot it. We had regular staff meetings by this point, and they quickly became miserable experiences for everyone, because I would use them as opportunities to tell people all the things I thought they had done wrong.

About 3 years into our work, I found out about a project that had not been tightly managed. One of our strengths as an organization, in my opinion, is that we learn from mistakes and we revise protocol and best practices with new situations as they emerge so that an individual's learning becomes organizational learning. We have developed, over time, negotiable and nonnegotiable activities throughout our processes. One of the nonnegotiable ones is the timing of getting the holes dug. We had learned that when you dig 30 holes that are 2½ feet deep and 18–24 inches wide, sometimes you run into the unexpected—old foundations, granite, underground systems that no one has in their records, etc. It's critical to get the holes done (or at least started) on day one of prep. That way, if you run into issues, you have 2 days to figure out a solution and the Build Day can still happen on time. Our partners building with us for the first time would have no way of knowing why some of our processes are inflexible, so they might try to get the project manager to forego a step or change the order of events. The onus is on the project manager to be firm and manage the nonnegotiable elements of planning.

On one build, that didn't happen. The project manager had never himself experienced a project with major challenges when drilling the holes. Naturally, the community didn't understand the importance of digging the holes on day one of prep, and they convinced the project manager to let this occur on day two, the day before the build. The project manager had been lucky. It worked that time without incident, so he came to the conclusion that this nonnegotiable was actually negotiable, and he continued to let the timing of digging the holes be decided by the circumstances of each project—until he hit a major underground issue on one of his projects and all of this came to my attention.

The importance of the timing of digging the holes was a very early lesson for KaBOOM!; it has been a proven best practice to us many times. And yet this person was unnecessarily putting the success of the definable-project-on-a-definable-timeline at risk for every build he led. He was making it up as he went and ignoring what we knew was a better way to operate. I was furious, and I lit into him in front of everyone at the staff meeting. "You can't just wing it," I yelled. "There are reasons why we do what we do! If you don't know, ask. You risked the project in every situation where you let this happen. Just follow the basic model!"

He understood the problem right away, but I kept going, and then I turned it into a group lecture. In hindsight I can see how wrong this was. It seemed like the most efficient way to communicate to a group: Point out one person's mistake, in front of everyone, and then no one else will make the same mistake. The concept actually does work, as long as you flip it around and publicly highlight all the great things people do, instead of yelling at them about their screw-ups. Praise in public, reprimand in private. But at the time I couldn't see that. I was impatient and I was immature.

It all came to a head in early 1998. We realized that we'd need someone to run day-to-day operations because I was on the road so much, and we had a candidate in mind, a man I'll call Eric. Eric had done some contract work for us—writing project manuals and other content—and he had done a very good job. He also had a solid background, with a master's degree from an Ivy League school, along with stints at other nonprofits. He seemed like an ideal fit for this role.

But almost right away, I could sense tension. It was nothing I could specifically point to, and we never overtly butted heads. But I would come back into the office from a trip and feel like there was something in the air. And I was right. We had a board of directors, a requirement for all nonprofits, and like everything else about KaBOOM! at the time, it was pretty informal—we were not tapping this resource in the way we should have. They were a group of people who would sign off on our financials and individually give me needed issue expertise. But their collective wisdom was not being harnessed in a strategic manner.

When the time came for our next board meeting (we were so young that this would be the first time they would actually meet in person), Eric sent a note to Kenny Grouf, the board chair, demanding that I be fired or else he and eight other employees would walk out. He had gone around and lined up allegiances against me. We only had 12 employees at the time, counting me, so if he followed through on his threat, we'd be left with just three.

Kenny called me right away and said, "We've got a problem." I felt completely ambushed and was furious. After ruminating a bit, I knew that I had to set my ego and my anger aside. I agreed that the board would need to resolve this as they saw fit. Kenny responded to Eric and said, "We'll talk about it at the meeting." That wasn't enough for Eric—he then raised the stakes by faxing his note to every member of the board. We had five people on the board at the time, and the good news is that all five attended that meeting. The bad news was I was facing the possible outcome that I would be ousted as CEO. This was my biggest crisis as a leader.

Initially, we didn't even know where we would hold the meeting. Our office had a small conference room, but we knew the meeting was going to be contentious, and the board wanted some privacy. A hotel conference room wasn't going to work—we didn't have the money. The headquarters of the American Bar Association was right next door, so we walked over and asked if we could use one of their conference rooms. We had gotten to know some of the receptionists and other staffers from being in the neighborhood, and they agreed to let us use the space for the afternoon.

Eric had a chance to go in and make his case to the board without me there. Then they sent him out and called me in. I honestly had no idea what was going to happen. Kenny said, "Look, he has some legitimate points. The organization is growing extremely fast, and it's putting a lot of pressure on people, on you, and on KaBOOM! as a whole. That said, we honestly don't see him running this operation. So you're free to sever his contract as of this afternoon." I asked about the eight employees, and the board said that if those people actually walked out, it would be a difficult transition, but that still wasn't enough for them to give in to his demands. You couldn't run a legitimate nonprofit—or any type of organization—through extortion, and they were prepared to make the hard decision and deal with the consequences. I felt a heavy load lifted from my shoulders. I remember looking around the table of the borrowed conference room; all eyes were on me. I was humbled by the support demonstrated in this decision and would later determine that they would not regret the trust they were placing in me.

I left the board members in the conference room and walked back next door to KaBOOM!, where I found Eric. He must have known what was coming—he didn't have much in his office, just some papers on his desk, nothing substantial to clean out or pack up. (Or maybe he was all set to take over my office.) I had rehearsed in my head what I would say to him and decided to make it clean and simple. Feeling a little like I was reading lines out of a script, I said, "Your services are no longer needed." I'd anticipated a showdown, but there was no argument, no angry eruption. The whole thing was very professional—he stood up and cleared off his desk, stuffed his papers into a soft-covered briefcase, shook my hand, and walked out. I felt a tremendous sense of relief.

The board gathered the entire staff in and explained their decision. One young woman broke down crying. That day, only two of the eight employees who'd sided with Eric walked out. Over the following

6 months, the other six would leave, two on their own and the other four were ultimately fired.

We were doing good work across the country—all 37 playgrounds for Kimberly-Clark would be completed on time and on budget—but internally, we were a mess. The attempted coup had put our entire venture in jeopardy. I came away from the experience knowing that this was no way to run a national, fast-growing organization. We would have to change the way we did things. I would have to change, too.

[6]

You Can Do Routine Tasks
without Doing Them Routinely

On a flight from Los Angeles to Washington not long after the attempted coup, I found myself seated next to a man named Pete D'Amelio. The name tag on his briefcase listed his title as vice president of operations at the Cheesecake Factory chain of restaurants. We struck up a conversation. Pete and his wife were expecting twins at the time, so he was newly interested in play—and we ended up talking for most of the 6-hour flight.

When the plane landed at Dulles, I asked him if he'd come by the KaBOOM! office and take a look at our operation, to see if he might have any advice for us. He had no experience with nonprofits, but his depth of operations experience made that a nonissue. We were lucky to get him involved. Pete ended up becoming our board chairman a few months later. (His version of this story: "Darell hornswoggled me, but I'm glad he did. I found it impossible to say no to him.")

Pete is obsessed by details, and he's good at standardizing the operations of an organization. He started his 18-year stint at the Cheesecake Factory as a restaurant manager, and he quickly worked his way up, ultimately becoming president and COO of the company. During his tenure, the chain would go from just four restaurants to more than 150, including 23 new locations that he helped launch in 1 year—13 in just 8 weeks. That kind of rapid growth only comes when the process of

opening and running restaurants has been analyzed enough to have all
the kinks taken out. And Pete had a knack for this.

He knew, for example, that every customer used an average of 1.2
napkins per visit, and that each napkin cost seven cents apiece. He
knew that every Chinese Chicken Salad had 12 mandarin orange slices.
Not 11, not 13, not a random spoonful. And he had a kind of "dashboard" on his computer, a spreadsheet that could give him precise
operational data on all restaurants and regions, which allowed the company to model its prices, spot problems, and expand quickly. Many
restaurant chains now operate with this level of precision, but at the
time, Cheesecake Factory was miles ahead of the industry.

When Pete joined our board, we needed that expertise more than
anything else. We had taken on some big projects, but we didn't have
formal processes for much of anything. We were still buying playground equipment from three manufacturers, for example, which
meant three sets of relationships that had to be maintained, three sets of
assembly instructions, three sets of invoices and tools and shipping
requirements and so on. (This is a lesson I probably should have learned
during the Columbus project for City Year, when we hired separate
manufacturers for two playgrounds that were less than a mile apart.)
During some builds, the project managers had to make multiple runs
to the local hardware store for last-minute fill-ins like bolts and wash-
ers. Pete used to say that we were flying the plane as we were still
designing it.

One wouldn't think that there would be a lot of parallels between
restaurants and playground-building, but there are. Both are primarily
experience-driven (a meal, a day of service), with a long list of resources
required in advance (food, playground components). Most important,
both experiences happen repeatedly, in ways that are largely predictable. Hundreds of people eat at Cheesecake Factory restaurants each
day, and hundreds of people were volunteering at each KaBOOM!
project. That repetition meant the process could be analyzed and
improved.

During one board meeting back then, Pete said that we should know exactly how many nuts and bolts a playground would require. Each component, like a slide or swing, needs a certain number, and the components were planned in advance, as part of the overall design. So there was no reason we couldn't figure out this number weeks ahead of construction for a given playground—or even the total required for a given year. That would eliminate those last-minute trips to the hardware store, speeding up our projects and saving us money. It would also let us jump on future opportunities in an intelligent way, because we would know exactly what we'd need.

In another meeting, Pete showed me the company's manual for how to open a new Cheesecake Factory restaurant. It was a thick binder with a timeline that counted down all the necessary steps, in methodical sequence, all the way to opening day. Every detail was in there—when each element had to happen, how long it should take, and what it should cost.

I realized that we needed to create the same kind of standardized process for our service. That way, everything we did at KaBOOM! would be consistent and reproducible and wouldn't change in critical ways from one project to the next. The companies that funded multiple playgrounds would get a consistent, repeatable experience that they would be able to count on. Improving the process meant that we'd become more efficient, wringing every last dollar out of the money our funders had entrusted with us and ensuring it was well spent on the project for the community.

More important, we'd start to amass and organize our collective knowledge—everything we'd learned about playgrounds and how to build them. To that point, a lot of the information got passed down like folklore, from one project manager to the next, and when those people left the organization, much of their knowledge left with them. Instead, we would document everything, analyze what worked and what didn't, and over time make the whole experience better.

So we made a very conscious decision that we would redesign the way we did things. We had to slow down and analyze our process in order to be able to speed up and replicate it. No more winging it, no more changing plans because a funder requested it or because a project manager wanted to take a pass on something. We learned this lesson the hard way, but we learned it.

At the same time, the process shouldn't turn into one long monotonous checklist. After all, we've been through this process dozens of times, but for each community it's the first and only experience with KaBOOM!, so we don't want to come across like flight attendants blandly reciting their lines before takeoff. There's a Boomerism that sums up this balance: "You can do routine things without doing them routinely." That means that while we have certain required processes and protocols (which are not negotiable), the community and funding partners also have some flexibility, along with the project manager, to customize each event.

Here is one example. On Build Day, we always start with a warm-up for volunteers. It's first thing in the morning, everyone's a little stiff, and we think it starts the day right if everyone can move around a bit before they jump into the actual construction work—plus we think it makes people feel a little silly, laugh a little, and get outside their comfort zone a bit. The warm-up becomes specific to that project, and it isn't cookie cutter. Sometimes people ask a trainer from the local gym to come by to lead everyone in a round of jumping jacks. But we've also had a yoga instructor serenely guide everyone through some gentle stretches. And on the other end of the spectrum, we've had hip-hop dancing, with speakers thumping out beats at 85 decibels. Routine things, but not done in a routine way.

▲　■　●

To the extent that Pete introduced these concepts to the organization, my wife, Kate, got them implemented. Kate and I met for the first time at a project she was managing through her organization, AmeriCorps

National Civilian Community Corps. It was Martin Luther King Day, and the project was very high profile, with President Clinton attending. I had given my staff the day off to volunteer at the project, and she and I met briefly that day. The service world is small, and we had each heard of the other and the work of our respective organizations from mutual friends. Kate and her Corps members had actually volunteered at several builds. After meeting that day, we ran into each other a couple of times over the course of the next 6 months.

But we didn't talk at length until a dinner we both happened to attend. One of the first KaBOOM! employees, Ian Fisk, hosted it. Ian knows a lot of people in the Washington, DC, service community, and he had a friend who was a chef, so once a month he would talk the chef into cooking a meal for 30 or so people. "I called it the Progressive Culinary Arts Movement," Ian says, "but basically, I wanted to make my friends come to me."

The meal was chronically late. We wouldn't eat until 9:30 or 10 on some nights, and because none of us had a lot of money back then and also because Ian is a progressive guy, the meals were vegetarian. I admit that I am not at all a vegetarian—sorry if that offends folks, but back then in particular, I was a meat-and-potatoes kind of guy, and eating a meal without meat just didn't make sense to me. I usually stopped for a slice of pizza or a burger on the way over to Ian's. (I wasn't the only one who did, but I think I was the only one who ever fessed up.)

At the dinner in July 1998, it didn't much matter that the food was late. Kate was there, and that was the night we really connected. Ian has a picture somewhere of the two of us talking on the couch. It was probably an easy picture to take, as we were there for most of the evening. I found her incredibly easy to talk to, and I was inspired by her life. In fact, if I had to create the perfect person for me, I'd come up with . . . her.

Like me, Kate comes from a big family, though in her case she grew up in Ohio, and she's still very close to her four siblings. She also has a long career in service, inspired by the example her parents set. After

several other jobs, Kate worked with abused kids at a residential facility
while studying for a master's degree in psychology. These were severe
cases, kids who had been taken from their homes because of repeated
abuse and neglect, and she left the facility each night wanting to bring
one of them home with her. "I called my parents some of those nights
to thank them for the upbringing they gave me. I realized how lucky I
was," Kate told me. The experience taught her firsthand that kids often
don't have a voice or much ability to change the conditions in which
they're raised. In that regard, they're victims of whatever situation they
happen to be in.

After 2 years in that position, Kate joined the Peace Corps, where she
served as a health educator in Cote D'Ivoire. She was the only non-
African in a village of 5,000, working to increase the survival rates of
young kids through immunizations and nutritional counseling for
mothers. When her assignment was up, she decided to live in DC
because it had some of the worst inner-city issues in the country—the
highest crime rate, the highest infant mortality rate, and so on. Once
here, she heard about the creation of AmeriCorps and grew passionate
about the idea of a slate of service programs that would similarly expand
the service opportunities in the United States.

Kate ended up at the National Civilian Community Corps
(NCCC), a new program at the time, which was modeled after the
Civilian Conservation Corps of the 1930s. It was an AmeriCorps program and was akin to a peacetime military service, with young people
devoting 10 months of their lives and staying on downsized military
bases, where they could be deployed to address the greatest local
needs. She was hired on at the Corporation for National Service at the
inception of AmeriCorps and was a part of the early team that helped
get the NCCC program up and running—first in recruiting the inau-
gural Corps, next as the national head of training and education, and
then starting up a campus in DC and, for 5 years, overseeing a residential program of more than a hundred 18-to-24-year-olds. Corps
members built houses with Habitat for Humanity, responded to
national disasters, and, by the way, worked on playground projects

with KaBOOM!. And now we were both at Ian Fisk's dinner party that night.

After a few hours of talking on the couch, I knew enough about her to know that I wanted to know more. The next day I paged her and asked her to go to a movie. It was the old kind of pagers back then, where it showed the text. I said, "What are you doing tonight? Want to go to a movie sometime?" After that, we started dating, and it became pretty serious, pretty quickly.

Kate would ultimately come to work at KaBOOM!, where she now runs the program side of the organization—meaning she oversees the playground-building component and everything that supports or is connected to that. I lobbied hard for her to come and work there, and she resisted for a long time, satisfied in her role at NCCC. Kate ended up deciding to leave NCCC, where she was working 80 hours a week, after a good friend of hers died from breast cancer. Shortly afterward, in the spring of 2002, I had a senior person leave us unexpectedly, and we were in a tight spot. I asked the board if we could have Kate step in (we were married by then, and we wanted everything to be completely transparent and aboveboard). She's been with KaBOOM! ever since.

KaBOOM! would not be the same organization without her. She professionalized the operation, and she was a driving force behind making sure we prioritized the communities as we worked with the corporations and other entities that fund playground projects. People give me a lot of credit for the things we've done, but everyone who's ever worked here knows that she's done just as much for the organization's success. More importantly, I wouldn't be the same person without her.

▲ ■ ●

When she started at KaBOOM!, Kate, like Pete, was struck by how we didn't have a lot of things written down. We were winging it. Her initial goal in documenting the process for building playgrounds was to make sense of it herself. Then she could standardize and improve it. And with Pete's insight, we applied that to the rest of the organization as well.

That was the beginning of the approach we used to improve our execution. Since then it's been a continuous journey that never really ends. We keep trying to get better and improve the way we do things. Today execution is probably the thing KaBOOM! is best known for in the nonprofit world, and we never take that for granted.

This process helped me make some changes in the way I operated around the office, and particularly in the way I managed people. For one thing, I got better control of my temper. To that point, it was something that impacted not only my relations with the staff but also our relations with outsiders. During one incident, which is funny only in hindsight, I was at a playground project in Chicago, prepping for a live television interview with a reporter at news station WGN. We were chatting before the cameras started rolling, and she twice referred to our organization as KaBANG. I gently corrected her both times, but when the interview started, she did it again. "I'm here live with the founder and CEO of KaBANG," she said. This was going out to television stations across the country—a huge opportunity to increase the awareness of KaBOOM!—and she couldn't get our name right.

I was so mad that I couldn't resist referring to WGN's competing station. "To all you WFLD viewers out there," I said, "here's what KaBOOM! is all about." It felt good for about 5 minutes, but the reporter was livid, and my name became infamous at the network, which impacted our coverage later on. Only later did I learn from my former mentor, Liz Thompson, that there's a time and a place to deal with situations like these, and that embarrassing a reporter and an entire news station on live TV wasn't the way to do it.

My temper showed up around the office as well. I had a hard time listening and allowing the collective ideas of the staff to add up to something more than my own personal vision. It took me a while to realize that those employees weren't the problem—I was. I was young and had almost no management experience, and I thought I could get the respect of employees by demanding it instead of earning it.

But as the organization grew, I eventually calmed down, gained more control over my emotions, and opened myself up to listen to the ideas of other people. I'm entirely self-taught as a leader, and I learned most of my lessons through trial and error (along with the criticisms of my staff—sometimes diplomatically presented, other times less so, but almost always legitimate). The most crucial of these lessons was that I needed to adapt to the strengths and weaknesses of my staff rather than expecting them to adapt to me. That can be a nerve-wracking transition for any leader, but only by confronting those vulnerabilities did I push past them and create a better organization, one where people want to come to work every day, and where I'm now leveraging the contributions of the entire staff. There's a tremendous power in that kind of collaboration. I'm not 100 percent there; it's something I continue to work toward.

[7]

Audacious Dreams

All throughout KaBOOM!'s history, we've faced situations where we committed to something without knowing exactly how we'd pull it off. At times, especially early on, it was a kind of challenge to ourselves. *Yes, of course we can build 37 playgrounds for you. You want five in one day? No problem.* Kate calls it "audacious thinking." You dream big, and if you're given the opportunity to achieve that audacious dream, you do whatever's necessary to make it happen. And you never let anyone down.

It was in the late 1990s and early 2000s that this element of the culture at KaBOOM! really started to solidify. We were growing at warp speed. Anderson Cooper did a 6-minute segment on KaBOOM! for ABC's nightly news in 1997. Al and Tipper Gore and Colin and Alma Powell showed up at a playground build together. That playground was part of a huge service event connected to the 1997 Presidents' Summit for America's Future, where all citizens and all sectors, including corporations, were being called on by all the living presidents to volunteer. To be a part of this at such an early time in our history was huge. In addition, Stride Rite developed a cause-marketing program in which the company developed a special KaBOOM! kids' shoe, with a share of sales going to fund playgrounds. Stonyfield Farm ran a promotion on their yogurt lids, and Fairytale Brownies and Odwalla each started similar promotions.

Through these cause-marketing programs, we were able to connect to a socially conscious audience as well as build our reputation and increase our visibility and name recognition.

At the same time, we kept aiming higher, and in a few cases we succeeded way beyond what we'd hoped. There are dozens of anecdotes I could use to illustrate this, but I'll only mention a few, which were all pivotal in our growth in those first few years and all underscore the importance of audacious dreaming.

Over the first 14 years of our history The Home Depot devoted more than $55 million to us to advance the cause of play and directly helped communities build nearly 800 playgrounds in our history, while indirectly supporting another 600 through challenge grants and similar programs. In fact, The Home Depot had been a partner beginning back when cofounders Bernie Marcus and Arthur Blank were still running things there.

During the first few KaBOOM! projects, I was coordinating with the company through its community affairs department, but as our relationship deepened, I managed to introduce myself up the corporate chain of command, until eventually I met Bernie and Arthur. Both men are extremely down-to-earth, despite the scope of their accomplishments. At the time the company had about 200 stores nationwide, compared to about 2,200 in 2010.

At one point, Bernie and Arthur were scheduled to be in Washington for a conference at the Marriott, across the street from our office on Connecticut Avenue, and they announced that they'd like to drop in. This was when we were still in the donated space we'd gotten through Marian Wright Edelman. We only had a handful of employees at the time, but we wanted to show that we were serious and could be trusted to work with one of the fastest-growing retail chains and most admired companies in America.

Bernie and Arthur were only in the office for 10 minutes or so, but we managed that experience like it was a visit from the president. Among other details, we arranged to have all our friends call in, so that the place would seem bustling and active. They came away satisfied, though in hindsight, we probably overdid it. We only had a few phone lines, which rang more or less nonstop while the two executives were there, making the office sound like we were running a telethon.

The postscript is even better, though. About 10 years after that happened, I saw Bernie at a playground build down at the Marcus Autism Center in Atlanta, the organization he founded and generously supports. I confessed to him that we'd staged that visit for them, and he told me they'd known all along! Not only that, but they respected me for doing it, as they'd done something similar back when they were just starting up. In one of their first Home Depot stores, they got a bunch of empty boxes from a supplier and stacked them on shelves behind their products so customers would think they had massive quantities of inventory.

I worried when The Home Depot faced its first major leadership transition in 2001 after 23 years. Would Bob Nardelli, the new CEO, maintain a partnership with KaBOOM!, or would he want to do something different? I, along with many others, wondered if the new CEO would value corporate philanthropy and foster the "giving back" culture that had been initiated by the founders and was now emerging as a core component of The Home Depot's culture.

I first met Bob at a KaBOOM! build in Washington, DC, a few months after he took the reins at The Home Depot. He was wearing pressed khaki pants—I was struck by the almost razor-sharp crease—and an orange (also pressed) Team Depot polo shirt. Within the first few minutes of our conversation, it was clear that he knew everything about KaBOOM!, the partnership, our history, and our reputation. Bob is wicked-smart, disciplined, and always well prepared. After charming me in our brief discussion, he got to work, really got to work.

I think that was the last time he wore pressed slacks or a pressed T-shirt to a KaBOOM! build, but it was far from his last build. I would guess that Bob has been to 30-plus KaBOOM! projects. He is the first to arrive and the last to leave, and he gets in and does the heavy lifting and the dirty jobs. He is a man who cares deeply about service and not only supported an ethic of giving back, but he fostered a culture of employee volunteerism throughout the corporation. The Home Depot-KaBOOM! partnership would go from $500,000 to a remarkable $10 million a year under Bob's leadership. Bob left The Home Depot in 2007 but has continued to be a champion for KaBOOM!.

After a significant 14-year partnership, in September 2010 The Home Depot Foundation ended our partnership.

▲ ■ ●

Then there's Target. In 1999 the corporation announced a Valentine's Day promotion called Million Hearts, in which it would donate a total of $1 million to five nonprofits. There was a twist, though: The money would be apportioned by a customer vote. Target distributed a ballot with its regular insert in the Sunday newspaper, and people used those to vote for the organization they thought should receive the most money. What's striking looking back is how much effort these votes required. When an organization wants to stage a similar promotion today, everything is online, and people vote with a single mouse click. Back then, people had to get the newspaper supplement, fill it out, drive to the store, and put it in the box.

I had met one of Target's community affairs managers at a Businesses for Social Responsibility conference, which is where I used to do some of my best prospecting. Arthur Blank was the keynote speaker this particular year, and I was there by invitation of The Home Depot. I convinced the Target community affairs manager we were worth looking at, and we talked about a few possibilities that ultimately didn't pan out. But when this promotion came up, we managed to get designated as one of the five nonprofits.

We were on a list with some very high-profile organizations, like St. Jude Children's Research Hospital, the Salvation Army, and the American Red Cross. Those all had national name recognition along with local chapters and affiliates and armies of volunteers. We were so little at the time that Target didn't even mention our name prominently. Instead, we were listed by our cause—the ballot read "Community Playgrounds (KaBOOM!)." But while we might not have had a household-name brand, we had a lot of hustle. And we had a secret weapon: Kim Rudd, the marketing manager I first met at the Chicago Park District, where I'd interned years ago.

Kim had worked at Leo Burnett, an advertising agency, before the Park District, and she has a fantastic marketing mind. I knew nothing about marketing at KaBOOM!—like so many other things, we were making that part up as we went along—but I recognized how good she was and how much she could contribute to our organization. We could be better with her, and I really needed that kind of talent. After I left Chicago, she and I stayed in touch, and when we started needing big-time marketing, I began lobbying her to come and work at KaBOOM!.

At the time, she had just had twins Gregory and Victoria, and she thought our young nonprofit was too much of a risk. As she put it: "To be honest, I thought it was cute that you started a nonprofit. And then when you would call in or stop by with these tales of having met Michael Jordan or the CEO of Discover, it was sort of like, Okay, Darell, sure you did. And then I started to wonder, how was he getting all this access? The stories became more like stories and less like tales. It went from skepticism to wonder to amazement. Look at what you are doing—how are you pulling it off?"

I used to call her and say, "Kim, I'm going to hang up the phone and call you right back, and I'd like you to answer the phone, 'KaBOOM!.'" I'd call right back, and she'd say, "Hello, Chicago Park District, this is Kim." This happened every time we talked, for months. Then one day I called her and said, "I'm going to hang up and call you back, and I want you to answer the phone, 'KaBOOM!.'" This time, she answered, "KaBOOM!, this is Kim Rudd." I was thrilled. I said, "Doesn't that sound powerful? Doesn't that sound great?" She joined us 6 months later.

Because of her agency experience, she helped us set up a system of billable hours at the organization, in which an employee's time equated to a certain value, and that value got pegged to specific projects. Employees had different values depending on their level of seniority and experience. We also set up a price structure for projects, with a rough idea of what each one would cost us, in both time and money. That allowed us to budget more effectively and justify higher fees to corporations for more complicated projects. It sounds simple in hindsight, but it was a big step for us.

Most important, Kim came up with some great marketing and PR promotions. For the Target contest, she ordered tens of thousands of candy hearts with our name printed on them. We also had 11-by-17 posters designed and printed up, with information on the campaign and instructions on how to vote. (The headline on each poster said, "Have a heart for KaBOOM!") For about a month leading up to the campaign, we basically shut down our playground operations and turned our full attention to getting out the vote—it was such a good opportunity to raise funds and make people aware of us.

The entire staff gathered around a rickety cafeteria table every day for a week and stuffed countless envelopes with candy hearts, a poster, and a handwritten note thanking people for their support. We mailed these out to communities and business contacts and basically everyone that anyone on our staff knew or had ever known. We also asked those people to pass the extra hearts along to everyone *they* knew. Hand them out at restaurants! Give them to co-workers! Leave a bunch at the gym! It was about as grassroots as a promotion like this can get.

Kate and I also voted in person, as many times as we physically could. You had to have the actual original newspaper supplement to vote (photocopies didn't count), so we asked people to collect them from neighbors and save them for us. I distinctly remember going to a 7-Eleven and pulling about 15 supplements out of the stack of Sunday papers.

My driver's license had expired a few years earlier, and because

I'd been so busy getting the organization up and running, I hadn't gotten around to renewing it. So Kate "chauffeured" me around in her silver Honda Civic, and we crisscrossed the region to drop these ballots off at every Target store within driving distance—places like Richmond and Charlottesville, hours from DC.

Each night after work during the weeklong period when you could vote, we would set off. At this time Target had only about 150 stores, and it was a logistical challenge to get around to as many as we could in our region because of the way they were spread out. This was before GPS, so we were using maps and finding our ways to the towns that had Targets. We'd park, run in, stuff our ballots, and run back out to the car to drive 50 miles to the next nearest Target. (By the way, I did eventually brave the DC Department of Motor Vehicles and got my driver's license again, though it would take years before I drove Kate around enough to balance this all out.)

Target executives later admitted that they thought we'd get a few percentage points of the vote, at most. They were more or less humoring us by including us with the other four giant entities. But when the counting was over, we ended up with almost 14 percent of the total, netting us a check for $137,000. Target was so impressed it launched another campaign in which we would build 17 playgrounds with the company, including 10 playgrounds in a single week, something we'd never done to that point. We are proud that we had been scrappy enough to hold our own against some of the most well-known non-profits in the country through sheer hustle. Dreaming big is important in the growth of any organization. Executing on the big dreams is even more important.

▲ ■ ●

Like everyone else in the United States, KaBOOM! was profoundly affected by the events of September 11, 2001. On that day we were scheduled for our first-ever senior management meeting. It was to be held at our office in the CNA Center in downtown Chicago (which they donate to us), and I heard about the terrorist attacks when I got there. The building was quickly evacuated, as was my hotel—people thought Chicago would be the next target. KaBOOM! had staff members flying around the country, traveling to and from various projects. As we were in the midst of trying to assess everyone's whereabouts and verify that they were safe, we were receiving calls from panicked families and friends. In the first few hours, we were scrambling to confirm that everyone was okay and communicate that back to their families. It took days—in one case, 6 days—before everyone was back to their respective homes. People on the staff in Washington were especially rattled—from our office, they could see smoke billowing from the Pentagon.

Even after getting through that day, we faced a very real question of how we were going to operate in the weeks immediately following. We had projects scheduled around the country, and we weren't sure they should still happen. Yet we pressed ahead. One was on the calendar for just 4 days later, September 15, in Seattle. We called the community leaders in that neighborhood, and they said the national tragedy was all the more reason to go forward with the playground. People wanted to do something positive, anything, in those first few days.

No flights were operating yet, and the originally scheduled employee responsible for that project was stuck in Los Angeles. But two of our employees in the San Francisco office, Melanie Barnes (who still works for KaBOOM!) and Tom Mitchell, decided with almost no advance notice that they would see it through. This is the sort of Boomer spirit that's prevalent throughout our entire team, and it makes me so proud to be involved with our organization. They rented a car at 3 in the afternoon and drove up the coast, almost 800 miles, stopping only to sleep at a motel for a few hours, and the build happened on schedule. Tom and Melanie reminisce about stopping at a gas station early in the trip and buying a Lee Greenwood CD. As they drove the rest of the way north, they kept replaying *God Bless the USA* cranked as high as they could bear it and sang along at the top of their lungs.

A few weeks later, on September 29, we had another project scheduled, this one in New York City. Again, the community decided to press ahead with construction. Sprint funded the project—2001 was the first year in a long relationship between KaBOOM! and that corporation—and our local community partner was the Restoration Project, the organization Bette Midler founded to revamp small public spaces around New York City. The site was in the Bronx, on a tiny slice of land between two huge public-housing buildings that rose up on either side of the site like the walls of a canyon.

I'll never forget that morning. We showed up at the site early, and volunteers started arriving around 8. To launch the event, the community had arranged for a police officer to sing the national anthem. He was wearing his dress blues, and he had a beautiful, powerful voice.

As the first notes of "The Star-Spangled Banner" rose up over the crowd of volunteers, windows in the buildings above us started to open. I wasn't sure what would happen. It was early on a Saturday morning, and I honestly thought someone might yell that we were making too much noise. Instead, residents in those apartments began draping American flags out of their windows. Others started to sing with the police officer. People were crying all around us. It was extremely emotional. And when the work began, residents came out of those buildings in droves to help. If I'd had any doubts about the timing of the project, they were gone—it was absolutely the right thing to do. This was an opportunity to rebuild something, and people in the neighborhood told me they were relieved to come out and get dirty and do something physical for a good cause.

▲ ■ ●

Perhaps our biggest corporate connection from those early days, and one I think led to our greatest achievement in terms of building a brand

and spreading joy to advance the cause of play—and certainly one that made us hip and "big time"—came from Ben & Jerry's. That company is now a division of Unilever; back in the late 1990s, it had a cultlike following. Founders Ben Cohen and Jerry Greenfield matched a fantastic product with ideological passion. The result was something consumers perceived as a *good* corporation, one you felt right about supporting for more than a good product, because they were doing good things with some of their profits. Ben & Jerry's was a brand that engendered trust among consumers. The company bought supplies from environmentally minded farms and donated 7.5 percent of pretax earnings to social causes. It also gave its franchisees a lot of leeway to support the local nonprofits they thought were most deserving.

The franchisee was Lori Johnston. Lori owned two Ben & Jerry's stores in Washington, DC—one in Georgetown and the other on Capitol Hill near the Eastern Market, a farmers' market in the city where vendors sell local food and goods. Lori and I had mutual friends when I moved from Chicago to Washington, and after she heard about the work we were doing at KaBOOM!, she became a big champion of the organization and a great friend.

At the Livingston Manor build, Lori donated Peace Pops (ice cream treats) for all the volunteers. She later donated bulk ice cream to communities to use as a fund-raising tool—they would sell it in cones and cups and keep all the proceeds for their playground. At one of our playground projects, Jerry Greenfield himself, the Jerry of Ben & Jerry's, showed up, though he wasn't as much of a hit as we all thought he'd be. When we told kids in the community that "Jerry" was coming, they were expecting Jerry Springer.

On the company's birthday, all franchisees held Free Cone Day, in which each location gave away ice cream, and any voluntary money that customers wanted to pay went to a local nonprofit. Lori chose KaBOOM!. We brought our team out to help scoop ice cream—and raised not only money but awareness in Washington by being Lori's designated recipient of Free Cone Day funds for 5 or 6 years.

Similarly, during the 2 day Congressional Family Picnic at the White House one year, I talked to a friend working for Mrs. Clinton and we were allowed to scoop ice cream from a Ben & Jerry's truck on the South Lawn of 1600 Pennsylvania Avenue. The truck was on tour around the country, and because I told them I could get it on the White House lawn, the company agreed to divert it to DC for us.

To make sure everything was perfect, Kate and I washed the truck ourselves. At the time, we lived near Capitol Hill, at 911 Independence Avenue, with an alley next door. We pulled the truck into the alley and scrubbed it from top to bottom with a mop. The truck was so tall that we had to borrow a ladder from one of our neighbors, a judge who lived across the street and down an alley.

The ladder was the judge's pride-and-joy possession; it had slides and extends and could also go horizontal. I had locked us out of our apartment on multiple occasions, including once when Kate's parents were visiting. One night, after we all got back from a nice dinner, I took a quick walk to the judge's for the ladder, so I could climb up to the roof of the porch to get in through an upstairs window. (This was in our first year of marriage, and I can only imagine what Kate's parents were thinking about their new son-in-law as I climbed up to a second-story window to gain access to the house.)

I was happy to have a better reason to borrow the ladder this time, and I repaid the judge with a few free pints of ice cream. That was protocol for us back then, and it's still a principal element of the culture at KaBOOM!: Hard jobs, dirty jobs, physical work—whenever something needs to be done, you jump in and do it, regardless of your title or seniority.

Lori took every opportunity in those years to talk us up to her network of Ben & Jerry's franchisees, and once she was named to the company's Franchisee Advisory Council, she was in direct contact with the management of the company. Through Lori, we were able to get a flier distributed in every franchise location in the country, listing 25 easy ways to make play better and more accessible in local communities. That was a huge win for us, and a way to get people nationwide excited about KaBOOM! and take local, direct action for the cause of play.

We organized a playground build in Key West, Florida, in conjunction with an annual meeting of Ben & Jerry's franchisees. They were a very fun, eclectic group of people, and the weather was absolutely perfect. We had one major glitch—the playground manufacturer had just changed the hardware for some of its fasteners, and they sent us exactly one Allen key that fit the new tamper-proof bolts. But that became a running joke and a way to foster morale. We more or less acted as if that mistake was intentional, and we designated one of the franchisees as the czar of the Allen key. She solicited favors from her comrades in exchange for a few minutes of use. (We modified our procedures because of that build, putting together standard tool kits with multiple copies of everything we'd need, to make sure we'd never find ourselves in that situation again. That was part of the system Pete D'Amelio and Kate helped put into place— document, analyze, improve, and do it constantly.)

Initially we thought that the Key West project would lead to franchisees around the country sponsoring builds in their hometowns, but many of them were already committed, understandably, to their own local nonprofit causes. However, the management at Ben & Jerry's had something better in mind: They offered to create an ice-cream flavor for us. It was virtually unheard of—no other nonprofit had ever had an ice-cream flavor named in its honor.

I knew exactly what we wanted—pop rocks! We had to have pop rocks. They would go off in your mouth with a tiny KaBOOM!. I'll confess here that I'd long fantasized about being one of the company's coveted "Free Ice Cream for Life" card-holders. Marian Wright Edelman had one of the cards, which let you bring friends to any location and order anything you want, whenever you want, for the rest of your life. That dream aside, the flavor would be a huge boost to KaBOOM!. It would generate tons of publicity, and Ben & Jerry's offered to donate a percentage of sales from that ice cream flavor to building playgrounds.

The food scientists found the exploding candy a little tricky: In early batches, the moisture content in the ice cream caused it to detonate prematurely. But after some further testing, they figured it out (white fudge coating did the trick). The flavor, called KaBERRY KaBOOM!, went on sale in 2001 and stayed on store shelves across the country for 2 years. Our flavor—and our cause—got talked up on the *Today Show*; Katie Couric raved about the ice cream. Our cut of revenue was enough to fund four community playgrounds. Four neighborhoods got a safe place for their kids to play because of ice cream.

▲ ■ ●

Our audacious dreams are alive and well at KaBOOM!; the most recent evidence to that effect is a partnership facilitated by Tina Barry, the executive from Kimberly-Clark who entrusted us to build 37 play-grounds in honor of their 125th anniversary, and who is now oversee-ing Corporate Affairs for Dr Pepper Snapple Group. Under her leadership, we have entered into a 3-year, $15 million partnership with Dr Pepper Snapple Group that will impact five million children by improving or building 2000 play spaces! The partnership is part of a larger Let's Play campaign, the goal of which is to get more kids playing and playing longer.

[8]

Transactions versus Transformations

As KaBOOM! got better at building playgrounds and managing a good volunteer experience, and more mature as an organization overall, we focused on refining the community component. We wanted to make certain that local residents were getting involved in the project early and staying involved throughout every phase—planning, designing, fund-raising, organizing, constructing, and maintaining.

I have come to see this emphasis on process as the distinction between a transaction and a transformation.

A transaction would be more efficient: We'd show up, build the playground, and leave. We could do this with a team of installers. Or we could retain the corporate funding and still pull off good volunteer days and team-build events but not try to leverage the community engagement. It would be easier for us and take a lot less work if we did it that way.

But the builds would be missing the genuine and meaningful spirit that comes from working side by side with community. Today, we see 86 percent of our projects maintained. That would certainly change if we parachuted a playground into the community. Building playgrounds in partnership with the community is richly transformative. Its effects resonate and extend far beyond the scope of a mere transaction.

To be honest, we really learned this lesson by experiencing its effects the few times we allowed ourselves to deviate from our model—times when the community partnership simply wasn't there.

The first instance of this was in Belfast, Northern Ireland. Through Mrs. Edelman, I got connected to then First Lady Hillary Rodham Clinton in the late 1990s. Mrs. Clinton came to a few playground builds that we organized with Mrs. Edelman and Stand for Children. This was pivotal for us. Mrs. Clinton had been an intern for Mrs. Edelman at Children's Defense Fund, and they have a very strong friendship based on mutual respect. Mrs. Clinton is genuinely curious and interested in others. She was not the least bit pretentious and immediately put me and the others around her at ease. In our first meeting, she asked thoughtful questions about our community-build model and how we got started. She quickly grasped the importance of the process of our work and the power that a playground could have in a community. Her follow-up questions honed in on the longer-term impacts; she was most interested in the community stories and in the public-private partnerships from which we derived our main funding.

On that first playground with Mrs. Clinton in Washington, DC, when it was time to work, she and Mrs. Edelman went about using ratchets and Allen keys and teasing each other as they worked to build a slide and a climber together. Fortunately for us, we made a good impression on her; our relationship has turned out to be one of the most pivotal ones in KaBOOM! history. Mrs. Clinton and many of her staff members continue to be tremendous friends and supporters.

A few months after her first experience with KaBOOM!, Mrs. Clinton invited me to accompany her to Northern Ireland, to look into a possible "peace playground" in Belfast. This was in September 1998, only a few months after the peace accords that finally ended the decades-long violence between Catholics and Protestants in that region. President Clinton was heavily involved in the peace process, and he was the first U.S. president to make an official state visit to Northern Ireland. The 1998 trip would be the last of his administration, when he would press for the accord to be finalized.

Mrs. Clinton's staff had been contacted by a group that wanted to build a playground where Catholic and Protestant children could play together, as a way of healing the divide between those groups. One study found that 70 percent of kids in Belfast ages 9 to 11 had witnessed a bombing or shooting firsthand, and children as young as 3 played games that re-created this sectarian violence. A member of the First Lady's staff called me and asked if I could come with her to Belfast.

KaBOOM! wasn't working internationally, and we didn't have the funds for me to take this trip; my trip was sponsored by a friend of the administration. Just a week after I first heard from Mrs. Clinton and her staff, I was on my way to Belfast. Only later did I realize that this abrupt and somewhat arbitrary decision on my part caused some ill will within the organization. Not only was I disappearing for a project that I didn't talk over or debate with anyone else, but we were suddenly an international organization. I think most people in my shoes would have taken this opportunity—it really was a once-in-a-lifetime one. But I could have managed the process differently. I should have given more consideration of what the trip and the prospective project meant and how we could pull it off.

Mrs. Clinton introduced me to the staff of PlayBoard, the Irish group, which has been around since 1985 doing a lot of good work to raise awareness of the benefits of play in Northern Ireland. Together we toured the site, a 3-acre patch of land called Musgrave Park in Belfast, which sits adjacent to a large hospital. Right from the start, I had more questions than answers. What was the role of KaBOOM! in this? How would we connect the two religious groups and get them to rally around this project? Even basic stuff like a design for play equipment still had to be decided. The more we talked, the less confident I felt about our ability to contribute.

For starters, PlayBoard was more sophisticated than we were and had been around longer. They were also local. But they had different ideas about how they wanted to operate. Mrs. Clinton understood the benefit of community-building and saw the power it could potentially have in this instance, and that was why KaBOOM! was there. Meanwhile, PlayBoard didn't seem interested in the community-building component, in which local volunteers organize the project and do grassroots fund-raising for it and put in most of the labor.

A more immediate problem was that they didn't want to work with the 20-something founder of a small nonprofit—they wanted to deal with the First Lady. Whenever I asked questions, they tended to give the answers to members of Mrs. Clinton's staff.

When we left Belfast a few days later, I still had almost no idea how the project was going to work and what our role would be. Mrs. Clinton saw a brilliant opportunity to use our model as a way to bring these communities together. But I was way too young and inexperienced to be involved in a project with this level of complication, not to mention the international component. KaBOOM! was not ready to try to build a coalition among two communities with such a deep-seated mistrust of each other, especially when we were so far away from them.

Once I got back to the United States, all of my phone calls to Play-Board's executive director went unanswered, and the people on Mrs. Clinton's staff started forwarding me diplomatic cables and e-mails that they had received directly from the Irish group. "What do you think about this?" the staffers would ask, and I would tell them that I hadn't received that fax. Not long after that, the executive director left (I heard about it weeks afterward), and PlayBoard subsequently had two more directors in short order.

To this day, Musgrave Park has a soccer field (or "pitch"), two bowling greens, and a well-tended garden, but no playground.

▲ ■ ●

After that experience, we were not in a hurry to try another international venture. But about a year later, I got a call from Katy Button, a friend on Mrs. Clinton's staff. She told me about the situation in Rwanda. The need was huge, and I think a part of me hoped to correct the mistakes I'd made in Belfast by getting involved and achieving success in Rwanda. As with Belfast, the opportunity was coming to us because of the First Lady. Mrs. Clinton believed that KaBOOM! and our model is what was needed.

In 1999 the Clintons hosted a series of dinners at the White House leading up to the Millennium, and in April Dr. Odette Nyiramilimo, a Tutsi woman from Rwanda, attended one of these celebrations. Odette was a survivor of the genocide that had taken place in that country in 1994. In all, roughly a million people were killed, 800,000 in the first 100 days.

As Philip Gourevitch captures so vividly in his book about the Rwandan genocide, *We Wish to Inform You That Tomorrow We Will Be Killed with Our Families*, the violence was barbaric, often carried out with machetes by people who knew the victims personally. "Following the [Hutu] militia's example," Gourevitch writes, "Hutus young and old rose to the task. Neighbors hacked neighbors to death in their houses, and colleagues hacked colleagues to death in their work places. Doctors killed their patients and school teachers killed their pupils. Within days the Tutsi population of many villages were all but eliminated, and in Kigali prisoners were released in work gangs to collect the corpses that lined the roadsides."

A member of the country's imperiled Tutsi ethnic group, Odette tried to flee the capital city of Kigali with her family, but they weren't able to get away. Instead, they found refuge at a hotel in the city along with hundreds of others. Their story was later recounted in the film, *The Hotel Rwanda*. Odette's husband was Hutu, and many people in such interethnic marriages were killed, but she and her husband survived along with their three children. Sixteen of her 17 brothers and sisters were killed, however, along with many others among her extended family and friends.

Many international observers came to Rwanda in the mid- and late 1990s, seeking to ensure that the people arrested for the killings were not being mistreated in prison. They thought that any retribution by the Tutsis would lead to continued ethnic violence. Yet few came to check on the country's orphans. Even though the killings—carried out by the very people the observers seemed most concerned about—had created roughly 300,000 orphans, more than any other country in the world at the time, no one seemed concerned about the well-being of those children.

Odette's request was simple: She wanted playgrounds at some of the facilities that housed orphans. She recognized that playing together could help kids get past the ethnic divides that had ravaged their country. Her early requests had largely gone unheeded, though she had managed to convince a group of German diplomats who were touring the prisons to send back some basketballs and soccer balls.

On the night of the White House dinner in April 1999, just a few hours after Odette spoke, I got a call at 1 a.m. from Katy Button, asking if I could come and meet with Odette the following day. She was heading back to Rwanda, but the First Lady thought we should talk before her flight. We met briefly—Odette is a remarkable woman, and she was excited by our model of community involvement. I could not even begin to imagine what these kids had seen and endured. I thought we could do something for some of the orphans of Rwanda.

Odette and I talked intermittently for the next year, and then she returned to Washington on another visit. This time she had plans in hand. A piece of property had been designated, and a local committee of volunteers had come together around the project.

I booked a plane ticket to Kigali in July 2000. The plan was that this first trip would be a fact-finding mission, in which we would finalize a lot of the details, and then we could return a second time for construction.

Kate traveled with me. Her Peace Corps experience and her ability to speak French would be invaluable assets. Odette met us at the airport, escorted by armed guards who would travel with us everywhere. They were very young-looking men, toting AK-47s, who were meant to be reassuring but in fact made me nervous. The International Rescue

Committee hosted us during our stay, where the staff served as de facto ambassadors for our playground project. That help was crucial, given the tremendous cultural and language differences. Technical barriers abounded as well. We were confident that shipping US-manufactured components over was not the right approach because once built, it would be difficult to maintain with local resources.

As it turned out, that was the least of our problems. In the time between my first meeting with Odette and our trip to Kigali, she had begun serving in the national government as the Minister of Social and Internal Affairs. This represented huge progress—only several years earlier, there were no women at all in the Rwandan government—but it meant she couldn't devote much attention to the playground. And the committee she handed it off to had very different ideas of what they wanted. When we met with its members, we realized that the vision for the site had expanded far beyond Odette's original vision. Almost unrecognizably so.

Instead of a single playground, the new plans included an auditorium, a fishing pond, trails for hiking and biking, a swimming pool, an exhibition area for local crafts, and, by the way, some play structures for kids. The property was no longer a small piece of land but now a massive plot of 20 acres. Instead of focusing on children who had been orphaned by the genocide, the new facility would serve all children—and adults as well. Instead of being located in areas that would serve great numbers of kids with equally great needs, the site was adjacent to a relatively wealthy area that was remote and accessible primarily by car. Most troubling, the people behind the project wanted to charge for access once it was completed. In just about every aspect, it was more like a country club than anything else.

At the same time, there was obviously a crushing need for assistance in the country. We saw horrific reminders of what had happened in 1994, like a church where the bones and splattered blood remained, evidence of the thousands of Tutsis who'd been killed after seeking refuge there. Everywhere there were kids so determined to play that they resorted to sticks, or toys they had made from trash, or soccer balls made of bunches of balled up plastic bags wrapped in twine. It was incredibly frustrating to see such a huge gap between what was needed for these kids and what the committee was proposing.

We came up with another solution—one that would be more feasible and more in line with the way KaBOOM! operates: a single playground to be built of metal components at an orphanage outside Kigali, and five more built of local materials like tires and wood in neighborhoods around the city. Those locally built sites would be easier to maintain and repair. We would leave plans so that they could be easily replicated by Rwandans at other sites once we had left, along with $25,000 to the International Rescue Committee to get construction rolling.

Yet even after we made that decision, the women on the committee continued to lobby for the larger, more ambitious project in the neighborhood they wanted. I realized that this fact-finding mission would probably be the first and last time we would travel to Rwanda. Even as we were heading home, a few committee members showed up at the Kigali airport to ask us to carry their revised plans back to the White House. They were looking for the transaction—the infusion of foreign funds that could be steered to the project they wanted, instead of a smaller, more community-oriented project that would help alleviate the suffering of a few hundred of those thousands and thousands of Rwandan orphans.

In the end, the cultural differences were just too profound, and the miscommunications confused our operations and what we would be able to accomplish. I think Odette's original goal was noble, and it was the right one for KaBOOM!. But, as with the ill-fated Belfast project, there was a sense of inflated expectations on the part of people hoping to receive assistance. To this day, when I see Mrs. Clinton, she asks me what we're doing for those children. It's one of my greatest professional disappointments that we weren't able to do more.

▲ ■ ●

The projects in Belfast and Rwanda were outliers for a lot of reasons. Both were international and high profile, and in both cases we didn't have a whole lot of control over the process. Yet as frustrating as those projects were to me, our 100th project—July 2000, a return to the Stoddert Terrace housing project in DC, the one where two children had died after locking themselves into a car back in 1995—was even more so, because I had a more personal connection to the community.

In the years since the kids died, we had accomplished a lot and built a lot of playgrounds, and yet conditions in that community hadn't changed substantially. The deaths of Iesha and Clendon had drawn a lot of media attention—yet instead of the conditions in the complex improving, people pointed fingers at each other and nothing really changed. Two years after the tragedy, there was still no playground, and no place for the children to run around. We wanted to fix that, and we were so intent on doing so that we set aside our usual approach, as we'd done in Belfast and Rwanda.

Instead of asking the community to compete for a project, and making it clear that they would have to do a lot of the hard work before, during, and after construction, we were determined to put up a playground in that neighborhood no matter what. We funded it ourselves, instead of partnering with another organization that would provide volunteers and most of the money. And while we did actually build a playground, it was a long, uphill battle that ended with mixed results at best.

The site lay smack on the boundary between two DC housing projects, each of which had its own bureaucracy that we had to navigate. There were two housing authority contacts and two separate resident groups, and the women who ran those groups couldn't stand each other. Each wanted its own playground that the people in the other building wouldn't be able to use, and they resented it whenever we tried to include both of them in the process. (One even asked why we couldn't build a gymnasium, instead of just a playground.)

During the planning phase, we realized that the community was not coming together, but we pressed ahead anyway. This all took place during the city council elections in Washington, and at one planning meeting, in which local kids showed up to help us design the playground, the woman who ran the resident association at Stoddert Terrace brought in the two candidates. They were obviously campaigning for votes, and the meeting quickly turned into a gripe session, with people yelling at each other. A community-built playground project here was clearly going to be a laborious process, but we were still so profoundly affected by the children who had died, in part because they'd had no safe place to play near their home, that we pushed onward.

When the work was finished, the lack of community involvement showed: Local residents didn't maintain the site the way other communities with KaBOOM! playgrounds do. It soon fell into disrepair, swallowed up by the blight around it, and we later thought that maybe we'd made a mistake. We'd succeeded in only half of our mission—a playground went up, but the community didn't coalesce around the project and the experience. It represented a simple transaction instead of a transformation. Our screening protocols nowadays would most likely preclude building in a place without some social capital, substantial infrastructure in place, and people willing to take on a project of this scope. Instead, we would build somewhere else, in a neighborhood that was more enthusiastic about it.

Mrs. Edelman talked to me about my frustrations, and some of the things she said to me about the Stoddert Terrace project stay with me to this day. "Even if the playground gets burned down next week, next month, or next year," she said, "for the time it was up, it was better for the kids than nothing." In other words, something that we considered only half a success represented a big step up for those kids. Even if the solution doesn't work long-term, it still represents a period in which their lives are a little better, and that's better than doing nothing.

▲ ■ ●

An 8-year-old girl followed Kate around all day on that build. She was endearing and in desperate need of adult attention, and she seemed at risk of falling through the cracks.

It was a weekday, and Kate asked, "Why aren't you in school?"

The girl said, "I'm tired, because I was up until 3 last night."

"What were you doing up so late?" Kate asked.

"Playing video games. I live with my grandmother, and she let me stay home from school."

It was hard to imagine how so many troubling elements could be packed into such a short conversation.

I think about that 8-year-old girl all the time, and how kids like her can miss out on a great place to play because of decisions we make from the comfort of our office. Kids rarely have a direct vote or voice in what happens to them, so adults and organizations tend to do things for them by proxy—and the proxy is usually their parents or the neighborhood in which they live. In some cases that means they'll continue to be punished, indirectly, because of the choices their parents make, and the cycle of dysfunction and poverty will repeat itself.

These are complicated issues, and there aren't any easy answers. Even today, with the benefit of a lot more experience in building communities and playgrounds, I don't think we have the perfect solution at KaBOOM!. You have to break the cycle for children, which means that sometimes you have to look past the actions of their parents and their neighborhood and do things that will benefit them directly.

The projects at Stoddert Terrace, in Belfast, and in Rwanda didn't fit with our approach, and people advised us against them. I came away from all three experiences with an understanding that some communities are so entrenched that the deep lines of division within them can't be healed—at least, not by the process of building a playground. Maybe they could be healed down the road, but if we tried to work with places like this before they were ready, we would fail.

Yet in a way, these experiences reinforced my belief in our strategy at KaBOOM!, that the most successful community projects don't come from the top down but rather from the grassroots up. We can do a lot at KaBOOM!, but only if we have people from local neighborhoods working shoulder to shoulder to reach their goal. Without that deeper level of engagement, it's not going to work. Handouts don't help. Even the power and resources of the U.S. government don't compare with what a small group of dedicated, passionate people can do in their own neighborhood by working together.

[9]

Play Matters

In early April 2002, I returned to Mooseheart. It wasn't yet 6 a.m., and the facility was still shrouded in darkness. I made the familiar left turn off Highway 31 and pulled out my ID to show the guard at the main gate by the field house. The man on duty had been a security guard back when I lived at Mooseheart. For a reason I never learned, he had a hook in place of one of his hands. He greeted me as an old friend, grasping my right hand with his left through the open window in a modified handshake and giving me a hearty "Welcome home, Darell!" Feeling like I was indeed returning home, I continued on into the center of campus. This wasn't my first return to Mooseheart—I had been back sporadically over the years, to see friends and to visit the Aireys—but this time was different. This time I wasn't just dropping in for a visit, I was returning with my organization, and we were coming to build a playground.

Back when I was kid at Mooseheart, in the 1970s and '80s, the play equipment had been serviceable but starting to show its age. There were actually two playgrounds: one on the edge of campus and another along State Row, near most of the residence halls. The closer one was more popular when we were kids, because it was so much easier to get to. It had separate stations, not the linked post-and-platform structure that's become popular in recent decades. There was a giant swing set with eight bays, a tiny house that five or six kids could fit into, monkey

bars, and a kind of gigantic treadmill, like a steel drum, with different
colored planks that formed steps along the outside. During my time at
Mooseheart, we used to climb on top and just run the hell out of it.

The more remote playground was gone by the mid-1990s, and in
2001 the school was forced to rip the second one out as well, leaving
the campus without any play structure at all. Why? Mooseheart has to
routinely get recertified under the Illinois state Department of Child
and Family Services, which has strict guidelines on playgrounds, and as
the thinking on safety requirements has evolved, more and more playgrounds are ruled out of compliance. On top of that, the school also
had insurance considerations—it was potentially liable for any child
who got hurt on a playground that was 30 or 40 years old.

Unfortunately, Mooseheart was forced to take the old stuff out
before it had money or a plan for how to replace it. This is actually a
dilemma many of our community partners face. At that time, the campus was going through a major upgrade of other facilities. Its steam
power plant and residence halls were being renovated, and the school
was getting a new multipurpose gym. Those projects were budgeted
and rolling forward, and there simply wasn't enough money left over to
replace the playground.

Thousands of schools around the country face the same situation
every day: When resources are scarce, how should they get distributed,
and where does play fall on that list of priorities? Unfortunately, many
people think of play as a luxury, not a necessity, so it often falls to the
bottom. Schools make do with outdated equipment or none at all.
The thinking is that kids are resilient, so they'll be fine in the end. This
raises some key questions: Is play really necessary? And if so, what purpose does it serve for kids?

▲ ■ ●

Many scientists have been asking those same questions lately, in an
attempt to figure out how play helps children develop, and a good

amount of scientific research shows that play isn't just running around and letting off steam. Important stuff is happening inside the brains and bodies of children while they do it. Exactly how it works still isn't totally understood. Research into play is seriously underfunded and has been under-respected in the scientific community. We know a little about its benefits, but there's far more that we don't know.

Part of the problem is that play is a broad subject; people have a tough time even defining it. Some call it "apparently meaningless activity" or say it's "the product of superfluous energy left over when people's primary needs are met." Others say it's what we're doing when we lose track of ourselves, which seems even more vague to me. Probably the best definition amounts to a list of descriptors: play is unstructured, freely chosen by the child, personally directed and motivated, active and engaging, and exploratory. There are also a lot of different types—like dramatic play, rough-and-tumble play, language play, and more. So it's understandable that there would be big gaps in the research.

Still, scientists have slowly begun to fill in some of those gaps. Over the past decade, thanks in part to medical-imaging technology, researchers have been learning more about the purpose of play. Stuart Brown, a psychiatrist and longtime researcher in the subject, has put together an organization called the National Institute for Play in Carmel Valley, California, which is attempting to connect the dots in terms of academic research in order to assemble a body of evidence about the importance of play. Two other groups pursuing the same goal are the Alliance for Childhood and The Association for the Study of Play.

The research as it relates to animals seems to have advanced sooner than that of children (similar to the way animal protection laws predated those for children). There's clearly a parallel in nature—you don't need to look too hard to see how frequently play shows up among animals, especially among mammals, some birds, and a few reptiles. Predator animals wrestle, from house cats to hyenas, tigers to terriers. Grass-eating prey animals like lambs and antelopes play at bolting—veering and sprinting away from invisible threats. Predator animals such as tigers practice hunting skills like stalking. They pounce on things, roll around with them, and bat them with claws. Even ants play-fight.

Most commonly this happens during adolescence, but some animals play as adults as well. Hippos do their version of synchronized swimming: back flips underwater. Ravens slide down a hillside covered with snow and then fly to the top to do it again. Bison run out onto the surface of a frozen lake and slide on all four hooves. In fact, if you wanted to *stop* animals from playing, in the lab or elsewhere, you'd have a hard time.

Of course, play is a bigger part of development for humans than any other species. There's evidence that children actually played in concentration camps during World War II. The big question is why. Nature tends to be efficient, and any wasteful activity quickly gets tossed, bred out over a few thousand generations. Play typically consumes anywhere from 2 percent to 15 percent of a young mammal's calories, which, during times when food is scarce, could be better used in some other way. So play must offer some advantages, or natural selection would have eliminated it.

One theory is that play is basically how children learn about the world and prepare to take their place in it. A 19th century German educator named Frederich Froebel, who is still one of the most influential thinkers on the subject, put it best: "Play is the work of children." It's how they prepare themselves to be grown-ups.

For most of the time that humans have inhabited the planet, there were no schools, no standardized tests, no organized teaching or classrooms or SAT prep courses. Even printed books are a pretty recent development, dating back roughly 600 years, which is nothing compared to more than 200,000 years of human history. Through most of that time, children learned how society worked through play. When a boy picked up a stick and pretended it was a spear, he was taking his first steps toward becoming a hunter. Today, kids hold wooden blocks up to their ears, pretending they're cell phones, but the principle is the same. These kids are trying out adult roles in order to learn how people function in the world.

In fact, that's a pretty good description of all play—it's a test run at life, without many of the consequences one faces as an adult. In much the way the play of young animals is related to what those animals will do once they've matured, for children, play is a stab at reality, a way for them to explore the world with the benefit of a safety net. This could explain why, in very broad terms, boys and girls play differently. Though there are many exceptions, in general, boys tend to tumble and wrestle and play with balls and other objects—practicing the skills their ancestors would have used in hunting—while girls typically play more social games that involve interacting through language and ceremony.

Play is key in social development, and it is also fundamental in brain formation. A newborn's brain is a mass of trillions of neurons. A small percentage of them get assigned to controlling involuntary things like heartbeat, reflexes, and body temperature, but the rest are just waiting for something to do. One science writer describes them as being like "chips in a computer before the factory preloads the software."

Many of these neurons aren't needed, and billions of them will die. But others will form synapses and connect to other neurons, becoming the paths for thought. Those synapses are formed by experience. That's the small-scale version of learning about the world by trying it.

When a baby is 2 months old, synapses start fusing in different parts of the brain on a pretty set schedule—physical movements at around 2 months (up until then, motions are mostly limited to sucking and involuntary reflexes), visual signals at 3 months, memories at around 9 months, and so on. Once babies are old enough to recognize physical objects, they will immediately start experimenting with them, which is the main way synapses get connected to each other.

"Play" at this stage is effectively a quest to gather sensory evidence (along with the language associated with that evidence) about the world and try to categorize it. Can the baby balance this block on top of that block? When the blocks are balanced, that success leads to a connection between neurons, which gets stronger through repetition. And that process happens at a fast pace in the first year of a baby's life— the brain scan of a 1-year-old will look more like that of an adult than of a newborn.

Even a child's babbling is a kind of experimental language play. All kids, regardless of what language they will come to speak, babble the same syllables. It's only through the reaction of the adults around them that babies learn the significance of certain sounds in their native languages. Just a few months after those specific synapses start to connect, that region of the brain will become mapped, and the language center of a baby who speaks Swedish will look completely different from that of a baby who speaks English.

The same principle applies to kids who are a little older. The period from age 2 up until about age 8 is when they play the most and—this probably isn't a coincidence—when synapses are being formed at the fastest rate. At this stage, the most active neurons are located in the cerebellum, which controls physical aspects like muscle control and balance. Play helps wire the parts of the brain that control movement.

As a child's muscle fibers mature, play—with its wide range of movements—helps establish the nerve signals to those muscles. It also makes sure that fast-twitch muscles (which are used for sprintlike movements) and slow-twitch muscles (used for slower, longer-lasting movements) form in the right proportion to each other.

How kids play also allows them to experience risk and the consequences of physical actions. It's where they get to push their physical limits (higher on the swing! faster on the merry-go-round!), which teaches them about danger and consequences. In adult life there are a lot of different types of risk—medical, financial, emotional. We protect kids from most of those, and for good reasons, but we may go too far in mitigating and eliminating risk, because managing through situations with risk is how children learn. Physical risk, as an example, is how they learn about the concept. *Reach for the next rung on the monkey bars, but if you don't make it, you might fall.*

In fact, you can make a strong argument that falling is part of the developmental process. It's only after being hurt that you develop some resilience and learn how to pick yourself up and try again (as opposed to never doing it again). In theory, hypervigilant parents could make sure that their child never skinned a knee and never suffered any minor injuries or physical hardships, but I don't think that kid would make it far as an adult, where the stakes are higher and where perseverance counts for a lot more.

The physical advantages of play are so deep-rooted that some of them don't kick in until years later. A few studies have shown that physical activity in young people helps prevent or delay the onset of diseases like high blood pressure and osteoporosis even when they're older.

And because play is a kind of physical learning, it turns out that kids who do a lot of it are better at what we think of as traditional learning, too. In one study, kids were broken into three groups. One was given a bunch of objects to play with (a pile of paper clips, a wooden board, a stack of paper towels, etc.). The second group was told to watch a researcher use those same objects and imitate him. A third was told to simply draw the objects. Next the kids were asked to come up with ideas for how those objects could be used. The group that had played with them came up with three times as many possibilities. Why? Play lets people become comfortable with unconventional solutions to problems. It expands the universe of options in a low-risk setting in which failure isn't a big deal.

The effects of play on a child's ability to learn—provided the child has sufficient access to it at the right stage of development—can be long lasting. In a well-known, long-running study, scientists at the University of North Carolina looked at different types of settings for children. Researchers there tested low-income kids from birth to age 5 in a highly stimulating environment with a lot of opportunities to play, compared to the standard home environment for those kids, with less room for play and more responsibilities due to a parent's work schedule. The researchers followed the kids as they grew up, all the way into their 20s. Those who played a lot in their early years ended up with improved reading levels and a greater likelihood of attending college. They even had higher IQ scores, averaging 105 compared to about 85.

That finding was supported by later research, the High/Scope Preschool Comparison Study, which followed 68 kids split between two programs at a young age. One was instruction heavy, and the other was play based. The IQ scores of all 68 kids initially rose, but by the time they hit age 15, the kids in classroom-heavy programs were more likely to show emotional problems and drop into special-education programs.

In fact, on top of the learning benefits of play come the social issues. There's a T-shirt with a phrase on it that comes from old report cards: *Plays well with others.* Irony aside, that's a big component of adult life. We're social creatures. And this is a fact kids first figure out on the playground, where they learn how to cooperate and compete, how to share, how to take turns, and what happens when they don't get these things right. They learn to experience conflict and solve disputes. They practice taking turns and playing fair, and they face consequences when they don't.

Much of this could conceivably be taught by parents, teachers, or other adults. But the lessons are longer lasting when kids figure them out on their own, and the social code of the playground deems these lessons self-reinforcing: *Share, or you don't get to play with us again.* A study of one elementary school found that the most liked kids tended to exhibit the most positive social behavior on the playground. They cooperated, they started games but could also follow if someone else took over, and they encouraged other kids by giving positive comments. The kids who were less well-liked didn't do any of these things. Another study, this one focusing on low-income, at-risk kids, found that those who were put into a play-heavy preschool became much more socialized, with effects lasting even into their 20s, and they had lower probabilities of job suspensions or criminal problems later in life.

Importantly, play helps kids behave better when they're back in the classroom. Why? They get to blow off a little steam, which makes them less antsy and more receptive to learning. This is self-evident to any parent who has cringed when the weather's bad because it means the kids are going to be cooped up inside all day. I can say without a doubt that I would not have made it through school without recess. And the science backs it up.

One recent study found that 8- and 9-year-olds who got at least one 15-minute break during the school day behaved better when they were back in the classroom. Another found that kids who play a lot tend to have lower levels of stress and anxiety as adolescents, and there's some evidence that it may help kids with ADHD lessen the severity of their symptoms. Play was even shown to help rehabilitate aggressive monkeys in the lab.

It's worth emphasizing that when these studies talk about play, they're really talking about *free* play, the unstructured kind, in which kids can do anything they want. They're not merely participating in games overseen by adults that have preset, unchanging rules. This type of play has its purpose, especially for older kids, and I want to be careful here about not setting up a false choice that says one type is better than another. In fact, there are benefits to all kinds of play. But for younger kids, the developmental benefits come from getting to make the rules and change them at will, so that there's enough variety for them to really engage. This is where they learn innovation, where they create a miniature version of the world and learn to master it, as a way to practice for the real world.

The bottom line? Play is pretty much exactly what young bodies were designed to do. And they won't become healthy adult bodies without it.

I should really add one last benefit of play, which can sometimes get lost amidst all the lab coats and clipboards—it's *fun*.

▲ ■ ●

About a year after the playground equipment had been ripped up at Mooseheart, I had a series of conversations in which the administrators there, including Mr. Airey, asked for my advice about getting it replaced. I was acting as a kind of informal consultant, putting them in touch with my contacts in the industry, but they hadn't made much progress. Money was still a big issue. And then I had another idea.

The fifth anniversary of KaBOOM! was coming up; we would commemorate it by building our 200th playground. We also had a kind of conference called the Playground Institute scheduled for the spring of 2002. We'd run these events before, dating back to the first one during that snowstorm in Wisconsin, where we gathered everyone involved in the 37 Kimberly-Clark projects. Over the following years, the workshops had become even more hands-on. We were no longer assembling samples of playground equipment in a cafeteria but an actual, permanent playground at a site nearby; this had become a standard part of the conference. Participants learned not only the latest ideas about playground construction but were also able to see those applied in the real world.

The event that spring was to take place in Oak Brook, Illinois, only about 30 minutes from Mooseheart. What if our 200th playground, the one associated with that conference, went up on campus? After all, I had a good playground during my time there, and now I could help provide the school with a new one. This was a bit unusual, in that I had such a direct connection to them, but in a very fundamental way Mooseheart fit the criteria of a KaBOOM! community partner—kids there needed a place to play and didn't have one.

It seemed like an opportunity to me. Who wouldn't jump at a chance like that, to return home to give something back? It was extremely poignant and meaningful to me to be able to give back to the community that had done so much for me.

I proposed the idea to Mr. Airey and the man who was then serving as superintendent, and they both jumped at it. The build would be part of the training, so the normal funding-partner model was changed up a bit, and the training participants would be replacing the corporate volunteers. Instead of finding a corporate funder for the project, the way

KaBOOM! usually works, I asked Playworld Systems, one of the big playground-equipment manufacturing companies and a longtime KaBOOM! partner, if they would donate some equipment. They generously agreed to offer $70,000 worth of equipment. This was far more in equipment than the typical KaBOOM! project. A few other vendors lined up as well—like the company that supplied mulch (technically known as engineered wood fiber), the wood chips that cover the ground as a safety surface for when kids fall.

We would have about 100 volunteers through the KaBOOM! Conference, and Mooseheart had a fleet of buses that we could use to transport them from Oak Brook. Kids and staff members at Mooseheart could do the community element—designing the playground and planning the construction process.

When I arrived before dawn on April 6, 2002, only a few people were on-site, getting things prepped. Over the next 2 hours, others began to filter in, and it began to feel a little bit like an episode of *This Is Your Life*. My sisters Dawn, Sherry, and Shirley (also Mooseheart alums) showed up for the day along with five of my nieces and nephews. Mr. Airey was there.

As the kids began to gather in the morning, I was struck by how much the student population of Mooseheart had changed since I was a student. In those days, the school had been more or less entirely white. In the years since, it had become far more ethnically balanced, with something like 30 or 40 percent of students now Hispanic or African American, a far better reflection of society as a whole.

Today, the students at Mooseheart have generally had far tougher family stories. For most of its history, including the time I attended, Mooseheart took in the children of more or less nuclear families, in which one or both parents had died. Back then, the biggest emotional issue for kids was grief. But since the 1990s, the facility has taken in children with much more complicated backgrounds—broken homes, parents with drug problems, kids who've been kicked out of their houses. A few Mooseheart children have come all the way from Africa, after watching their parents die in civil war massacres.

Because of these experiences, kids and staff there today still deal with grief along with far more complex emotional issues, meaning the discipline and standards have had to evolve as well. I felt proud that the school had opened its doors in that way. Mooseheart is an evolving institution. It's a much different community than when I attended, but it appropriately reflects the changing social problems of our country.

As I looked around the campus that morning, I also noticed all the physical changes that had occurred. The hospital was gone, the auditorium was gone, and Ohio Hall had been torn down. Once-vacant spaces were now full, and other buildings looked completely different than they had during my time there.

Nowhere was this more evident than at the school. Kids in all grades at Mooseheart, kindergarten through 12th, attend school in a single building, complete with a new multipurpose gym. When I attended, we all used to walk back to the residence halls for lunch and then return to the school once we were done eating. Now there was a cafeteria. I teased the current students and administrators, saying, "These kids have it easy." But I thought it was awesome that the school hadn't settled—the kids there were getting the best of everything.

By 8 a.m. about 200 people had arrived. I climbed up the mulch pile and took the microphone. "Everyone wants to be able to do something for their own hometown," I said. "This is a great opportunity for me to be able to give back, and I'm glad you're all helping me do that, and now you will have the tools and inspiration to do the same thing for your own community."

And then we got to work.

The weather that day turned out to be absolutely perfect. April can be tricky in Chicago, but it was cloudless and cool, just about ideal conditions to build a playground. Because Playworld Systems had been so generous, the site would be about twice the size of a typical playground. I wish I could say that I worked hard that day, but really I was pulled in a thousand directions. The administrators took me around to meet with students, and they said, in every single introduction, "This isn't just another guest. This is someone who grew up here, played on those sports fields, slept in those dorms, and has gone on and look at what he's doing now. This is an alum of this place."

The build was more like a party than anything else. Because so many kids were too young to work on the playground, we had other activities for them. In the years since then, we're tried to use this as an opportunity to have the kids learn about service by taking on some kind of small-scale community project. But back then we had an inflatable house called a Jumping Jack, cotton candy, a popcorn maker, and face-painting for the youngest kids. During my tour of the new gym, I jumped into a game of dodgeball—one of the favorites from my childhood.

When it came time to cut the cake, someone realized that it actually had the wrong number written in the icing. Instead of "200th" playground, it said "2,000th." So there was a mad dash while someone found a knife and scraped off the extra zero. (This was pretty funny, and I took it as a good omen. As I write this book, we're getting ready to celebrate the actual 2000th build in the spring of 2011—1,800 builds in the 9 years since that day at Mooseheart!)

After it was all over, the local Moose chapter from Batavia, Illinois, came in for a corn boil—a giant cookout of corn and burgers and baked beans, and mounds and mounds of coleslaw. By then most of the conference participants had left to catch flights home. It had been a long day for me, but I wanted to stay a few more hours. The playground was gleaming. It felt like one of the most meaningful things that I had even accomplished.

[10]

It Only Takes a Single Spark
to Start a Fire

I was on a Northwest flight into Gulfport, Mississippi, just a few weeks after Hurricane Katrina had torn through the Gulf Coast. The flight was almost empty, and no one talked during the trip. I couldn't help wondering why the other people on the plane were going to the Gulf. At the time it was the only flight into the region—connecting through Memphis, one arrival a day—and I spent most of it looking out the window.

I couldn't see how bad the damage really was until the plane started to descend. As the plane's engines slowed, I saw blue tarps covering damaged roofs. At first it was just a few here and there, then more, and pretty soon they started to outnumber the intact roofs.

As the plane got closer to Gulfport, I saw something even more ominous: Beyond a certain point, the blue tarps disappeared. That made no sense. The destruction was clearly getting worse the closer we got to the coast—I could see that more and more houses were damaged. Had the relief workers run out of tarps?

Then I figured it out. The blue tarps simply weren't needed this close to the center of the storm's damage. Along the coastline, there weren't very many homes left to protect.

▲ ■ ●

Like some people, I had initially considered Katrina a distant issue—a tragedy that affected others but wasn't likely to impact my life. At most, it was a personal inconvenience. Kate's parents were celebrating their 50th wedding anniversary with a cruise. All five of their children and their children's families came, and we were to depart from Port Canaveral, which is on the Gulf side of Florida, near Orlando. Because of the approach of Hurricane Katrina, the ship was diverted, and we had to take a 5-hour bus ride from Orlando to Fort Lauderdale to meet it, something we considered a major hassle.

During the cruise, we followed news of the hurricane, and as the storm made landfall, there was a sense that a major disaster had been averted, at least in New Orleans. But then the waters kept rising, the levees ruptured, and all hell broke loose.

By the time we were back in Washington, DC, it was clear that the disaster in the Gulf Coast was of Biblical proportions. The storm surge destroyed a 90-mile strip of the coastline like a massive snowplow. Hundreds were dead. Towns were wiped out. Riverboat casinos in Biloxi had washed all the way up onto Highway 90, a few hundred yards inland. Thousands of homes were not merely blown down. They were blown *away*. The only signs that they once existed were crumbled foundations and driveways that led nowhere.

There was a tremendous need for assistance and, like others around the country, I wanted to help. Yet I wasn't sure whether KaBOOM! could get involved in any meaningful way—at least not right away. Before we can get communities organized, we need basic infrastructure in place, like electricity and running water. Playgrounds are time-intensive projects, usually involving 3 to 6 months of planning, and the people who were suddenly made homeless by the storms didn't seem likely to be able to commit that much time.

But a few weeks after Hurricane Katrina, we heard from a woman named Ginny Reynolds. Ginny was born and raised in Bay St. Louis,

Mississippi, a tiny town on the Gulf of Mexico about 20 miles west of Gulfport. When Hurricane Katrina hit, she was living in Connecticut, but she had vivid memories of an earlier storm, Hurricane Camille, which battered Bay St. Louis back in 1969, when Ginny was 9 years old.

Camille was one of the worst storms in U.S. history, even more powerful than Hurricane Katrina. Category 5 hurricanes almost never make landfall, but Hurricane Camille slammed into the coast with winds of about 200 miles per hour, and it hit in a more concentrated area than Hurricane Katrina—as Ginny put it, "Right straight over our home." Her family rode out the storm at a small hotel owned by someone who worked at her father's boatyard. When the walls of the hotel started coming down, they moved to a different building—the main house of the employee—where the walls remained intact but the windows still blew in. It was the first time she had ever seen her father truly afraid. Still, she considered herself lucky: Many of the children she knew from school were home when the storm hit, and some of them died.

After Camille, it took about 10 years to repair Bay St. Louis. People in town figured out a way to go on. A tugboat that had washed up onshore was turned into a gift shop. But locals, especially Ginny Reynolds, never forgot. Looking back years later, she remembers being infuriated that the local playground was never rebuilt, that the kids of the region became an afterthought in the wake of the storm.

The perception—which is still widespread today, though just as wrong—is that kids are resilient during major crises and that when parents have a lot of other worries, they can't spend time thinking about where their children are going to play. "They'll be fine," the thinking goes. Ginny remembers the vast debris piles becoming their playground after the storm. Massive live oaks lay across yards like beached whales, and the kids built tree houses in them. It was all extremely unsafe. "Stepping on nails was an everyday occurrence," she told me.

When Katrina hit, Ginny recognized that it gave her a chance to right a long-standing wrong. She had learned about us from a childhood friend who had organized and built a playground in Massachusetts and come across KaBOOM! during her research. Ginny sat down and wrote us a letter. Would we help her build a playground in Bay St. Louis? I communicated my doubts to her, but Ginny was persistent, and I agreed to at least go take a look.

▲ ■ ●

She met me at the airport. Ginny has a soft southern accent and quick sense of humor that tends toward the ironic. As I had already learned and would have proven to me over and over again, she also has a no-nonsense approach and can-do, will-do attitude that can move mountains. There were no rental cars to be found, but Ginny's father still lived near Bay St. Louis and had a spare that she borrowed. We drove west from Gulfport, through towns like Long Beach and Pass Christian and Waveland. All day we slalomed around debris or around parts of the road that had been washed away. There were a lot of places we simply couldn't get to. New Orleans, another 45 minutes to the west, was out of the question—it was still closed down by the National Guard, and half of the four-lane Interstate 10 bridge had washed away into the Gulf.

An eerie silence had fallen over the whole region. People were numb, crying, or both. Trees were stripped of leaves and peppered with sheets and blankets and clothing that had snagged on branches. A few homes were still standing, but they were filled with muck. Ginny's family home—which they had rebuilt after Hurricane Camille—had been reduced to a handful of bricks. In fact, many homes, especially near the water, were completely gone. No debris, nothing. They had been knocked down and dragged out to sea by the storm surge.

The site of the old playground in Bay St. Louis was in City Hall Park, a few blocks from the Gulf. The entire park was covered in wreckage, including giant branches, cars, and parts of buildings. It looked like a scrap pile, 40 to 50 feet high in places. I remember thinking, "Here? This is where you want the playground? And when is this supposed to get done?"

Already you could see a big difference between private-sector and public-sector responses to the storm. Blocks from City Hall Park, a set of privately owned railroad tracks runs across Saint Louis Bay, the large body of water that separates Bay St. Louis from Waveland, the next town to the east. The rail company that owned that bridge started repairing it immediately, and it was functional again in about 6 months. Meanwhile, the auto bridge across the bay, the one used by ordinary citizens, got caught up in the post-storm bureaucracy. The debate went round and round. Rebuild it here? Two lanes? Four lanes? It would ultimately take 2 years for the new bridge to go up. If something as crucial as a bridge got handled this way, it was clear that parks and playgrounds would be far, far down on the list of local priorities.

If Ginny had lived there during Hurricane Katrina, she probably wouldn't have been able to devote much attention to a playground, either. She would have had bigger concerns on her mind, like finding a place to live. But because she had moved to Connecticut, she had the resources to fight to get us involved. We say at KaBOOM!: "It only takes a single spark to start a fire." Sometimes people look at a situation and say, *That's just the way things are.* People get overwhelmed by the depth of a problem, especially if it doesn't have any obvious fix. But to solve that problem, you need to think of all that pent-up energy as fuel. The worse a situation is, the more primed it is for a single act to galvanize.

This comes up again and again in our work at KaBOOM!. Primarily we work in communities in need, and in most cases that stems from an economic deficiency, but in the Gulf region it was more of an infrastructure deficiency. Still, the principles are the same—fixing a problem requires some ignition. It needs a spark, and anyone can be that spark. It's all too easy to remain passive and think that someone else is going to fix things. Instead, people need to step forward and be the sparks that ignite change. For the Gulf region, Ginny Reynolds was that spark.

▲ ■ ●

By the end of that trip, I realized that Ginny was right and that KaBOOM! had to get involved. Anyone would. After bearing witness to what I saw on that trip, you couldn't *not* get involved. Even though I was convinced, I still had to convince others, and that's where I ran into roadblocks. "A playground?" people asked, once I was back in Washington. "The people in the Gulf don't need a playground. They need two-by-fours. They need generators." We have very solid relationships with our corporate funders, but when I called them to ask if they'd contribute money to the project, they all felt the same way. "It's too early for a playground," they said. "Those people need to get back on their feet first."

A few said that we should build something in New Orleans, as that was where much of the media coverage had been focused. I didn't rule that out, but I knew that the storm had left a 90-mile swath of destruction along the Mississippi coast and that those towns needed just as much help. We also tried getting money from foundations, most of which declined (some politely, a few somewhat curtly, and one that actually insinuated that KaBOOM! was trying to capitalize on the storm to advance our own cause; I still get livid when I think about that conversation). In all, it seemed that everyone was projecting what they thought was needed in the Gulf region, instead of listening to the local people on the ground.

Finally we decided to put up our own money. KaBOOM! playgrounds typically cost about $75,000, and more ambitious designs can go into the hundreds of thousands. We had just raised some unrestricted funds through a nonprofit contest that Amazon.com had sponsored to celebrate its 10th anniversary, and our staff made heroic efforts to ensure that we got as much money as we could, reaching out to everyone they knew and even making personal donations themselves. The funds were unrestricted, so we could use them wherever we saw the greatest need. I made another planning trip to Bay St. Louis around

Thanksgiving, and we scheduled the construction for December 17, 3½ months after Hurricane Katrina.

Some people who hadn't been to the Gulf wondered if this was too close to Christmas. In normal circumstances, it might have been a challenge to pull off a build so close to the Christmas holiday. People just didn't realize how much had been lost and how irrelevant a concern about trying not to impact the holiday season was for the residents of Bay St. Louis. No one who had been hit by Hurricane Katrina was going to have a traditional Christmas. Few stores were even open by this point. People were still eating meals in the Salvation Army tent or at "Katrina's Kitchen," a volunteer program set up in the washed-out Wal-Mart parking lot that was feeding 2,000 to 3,000 people a day. Most likely the people of Bay St. Louis would stop working for a few hours on Christmas, put down their crowbars and shovels, and say another prayer of thanks that they were still alive.

Jo Gilmore, a woman Ginny had grown up with, still lived in the area and agreed to work on the project. Everyone in Bay St. Louis was focused on reducing the misery, and Ginny and Jo came at the problem in another way: They focused on creating joy.

As with all KaBOOM! playgrounds, we asked local kids what they wanted to see on the site. This time things were a little different. The meeting was held on a large slab of a fractured tennis court, surrounded by a fence that was falling down. Ginny and Jo put a table out and brought some kids over from a nearby school. We got some heartbreaking design elements. Almost all of the kids asked for roofs to cover the playground, and others asked that it be built high off the ground so it wouldn't get flooded in future storms. One wanted a sign that said, "No Katrina allowed." Together we decided on the major elements, and they chose their colors—purple, teal, and beige. And then the planning got under way.

Jo helped us tremendously during this phase. Like Ginny, Jo had vivid memories of Hurricane Camille blowing through Bay St. Louis back in 1969. Her family rode that storm out at her father's law firm in town, but when they returned to their house, it was gone. Nothing. (Her parents later moved to Kiln, Mississippi, where their new home was reduced to a shell by Katrina.)

As for Jo and her husband, Tim, they lived about 10 miles north, in a town called Diamondhead, Mississippi. Their house was elevated—they parked their cars underneath—but it was right on the bayou, and the storm surge came up as high as their first floor, ravaging the bottom half of their home. Jo was extremely busy in the months following the storm, trying to find shelter for her family. She couldn't get a FEMA trailer, because the government was only putting those on streets that had electricity and running water, and their section of Diamondhead had no functioning plumbing. Ultimately they bought a smaller house nearby, which they lived in while gutting and renovating their original home.

Tim works for a real estate company and travels around the country, so he theoretically could work from anywhere. His company offered to set the family up a few hundred miles north, in Alabama, where they could have left the whole mess behind and started a new life. "We thought hard about it," Jo told me, "but we realized that this region was going to need a lot of help, and we wanted to be part of the rebuilding effort."

I thought that was incredibly courageous—that these people could set aside their own self-interest to do the hard work necessary to put the community back together. In the aftermath of Hurricane Katrina, we would see other people make these kinds of decisions again and again. Sure, some people left. Many of them didn't have an alternative. But a lot of people stayed, not merely to rebuild their own homes but to rebuild their communities, both physically and emotionally.

Jo became the on-the-ground person for the playground project in Bay St. Louis, and she lobbied for it at every opportunity. For the first months after the storm, the county held weekly meetings to make announcements about relief efforts, how services were going to be restored and the like. Jo attended every meeting, asking for a few minutes to talk about the playground project.

"At first some people at the meetings were not receptive," Jo told me. "People would look at me and say, 'Why would you bother with this? It's such a low priority. I'm living in a tent, and you want me to worry about a playground?' But gradually they started to come around. My husband, Tim, and I thought it was the kind of thing that could really change people's attitudes about the cleanup, and eventually it did. Especially as it got closer and started to become real. I would bring the plans with me to these meetings, and people really started to get into it. There was absolutely no new construction going on, and when people saw the plans, their eyes just lit up."

▲ ■ ●

We didn't know what to expect on the morning of December 17. We were hoping to get 200 volunteers, but it would be understandable if we couldn't hit that number. Unlike typical KaBOOM! builds, where we get about half of the volunteers from the corporation that funded the project, the Bay St. Louis playground would be built entirely with labor from the local community. Thousands of people in town were adjusting to living in FEMA trailers (where many would remain for years) or, worse yet, waiting for one to arrive and driving 100 to 150 miles a day back and forth to their damaged homes. The day was rainy and just above freezing that morning. That kind of weather deters some volunteers from a typical build, and I quietly wondered if a low turnout would be interpreted by some skeptics that a playground was not a priority as the residents of Bay St. Louis went about rebuilding.

At least the site was ready. In the previous few weeks, the person who ran the local parks and recreation department (a one-man staff, Jimmy Loiacano) recruited volunteers to remove all the debris from the site, and by that morning, it had been cleared to the ground. In fact, the construction site was *raked*. It was pristine.

People started showing up at 6:30 a.m., and by 8 we had 200 volunteers on the site, which is a very solid number under any circumstance.

An hour later we had 400, and during the course of the day, more than 600 people would turn out. There were lines at the registration tables, which provided the first opportunity of the day for old friends to hug each other and begin to get caught up with one another's lives since the storm. I wasn't sure we'd have enough tools, but many of the volunteers showed up with the tools they'd been using for weeks to gut their homes or clean the debris from the foundations. We later learned that a lot of people who had left town after the storm, living temporarily in nearby cities like Jackson or Baton Rouge and wondering if they should leave Bay St. Louis for good, returned home that day specifically to help build the playground.

Jo Gilmore was there, of course, though we didn't find out until later that she'd gotten no sleep the night before. Her two sons had been in a car accident. Another kid had to be airlifted because of a concussion and some broken ribs. Their truck was totaled. At 1 in the morning, literally hours before construction was supposed to start on the playground, Jo and Tim were in a hospital waiting room. Once they got word that everyone was going to be okay, Jo drove 45 minutes to a Krispy Kreme in Gulfport to pick up a few hundred doughnuts for the playground volunteers, went home to take a quick shower, and showed up at the project on time. She could have handed that responsibility off to someone else—most people would have—but she didn't. She took care of it herself.

Mayor Eddie Favre, who'd been governing Bay St. Louis for more than 15 years, made a giant batch of his famous jambalaya, and members of the city council served it to volunteers. When we realized how many people they'd need to feed, they went home, cobbled together whatever items they had, and made another batch. A group of kids from the nearby school came by to sing to us—songs they had written just for the day. Then another choral group came to the site, singing Christmas carols. They had come all the way from New York City because they remembered all the wonderful volunteers who had flocked to the city to help out after 9/11, and they wanted to return the favor in another part of the country that needed help, so they had come down to the Gulf.

Another friend of Jo and Ginny's from the neighborhood, named Mike Maggio, came as well. Mike had left Mississippi years prior and become a judge, but he'd driven nearly 8 hours from his home in Conway, Arkansas, to work on the playground. He brought his son, Nick, who was 7 years old. Normally we don't allow kids on the site during construction, because it can be dangerous. But Nick struck me as particularly focused for his age and was earnest in his desire to be helpful and accomplish something important. He seemed to grasp the poignancy of the impact of this storm. And on this build, frankly, there were no rules. Nick was mixing concrete, fetching wheelbarrows, helping out everywhere. He's in a lot of the photos, a small bundle of energy and a reminder of why the project was so important.

Ultimately, we didn't have enough jobs for all those volunteers, but people spread out to pick up trash and debris along the railroad tracks nearby. Or they fixed up the gazebo in the park. Or they simply danced. Many people told me that although they had known who survived the storm and who hadn't, many of the families of Bay St. Louis hadn't seen each other in the nearly 4 months since then. The playground project was the first time that they'd had a chance to reconnect and the first real reason they'd had to smile and laugh. There was a lot of crying as well. And the project gave all those families the hope that they could rebuild.

At the end of the day, we had a beautiful playground with four swings, a slide that could handle three kids at once, a miniature teahouse, a sandbox, and even a zip line. It was the first permanent structure to be built in the town since the storm had hit, and some speculate that it was the first permanent structure to go up along the entire Gulf Coast. Everyone in Bay St. Louis had a tremendous amount of work to do to put their lives back together, but they set that aside to tap into their shared sense of history and rebuild a space for the community. That park became a central hub and gathering place for people in town—not only during the cleanup but even to this day.

Just a week after construction, many Bay St. Louis residents spent Christmas Day at the playground, grilling their holiday dinner and watching their kids and grandkids have fun. They would later celebrate Easter there as well. No doubt, the park was better than a FEMA trailer, but the effect was greater than that. The park became the place to socialize with friends and family, and the place to celebrate the sense of accomplishment and possibility instead of focusing on the heavy lifting that was ahead.

Something else significant happened that cold, drizzly day in December 2005. Standing on the playground site, a small gem surrounded by devastation, I felt like the Bay St. Louis project would be another pivotal juncture in the evolving history of KaBOOM!. In the weeks leading up to that project, I'd talked to my senior management team and board of directors about doing more for the Gulf region. Some people were hesitant, for understandable reasons. The project was harder than I thought it would be—logistics in the Gulf were tremendously complicated, and fund-raising was another big hurdle. If we wanted to do another playground in the region, neither of these was likely to get easier.

Yet now that I'd witnessed how meaningful it was to people in the wake of Hurricane Katrina, I knew we had to come back. The community spirit can overcome a lot of practical problems, if you organize people around the right goal. We would build more—I didn't know precisely how, but that had never stopped me before.

So during the small ceremony at the end of the day in Bay St. Louis, I stepped to the microphone and told the crowd that we were committed to helping rebuild the towns along the Gulf Coast. Not just with one playground, and not even with 10. Instead, I said, we would build 100.

▲ ■ ●

In the end, KaBOOM! didn't build 100 playgrounds—we built more than 140 (and counting) across the post-Katrina Gulf. We called the program Operation Playground, and we mobilized about 25,000 volunteers in all. (One of them once asked, "Does KaBOOM! do levees?") I consider our work in that region among our greatest accomplishments as an organization. It certainly had the greatest impact in terms of transforming towns.

By the end of 2010, we had raised $9.9 million from corporations like Motorola, ING Direct, and Starbucks along with other organizations like the Marriott Foundation, Fannie Mae, and NBA Cares. Jim Barksdale, the former COO of Netscape, lives in Mississippi and became a major contributor as well. He heard about our work in the region, and he called me and said, "There's a lot of jokers down here, but you get stuff done. How much could you get done with $500,000?" His pledge came in the form of matching funds, and we had to raise the initial capital outside the Gulf.

We did direct-mail appeals nationwide, and I talked to everyone I could—hundreds of corporations and philanthropic groups. More than 1,000 individual donations came in. A Brownie troop in New England did chores for a month to raise money for Operation Playground, and middle- and high-school students in Massachusetts did a 24-hour walk-athon to raise $10,000. A Maryland teenager asked his bar mitzvah guests to help him raise $15,000. We were able to raise the $500,000 to secure the matching funds, and Mr. Barksdale later pledged an additional $1 million.

On the 1-year anniversary of the hurricane, we built 10 playgrounds in 4 days. Playworld Systems donated $250,000 worth of equipment for those 10 communities. I was in my hotel room one of those nights and turned to WLOX, the local ABC affiliate in southern Mississippi. The station had given us great coverage and helped spread the word about our projects to recruit volunteers. That night one of the newscasters said, "KaBOOM! is at it again. They're putting up better playgrounds than we had before Katrina."

Our 50th project in the Gulf got a lot of attention—it was at a school in New Orleans, and *Live with Regis and Kelly* showed up to cover it. Marge and Reg Morkin, a couple who have become very dear friends and who are the owners of the guesthouse in Bay St. Louis where I and some Boomers stayed during our first project in the region, were two of the many volunteers from earlier projects who came to help out at our 50th. Reg even got to shovel mulch with Regis.

First Lady Laura Bush participated in our third Operation Playground project at Hancock North Central Elementary School in Kiln, Mississippi. This was particularly meaningful in that two First Ladys from consecutive administrations were demonstrating their support to our cause by participating in KaBOOM! builds. Mrs. Bush was extremely warm and gracious. When it was time for her to go, her team was pushing her to leave to get to the airport. They all got in their cars, and as the motorcade was exiting the school, they turned a corner and Mrs. Bush saw a large number of the kids lining the fence along the back of the school, hoping to catch a glimpse of her. She had the motorcade pull over and got out, greeted the kids, and walked the fence line.

We even had a wedding during Operation Playground. In early June 2008, at a build in Picayune, Mississippi, two volunteers stopped construction—very briefly—and got married in a short civil ceremony. It was a highlight of the day, and it made the project even more emotional than usual.

Mike Maggio and his son, Nick, who had helped at our first Gulf playground, kept on helping after that. The two drove all the way from Conway, Arkansas, for seven more KaBOOM! builds, and Mike built another playground in Conway on his own, without any assistance from us.

We know how important play is, and we'd never seen it illustrated more vividly than in the Gulf. The projects clearly served a therapeutic function for kids whose lives had been turned upside down by Hurricane Katrina. After our build in Kiln (the project Mrs. Bush had attended), the school's principal wrote us a letter: "The psychologists in our area have been doing studies on kids in the schools in our district, and they reported seeing things that you generally only see in adults. This includes things like thoughts about suicide, murder, and other types of violence—truly terrible things. But, they also reported that they didn't see those things in the kids at North Central Elementary and they attribute a lot of that to the playground—having a safe place to play, something new to look forward to, and really just the opportunity to be a kid."

We heard this again and again from parents who told us about the acute need for their kids to have someplace to play. In fact, KaBOOM! was given an award from the National Association of School Psychologists, in recognition of the contribution we made toward play and children's health in the region. That association even funded another playground project with us, at Live Oak Elementary School in New Orleans.

Tony Recasner, principal of S. J. Green Charter School in New Orleans, credits the KaBOOM! playground as being the key change that brought other big upgrades to his school. S. J. Green was a relatively new school—it operated in an existing high school building, so there was no playground on the property. Tony couldn't change things inside the school as quickly as he wanted, but he thought a bright, beautiful playground, visible to everyone who passed by, would make a statement that this was a place for young children. The storm complicated those plans.

Tony also inquired about creating a partnership with Edible Schoolyard. That's the venture launched by chef Alice Waters of Chez Panisse in Berkeley, California. Edible Schoolyard is a comprehensive program in which students maintain a garden on school grounds, and the administration integrates food into classroom lessons and even changes the lunch menu to incorporate products from the garden. The goal is to get kids more connected with their food and to develop healthy eating habits at a young age.

Alice had never before replicated her Edible Schoolyard program. She was keenly aware of how much work the program takes and the incredible commitment needed at several levels to make it successful. Initially she was skeptical that Tony would be able to pull it off, especially given the devastated condition of the school grounds following Katrina. But after the KaBOOM! playground went up on the property in May 2006, she traveled to the school again and changed her mind, based on the work he'd done with us. As a result, Tony's school became the first affiliate Edible Schoolyard in the country. He hasn't stopped there—Tony recently created a partnership with the NFL's community outreach program and put in a half-football field with artificial turf.

KaBOOM! built the 100th Operation Playground project on June 14, 2008, back in Bay St. Louis, at MLK Park, a few miles from the place where it all began, and we invited volunteers and community leaders from all 100 of the projects in the region. Jo Gilmore was there, and Ginny Reynolds and Mayor Eddie and the Morkins. The day became a celebration—a lot of hard work, a lot of joy, and a lot of laughter.

▲ ■ ◆

One of the most personal builds we have done was at the Geraldine Boudreaux Elementary School in New Orleans. The build was in memory of Jeff Prout, who had attended the school. He was one of the casualties of Katrina. His mom, Linda, has been on 30-plus KaBOOM! builds and is one of those very special people who walk the earth. Linda and her husband, Lee, sponsored the building of the playground in April 2009. In August 2010 I accompanied Linda to her son's playground, and we released butterflies in his memory and sat on a bench enjoying the moment. Of all the meaningful moments associated with our work in the Gulf, this is one of the high points for me.

In spite of all we accomplished, anyone who's been to New Orleans recently and ventured out of the tourist areas knows that the region has still not fully recovered, and the recent oil spill has only made things worse. There remain streets in the Lower Ninth Ward that look deserted, filled with abandoned homes and overgrown properties. Yet the story is long gone from the front pages of newspapers, and most of those organizations have moved on. Immediately after Hurricane Katrina, many nonprofits and other groups flocked to the city and swore that they'd keep working until it was completely back to normal. They did a lot of good work, but then they packed up and left.

The citizens of the Gulf regularly shared with me the worry that they would be forgotten. I had taken it as a personal challenge. How could we be different? Could we sustain a presence building playgrounds until we had created enough great places to play within walking distance for all the kids of the Mississippi and Louisiana Gulf Coast? We would certainly try. To help people remember, we printed new purple shirts for all of our project managers. On the back they read, "We Have Not Forgotten" in bold orange letters across the top. Underneath, they said "Operation Playground." The Boomers wore them while building playgrounds in communities across the country. People would ask, "What's Operation Playground?" And we would have the opportunity to tell them about the continued need in the Gulf.

About 2 years after Katrina, Kate and I spent a weekend visiting some KaBOOM! playgrounds in the region to see how the sites were holding up and what kind of use they were getting. It was a punishingly hot August weekend. We started at the furthest point east, Pascagoula, and then doubled back to Biloxi, where we had put up a playground in a place called Beck Park. I had received a letter after that project was finished from a local family who had lived for decades near the park. After Katrina they had decided to sell, but when they saw that the local playground was being rebuilt, in the site where their children and grandchildren had played, they decided to stay and help the town rebuild.

The play space was in great shape—clean, no litter, no structural issues with the equipment, no graffiti—and there was more good news. A group called Architecture for Humanity had come in and designed a police substation for the park, in what had previously been a bathroom, complete with solar panels on the roof. Architecture for Humanity also built a shaded sitting area made out of reclaimed wood. And Hands On Network, a national volunteer group, had worked with volunteers in the neighborhood to put in community gardens—small plots where families could plant vegetables and flowers. It all looked fantastic.

At Miramar Park, another site in Biloxi, the equipment was also in great shape and we were delighted to see how it was being used: A huge family reunion was under way, with kids running and climbing on the playground, and a picnic table loaded with potato salad, hot dogs, and watermelon.

From Biloxi we worked our way west along Highway 90, stopping at each of the coastal towns that dot that route. And with each playground we saw, we realized that similar things were happening at these KaBOOM! sites. All along the trip, we saw the parks and playgrounds being put to the best possible use, as local gathering places where adults could gather and children could play.

At a park in Gulfport, there were two birthday parties going on at the playground. Cars were parked for blocks away. Before the involvement of KaBOOM!, the space had been referred to as Druggie Depot, because for years it consisted of nothing but a crumbling basketball court and a picnic table where dealers would hang out. Now it was a focal point in the community and a safe place for kids and families.

At War Memorial Park, a beautiful, tranquil space filled with hundred-year-old live oak trees, in Pass Christian—a Mississippi town just across the bridge from Bay St. Louis—the playground that had been obliterated by the hurricane had had swings that were oriented so kids could look out onto the beach and the breaking waves of the Gulf. When we came in after the storm and led this Design Day for the project, we asked the local kids and parents what they wanted in a newly rebuilt playground. They were adamant about the new swings being oriented the same way. Upon our return visit there, we saw kids enjoying the view.

We finished the weekend at two sites in New Orleans. Joe Brown Park was packed with families. At Taylor Park, located in the Central City neighborhood, a full-scale block party was in swing, one of the biggest events we'd seen all day. People were playing softball and cooking on grills. Someone had put together a crawfish boil. And most important, dozens and dozens of kids were running around on the playground. It was a complete celebration of life.

The weekend of playground revisits underscored that the playgrounds were a central element in getting those places reestablished. They were part of the comeback, and play wasn't a luxury that could be put on the shelf until later—it was essential.

Though that day represented a small victory in a larger struggle, as we drove through the Gulf, I couldn't help but feel proud. All those places—entire parks filled with families and neighbors and laughing children. They were communities that had been brought back from the brink.

[11]

It Starts with a Playground

Mixing concrete is a hard, messy job. Each bag weighs 80 pounds, and we typically go through 280 in a given day. Sometimes volunteers have some construction experience, but on one build awhile back, many of the people mixing concrete were absolute beginners who had never even seen a bag of the stuff before. I could tell they needed help.

We're ready for this. After all, even if you're experienced at construction, you'll likely be learning things on a KaBOOM! Build Day, because odds are that you've never built a playground before. Part of the success of our model is that people are randomly assigned to tasks, so you get folks outside their respective comfort zones and doing things that maybe they have never done before. We expect this, and we have a system in place to ensure quality.

In about 45 minutes of training, build captains learn enough to oversee the various projects. At every build, at least one professional installer from the playground equipment company supervises construction and ensures that it meets the manufacturer's specifications so the warranty will be in place. We also have two project managers on site who move around and supervise the entire series of events and all the work.

Simply lifting something that weighs 80 pounds off a pallet and into a wheelbarrow is more than most people can manage on their own, which means they have to team up and start working in pairs. Next, volunteers have to split the bag open, mix the gray, chalky dust with water from a hose, and stir the resulting slurry with a hoe, like mixing a giant batch of cake batter. A concrete wheelbarrow holds two bags plus water, and when it's fully mixed, the whole load weighs more than 170 pounds. Those wheelbarrows have to be pushed over to where the playground is going up, navigating around volunteers hauling mulch, and then the concrete gets dumped into the hole where each component is being built.

That process has to happen over and over again throughout the day—for a typical playground, it happens 140 times. Because this is so much work, volunteers usually figure out that it's most efficient to get a system going. The rhythm of the concrete team plays a key role in ensuring that the holes get filled on time, the play structure itself can go up on schedule, and everything else in these massive, 1-day projects can keep moving forward.

On one build years ago, I immediately noticed that the concrete team hadn't figured out the right sequence for the steps, and many of them were standing around, unsure of what to do next. The hose was leaking, turning the ground into a mud bog and making the few loaded wheelbarrows that much harder to push. And for the rare batch that was being completed, the volunteers were being sent back when they got to the holes because the concrete hadn't been mixed correctly and was too soupy. Concrete that is too wet takes too long to dry, jeopardizing the playground's structural integrity, a risk we can never take.

The clock was ticking. We were due to finish the entire project in an hour and a half, and we still had a lot of bags of concrete sitting untouched on the pallet. To the relief of the build captain, and frankly the whole team, I took charge. I was in a purple KaBOOM! T-shirt, so they immediately trusted that I knew what I was doing.

"Grab your wheelbarrows and line them up side by side facing the same direction," I explained. I created a rough assembly line, assigning two volunteers to haul bags over. I gave one person the hose and gave him a nickname: the "Water Boy," which quickly caught on. He began working his way down the line of wheelbarrows, and people started yelling, "Water Boy, let's get going! We need you over here!" Each wheelbarrow had two people on either end mixing the concrete using garden hoes, which work so much better for this than shovels. One volunteer became the "inspector." That person was responsible for making sure that every wheelbarrow was thoroughly mixed to the right consistency before it got sent over to the playground. The batches of concrete suddenly started coming out a lot better and faster. Once we got the kinks worked out, the volunteers started having fun.

It's not the most glamorous job, but when the concrete team is working smoothly, when people start getting dirty and working hard, other people suddenly want to come over and join them. I've seen this happen over and over again. The music's playing, the concrete team is yelling, making noise, teasing each other (especially teasing the Water Boy or Water Girl), and people who aren't doing that feel like they're missing out. The other jobs aren't as hard, but they aren't as much fun, either. I love being on the concrete team, and if I'm going to be at a build, most project managers know they can rely on me to take over this dirty task and get the team running smoothly and having fun.

Invariably someone will ask, "Why not just use a concrete mixer?" Companies make backyard models, which you just plug in, add the ingredients, and out comes perfectly churned concrete. The reason, in a nutshell, is that the experience just wouldn't be the same. The point isn't simply creating a playground but getting people to work hard, side by side with strangers, on a tangible project that improves the neighborhood. Not having any problems to solve, not getting dirty, not sweating shoulder to shoulder, not struggling a little bit would turn the whole thing into a simple transaction. What makes the KaBOOM! playground builds special is the fact that it's all about teamwork and what people, without machines, can do together.

I once had a woman in an inner-city neighborhood ask me why KaBOOM! was different from all the other nonprofits that came to her and made grand promises that sometimes did not come true. *Why is this playground going to be different?* she wanted to know. I said, "It's different this time because KaBOOM! isn't building the playground—you are. We'll be there with you, and we'll help you, but you're doing the work."

In other words, getting a group of neighborhood volunteers organized around a specific goal is as important as anything else we do. If a playground were to somehow go up without the community being actively involved—if, say, we did the bulk of the work ourselves, or we used industrial equipment instead of local muscle, or if the corporate volunteers built the project without engagement from the community—we would consider that a failure. The process counts as much as the playground, and part of that process is stripping out the advantages of technology and getting people, many of whom have little construction experience, to roll up their sleeves and work together.

We have two primary aspects to our mission at KaBOOM!. We want to turn a patch of dirt into a beautiful new playground to create better play opportunities for kids, and we want to help transform the community. The real change doesn't come from the events of that single day. Instead, it comes from all the planning and organizational work leading up to it, and the way that those skills get applied to other local projects afterward. The objective isn't merely a physical change to a single piece of land but a civic transformation.

The basic philosophy at KaBOOM! comes down to three key elements, specifically:

1) Convening People Around a Collective Cause. Too often, people in a neighborhood are at odds with one another, creating a fractured sense of community. Rallying people around children and the cause of play is powerful; social barriers are crossed for the greater purpose of taking action and fighting for something positive.

2) Achievable Wins. There are dozens of small victories built into our process. For each "win"—when a person gets four wheelbarrows donated for the day, for example, or when another person figures out a way to involve kids from the local school—someone is celebrated and applauded for making it happen. The individual responsible for the win

is lifted up and celebrated. The completed project—the playground—is the final, big win for the entire community.

3) Cascading Steps of Courage. The success of the project is a powerful and tangible transformation of a physical space, and it happens in a relatively short period of time through the hard work of the people who live there and in partnership with others who care about the community. The completed playground creates a confidence that comes from the recognition that individuals can make a difference, that they have a voice, and that the power to make other changes and upgrades happen in the community lies within their grasp. What they do next is viewed as the cascading steps of courage.

That is the KaBOOM! Theory of Change.

The manifestation of this last step of the Theory of Change is witnessed through "ripples," the word we use for all the follow-on effects after a playground goes up. We don't take credit for that term. It comes from a speech Robert Kennedy gave in 1966 in Cape Town, South Africa. At the time, the country was in the grip of apartheid, and Kennedy called on the country's citizens to take action against racial oppression. The subject resonated in the United States, too—America was in a bitter civil rights struggle when Kennedy gave that speech. City Year adopted the concept of "ripples," and we borrowed it from them.

Kennedy said: "Each time a person stands up for an ideal, or acts to improve the lot of others . . . he sends forth a tiny ripple of hope, and crossing each other from a million different centers of energy and daring, those ripples build a current that can sweep down the mightiest walls of oppression and resistance."

Ripples are what KaBOOM! is really about. We measure our success by looking at what happens after we leave. We like to say, it starts with a playground. That philosophy goes back to our earliest days.

In 1997 during the Presidents' Summit for America's Future, we were one of many organizations to take part in a massive service project in Philadelphia, which involved about 3,000 volunteers spread out over

6 miles of activities. Many of the people were doing important things like collecting trash and sprucing up parks, but the fruits of their labor were invisible to casual observers. In comparison, the playground project was incredibly tangible.

Because of this we got a lot of attention, culminating with the participation of then Vice President Al Gore and former Chairman of the Joint Chiefs of Staff (and future Secretary of State) Colin Powell during the Build Day. It was the first time we had to organize a press pool, arrange for a mult box (an electronic device allowing multiple media outlets high-quality audio), and coordinate on security with the Secret Service. Both men got to work and worked hard. At one point they were both standing on a 6-foot deck helping to precariously lift a 200-pound steel roof onto the structure. I was impressed and also amused (and a little anxious) as the Secret Service detail was going nuts!

Our project there was in the Nicetown neighborhood of northern Philadelphia, an extremely tough part of the city at the time. The Build Day turned out great, but a few mornings after the playground was finished, it got tagged with graffiti. Our community partner for that project was a nonprofit across the street from the site, run by a woman named Juanita Hatton. Juanita went out and cleaned up the graffiti herself. A few days later, the playground was tagged a second time, and she again cleaned it up herself. The same thing happened, again and again for 5 days straight, until she ultimately wore down the graffiti artists. From that point on, the playground stayed graffiti-free.

Juanita designated local kids to be captains of the site, with orders to report anything unusual to her. Ted Adams, the project manager, told me about going back a few months after construction to check on the playground. It was in immaculate condition, and he could tell that members of the community were still looking out for it, under her guidance. "We walked over to the playground together," Ted said, "and there was a broken juice bottle. Some kid saw her coming and ran over and picked it up before she even said anything." Some Boomers have followed up on this playground several times over the years, most recently in 2010, 13 years after construction, and it was still in great shape. Kids from a Boys and Girls Club nearby use it every day, and they have regular service days to repaint benches and plant trees. It's become a part of the community. Many communities struggle with establishing ownership of their parks. Sustaining them takes people like Juanita Hatton who take action, enlist others, remain consistent, and retain visibility.

That's a crucial end result of the way we work—the community takes care of the space because they *own* it. KaBOOM! didn't give a playground to the Nicetown community. Instead, everyone involved chipped in assets and labor and donations, and we helped the people in the community organize and build it themselves. Local kids designed it, their parents helped choose specific components, volunteers led the planning committees and hunted down tools and food and a DJ—and on the day of construction, they all came together to do the work. So it only makes sense that they would want to protect it afterward. (The Philadelphia Eagles football team participated in the build, and they were so inspired by the experience that they started building a playground each summer during training camp completely on their own, without the help of KaBOOM!, a nice example of a ripple.)

KaBOOM! conducts revisits each year to about 25 of our alumni playground builds, specifically those that are at least 2 years old. We try to meet and talk with people who were involved in the project. We hear some good stories from these revisits that are documented in our database. Minimally, the revisit is an opportunity to see how well the playground is being maintained. We rate the playground as "passing" or "failing" using specific criteria. Currently, 86 percent of our playgrounds pass, as the Nicetown one did when we conducted revisits in 2007 and 2010. We are proud of that number, and we continue to work to see it increase.

▲ ■ ●

In 2002, in a quirk of timing, New Haven, Connecticut, had two playgrounds under construction at the same time: one through KaBOOM!

and our community-building approach, and the other through the standard method in which outside contractors had been hired. In 2006 I talked to Hannah Sokel Holmes of the New Haven Housing Authority, and she described what happened at the second site: "We had trouble with things like kids throwing stones at contractors, and people knocking down the temporary fences during construction," she said. "None of that happened at the KaBOOM! project. With the other project, we talked to the community about what the builders were trying to do for them, but they weren't truly involved. They didn't get to make any of the decisions; they didn't get to design it or plan it or build it. That other playground is trashed today. The community-build playground, our playground, is well-maintained, while the playground that was professionally installed is in horrible disrepair."

There are some people who can't differentiate between the two approaches and are skeptical about the whole enterprise. I see this firsthand, when I talk to potential funders who don't think they can make a lasting difference in what they perceive as a "bad" neighborhood. Unfortunately, sometimes residents of those communities start to believe that themselves.

When we helped build two playgrounds in the North Side neighborhood of Pittsburgh in 2008, the projects got covered in the *Pittsburgh Post-Gazette*. We were happy for the coverage, but the writer spun the story in a way that underscored the persistent low expectations people have for communities like that: "Residents of those neighborhoods, plagued by vacancies, crime, blight, and vandalism, say children need safe places to play but that the effort and expense may have been for short-lived gain," the story read. "'It's nice they're doing this,' said Don Boggs, while watching the swarm of activity during the build on Spring Garden Avenue Tuesday. He has lived in Spring Garden all of his 46 years. 'But I'd be amazed if it lasts more than 6 months.'"

The two playgrounds are still up and still in great shape, more than 2 years later. There is no question that there were normal and relatively minor issues that happened in the first few months following construction. But they were addressed quickly, which is key to any community that is both "maintaining" a playground and "maintaining ownership" of the playground. A bolt came loose and was quickly replaced. A plastic element that listed sponsors was vandalized and replaced. Graffiti on the playground was quickly removed. The community organization we worked with for one of those playgrounds even managed to get a vacant house next door demolished after the playground went up. Another ripple.

There's a line of thinking that says if things *have been* bad in a certain community, they will *always be* bad. A poor community will never be able to improve its circumstances. That sort of thinking frustrates me, because I know that individuals and organizations and communities can and will rise to challenges, as long as the challenge is presented in a way that asks them for their very best. I've seen it firsthand throughout my life.

In Durham, a group of neighborhoods near Duke University had been bickering with each other (and with the school) for years before they built a playground through KaBOOM!. It was on the grounds of an old school, Lyon Park Elementary, which had been abandoned after desegregation and left to rot for decades. A group from the community put together a $6.4 million bond referendum, which passed in 1996, to gut the school, renovate it, and make it home to a cluster of nonprofits—GED prep, a health care clinic, vocational training, a day care center, programs for seniors. But after all the money was gone, there was no playground for the day care kids. The center opened in 2002.

When Duke started to reach out to these communities in 2000, the meetings turned ugly. Mayme Webb-Bledsoe works in the community affairs office at Duke (and grew up in the Lyon Park community). "It was like a civil war," she told me. Some people in the neighborhood had employment disputes with Duke, or property disputes, or just something going wrong that they didn't like, and they came to these sessions ready to vent—loudly. "It would last 3 or 4 hours, and they didn't want to talk to us—they just wanted to yell," Mayme said.

Our project there took place on February 21, 2001. Durham usually has pretty mild winters, but on that day there was snow, thunder, and lightning. In spite of less-than-ideal circumstances, this was the first tangible project that the six neighborhoods surrounding Duke were able to come together on and successfully complete. It gave them a sense of what was possible, Mayme said, and after that they were off and running. In the past 7 years, the residents, in conjunction with several partnerships, have built more than 40 houses and refurbished countless more in the area adjacent to the Lyon Park playground. They have built another two playgrounds, one with KaBOOM! and one without. With funding from Duke, they also completed a 32-unit housing facility for seniors.

▲　■　●

One morning in the early spring of 2006, I was sitting at the airport in Atlanta, waiting for a flight to Jackson, Mississippi, where I was scheduled to meet with Jim Barksdale, the technology entrepreneur who'd given KaBOOM! $1.5 million for our work in the Gulf region after Hurricane Katrina. He wanted an update of how his contributions were being used, and I was looking forward to the meeting in part because I really respect Mr. Barksdale and enjoyed being with him, and also because I had a lot of good news to report.

I was sitting at the gate, drinking a much-needed coffee and checking my BlackBerry, when I was surprised to see another KaBOOM! employee, a longtime project manager named Erica Liberman, who happened to be booked on the same flight to Jackson. Erica was traveling to Mississippi to run a Design Day at an elementary school there.

In 2002 we had 12 employees. Four years later, we were above 90, all working on a range of different initiatives and projects, many of which include frequent travel. Unlike the old days, it's impossible for me to know what everyone's doing and where they're going. In fact, this has been a major shift as a result of our rapid growth. We could no longer hold staff meetings by gathering around a small conference table, and my job had significantly evolved. Instead of managing playground builds like I had done in the first year, I was now managing managers, and I was far less involved in the day-to-day operational details of the organization. I still attend a number of playground builds a year, but much more of my time is spent meeting with funders and plotting overall strategy.

At the gate in Atlanta, I recognized a chance to get down to the ground level again, if only for an hour or two. I called Mr. Barksdale's assistant and asked to push our meeting back so that I could attend the Design Day.

Erica and I showed up at Pecan Park Elementary School in Jackson mid-morning. The school sits on Claiborne Avenue, about 2 miles northwest of downtown. The double-sided marquee in front welcomed KaBOOM!.

In the lobby on the wall, displayed on a bulletin board, was a giant anthill made of brown construction paper, which the school was using as a way to track fund-raising for the project (which is really much cooler than the traditional fund-raising thermometer). Each family or person who made a donation was represented by a red paper ant—the goal was $10 per family. In addition to parents, the school had received donations toward the playground from the postman, maintenance workers, delivery people, even the FedEx guy. I found out later that they managed to raise the whole $10,000 in a month!

Erica introduced me to the principal, a dynamo named Wanda Quon. I don't think Wanda believed Erica's story that the CEO of KaBOOM! just "happened" to spot her at the Atlanta airport and tagged along for the morning. Wanda just smiled and changed the plans a bit, so she could give me a tour around the school. We ducked our heads into classrooms, and I met many of the teachers. Pecan Park has about 500 kids, and I was amazed by how much Wanda knew about them. Not just their names, but what their families were like, who had older brothers or younger sisters in the school, whose mom made the best brownies for fund-raisers, which dad could be counted on for a spring cleanup day—everything worth knowing, she knew, and she made it all seem effortless.

Jackson is an inner-city community, and people move in and out frequently. About a third of the student population typically changes during a given year, so it's sometimes hard to build up a lot of social capital among parents there. Wanda is a rock of stability, though—after a lot of years teaching in Jackson's public schools, Wanda came to Pecan Park Elementary in the early 1990s and became principal 12 years ago. In fact, she's been at the school for 18 of its 21 years in existence.

Design Day was a blast and a reminder to me how much these projects mean to the kids. Every single kid in the school had made a drawing of the dream playground he or she wanted to see—just like Ashley Brodie had done all those years earlier, at the Livingston Manor playground in Washington. We couldn't have the entire school come to Design Day, so the kids in each homeroom had drawn names out of a hat to send a single lucky representative—25 in all. Those 25 wanted swings, swings, and more swings along with slides and benches. One 6-year-old named Dontavius asked for "a talking tree that only speaks good words." (Magic trees like that are tough, but we did incorporate a special tube that lets kids from one side of the playground talk to those on the other side.)

The meeting wrapped up with cheers and thank-yous, and I left for the meeting with Mr. Barksdale, feeling completely lucky for the chance meeting at the airport.

Of course, I kept in touch with Wanda and got frequent updates on the project as it moved forward. The school had to remove some outdated wooden play equipment in the schoolyard, including the hard surface underneath, which was the source of a lot of scrapes and bruises and nurse reports—almost one a day—for kids who'd gotten hurt jumping down onto it. The kindergartners were fascinated by the giant trucks that came to remove the equipment, and their teacher worked it into their lesson that day, asking them to write stories about what they had seen. One downside: Those same kids showed up at school the next day, expecting to see a gleaming new playground in its place. One girl was so disappointed that she started crying. The teacher had to explain that the KaBOOM! equipment wouldn't go in for another 2 weeks. But excitement was definitely mounting.

Once the day of construction finally came—May 18, 2006—more than 200 local parents and volunteers showed up along with central-office people from the school and the district, janitors, and even a local SWAT team.

It was a weekday, and children at the school were jumping out of their skin. The teachers staggered the classes so that each one could come outside for a stint to watch the progress and do cheers for the volunteers. The local news station recorded a segment to air that night, and three Jackson radio stations did live feeds during construction. It all helped connect Pecan Park to the larger community. "The build showed that even though we're a Title I school in inner-city Jackson, we've got positive things going on," Wanda told me.

But then the ripples started. Wanda had bigger plans for the school yard than just a playground, and first up was a walking track around the perimeter. That year, 2006, Mississippi had been named the fattest state in the country for the third straight year, and Wanda thought that teaching her students some of the elements of a healthy lifestyle could reverse that. She thought she could break the cycle. Early research into the cost of a walking track left her a little daunted, though. Estimates from local contractors for a simple quarter-mile track, 6 feet wide, ran about $61,000.

At the same time, the foundation run by Blue Cross and Blue Shield of Mississippi launched a program to get people in the state to exercise. When Wanda heard about the program, she immediately signed her school up. Schools had to log the mileage that they walked, but the program offered grants of $3,000, which she used to buy computers that could keep track of all that. It was a small help, but over time the lack of a walking track became a problem. The school property takes up an entire city block, with a fence around the back and a sidewalk on only 2½ sides of the perimeter. When kids walked the rest of it, they were in the street.

She applied to the foundation to give her a grant for the walking track, but representatives told her that $61,000 was too much. So she stopped calling contractors and started calling asphalt companies directly. After all, contractors would have sub-contracted the job out, so they were effectively middlemen that she could eliminate. That got the price knocked down to about $45,000, an amount that the foundation agreed to cover. The track went up in the late spring of 2007, about a year after the school's Build Day.

It isn't an oval, which would get boring for kids over time. Instead, the track meanders around past the playground and up the hill near an outdoor classroom before winding back again. "The kids use it almost every day," Wanda told me. "They love it." Since then, a few other schools in Mississippi have gotten similar grants for walking tracks, but Pecan Park was the first in the state.

Wanda was just getting started. That fall she applied for another grant, $58,000 from the Mississippi Department of Education to provide fresh fruit and vegetables for students at Pecan Park. One snack for every student, every day—strawberries, pears, plums, nectarines, whatever's in season. (Wanda told me that the program even benefited teachers by introducing them to exotic stuff like kiwis: "Some people on my staff had never eaten one," she said.) The grant provided enough money to purchase a refrigerator to store everything along with carts to deliver the fruit to individual classrooms. Since then, parents have told her about trips to the supermarket when kids hit the produce aisle and ask, "Mommy, get some of that."

And there's more. Wanda got yet another grant in the summer of 2008 to put in fitness equipment along the walking trail. It's a set of seven stations, including a vault bar, horizontal ladder, pull-up bars, sit-up station, and more. Total cost: $24,000, which includes $16,000 for equipment and another $8,000 for installation. Pecan Park's phys-ed teacher attended training on how best to get children to use each station. As a result, the body mass index of kids at Pecan Park has been going down.

What else? Where do I begin? Pecan Park held a play day in September 2009—kids played games like Duck Duck Goose and learned the hand-jive dance from Grease and had relay races where they had to pass a football from one kid to the next using only their forearms, no hands. Wanda took the opportunity to finally put in the stepping-stones that were designed on the Build Day more than 2 years ago. "When you look at our campus, you'd think that all the components were laid out as part of a master plan," she told me. "They all fit together. The walking track circles by the KaBOOM! playground and behind the outdoor classroom. The benches are dotted along the track, and the fitness equipment area is accessible from the playground and the walking track."

In all, Pecan Park raised $175,000 from grants and other sources for the school and its children. And it became a model for Jackson schools. One fan came all the way from the White House to check it out. In March 2010 First Lady Michelle Obama traveled to Mississippi to meet Wanda Quon and hear about all the things she'd been able to do to make the kids at Pecan Park a little healthier. Mrs. Obama had already volunteered on a KaBOOM! project in California, so she knew the kind of work we did. She used the visit to Pecan Park as an exemplary model to highlight her campaign to reduce childhood obesity, called "Let's Move."

▲ ■ ●

Wanda Quon didn't just work to improve her own school. Jackson is about 170 miles north of New Orleans, and she drove down to volunteer at other KaBOOM! projects in the area after Hurricane Katrina. She and her librarian came to the 50th build in New Orleans, with

Regis and Kelly, and she and her husband drove to Bay St. Louis for the 100th project. "That was an adventure," she told me. "He had been training for his first marathon, but he broke a bone in his foot, so he had to wear an air cast and couldn't train anymore. He really didn't want to go to the build, but I told him he'd enjoy it. And he did. There's pictures of him hauling mulch in his air cast."

KaBOOM! does not consider taking on a project in Jackson without talking to someone like Wanda Quon first. She's a great example of a KaBOOM! alumnus, folks who serve as extensions of KaBOOM! in their respective communities and take actions to help ensure that all kids have great places to play. Wanda is now mentoring other people in the community who want to create play or wellness programs aimed at kids. That helps build up the community's social capital and helps kids stay healthier. As Wanda puts it, "If we can convince kids when they're young, we can make real changes."

And to think, it all started with a playground. As Wanda puts it, "If it weren't for the KaBOOM! project, none of these things would have happened."

[12]

A Better Us

In July 2003, in an Atlanta neighborhood known as Virginia-Highland, a man named Brad Cunard was driving home with his family one afternoon during a violent rainstorm. While they were stopped at a traffic light, a 100-year-old oak tree blew over and crashed onto the back of their Toyota Highlander. Brad survived, but his wife and two sons, ages 5 months and 3 years, were all killed instantly.

The freak accident stunned the entire city. People in the Cunards' community immediately wanted to reach out and help, but they weren't sure what to do. A neighbor named Cynthia Gentry stepped forward. Not only did Cynthia live next door to the Cunards and know them well, but she also had organized arts festivals in the city, so she was the kind of person who could get things done.

A few ideas floated in, and then someone proposed upgrading the swing set at the local park. The Cunards had spent time at John Howell Park near their home, but the entire site needed an upgrade, especially the playground. "It was pretty sparse," Cynthia told me. "Much of the plastic was covered in mold, and the ground was covered with mud. There was nothing for anybody over 4 or 5. People never used it anymore, and the park area surrounding it was run-down." The swing set was a small step, but the community figured that it would be relatively easy to replace. They didn't have any larger ambitions beyond that.

A week and a half after the accident, Cynthia presented the idea to

Brad, to make sure it was the kind of tribute he wanted. In fact, he loved it. "He said, 'People will remember my family forever, with a smile on their face, because they're at a playground,'" Cynthia said.

Now that everyone was lined up in support, the next question was how to get the structure built. No one in the neighborhood had any experience working on play equipment, and Cynthia had never organized any kind of physical project like this one. Someone in the neighborhood knew about KaBOOM!, but the trendy Virginia-Highland neighborhood wasn't the kind of place where we typically devote our energy and attention; our resources are directed to lower-income communities, which this wasn't. This neighborhood had been a force in Atlanta politics for decades. If they were going to build a new swing set, they would have to assemble the organizational skills and financial resources to do it themselves.

But as it turned out, there was another way that KaBOOM! could get involved.

▲ ■ ●

How can you inspire passion on a national scale? How can an organization spread its knowledge and expertise so that people can leverage that information on their own? More directly, how can that organization turn its mission into a movement?

These were the questions facing KaBOOM! around the time of the tragedy involving the Cunards, and I spent a lot of nights staring at the ceiling and thinking about ways to solve them. The organization was at an inflection point. We had grown rapidly in our first decade, and we'd put up some solid numbers—building more than 1,000 playgrounds and giving hundreds of thousands of children a safe place to run around and make new friends and exercise their bodies and minds. Yet, as substantial as that sounds, I knew it wasn't enough.

The KaBOOM! leadership team was hammering through a lot of these issues as we focused on a "Going to Scale" strategy that would plan our growth for the next 5 to 10 years. We were simultaneously developing a dashboard—like the one Pete D'Amelio used at Cheesecake Factory—that would help us track how we were doing on specific goals, using ratings of efficiency, leverage, and value as our guide. The issues of direction and how we could be most effective were bubbling up in a lot of different ways.

There are simply too few playgrounds in the country, and many of those that do exist aren't well maintained or safe for kids. This problem has only been compounded by the recent recession, which has forced revenue-starved municipalities, parks departments, and schools to make tough choices between operating expenses (like employee salaries) and capital expenses (like the local playground). So these schools and parks try to make do by pushing aging equipment past its prime. This can happen even in relatively well-off areas, like the Virginia-Highland neighborhood in Atlanta.

Even if we knew that every one of the thousands and thousands of playgrounds in the United States was perfectly fine today, the components typically only last for about 15 years, so every year you'd need to replace a big percentage. At KaBOOM!, we're pretty busy trying to build 200 each year, which means that we will never, ever catch up.

A reasonable question might be why KaBOOM! can't simply build more. Basically, it comes down to cost and logistics. We currently have 18 project managers, each of whom is limited to overseeing 15 playgrounds a year. These are time-intensive projects that almost always involve travel, and we're constrained by the seasons, since it's hard to attract volunteers and build outdoors in many parts of the country during the depths of winter.

While KaBOOM!'s focus is on lower-income communities, there's a need for play in communities of all income levels. And we were increasingly being asked to step into middle-income communities to help build a playground. This became another consideration as we looked at our impact and our scale. The Virginia-Highlands of the world could benefit by having a new playground, and they could benefit more by planning and building it with community volunteers rather than outside contractors.

In theory, we could hire more employees, but you'd have to bring in a battalion if you wanted to get to sufficient numbers. Even a thousand playgrounds a year would not be enough. Also, a bigger staff creates its own set of problems—you need more office space for those people, which would significantly increase our overhead costs. And when the economy goes through its inevitable contractions, we'd have to scale back again. KaBOOM! has never laid off employees because of economic conditions—even during the recent recession—and we hope we'll always be able to say that.

Other nonprofits have faced this issue, and many decide to grow by expanding through some type of chapter program or franchise system. Habitat for Humanity, for example, has about 1,500 affiliates in the United States, plus many others overseas. But ultimately we decided against those approaches. There was a risk that they would dilute our energy and passion for community-building and play, instead of concentrating it. We would have less interaction with local neighborhoods and communities because we would be adding a layer of administration and bureaucracy between them and us. And frankly, I had seen communities build playgrounds without the direct support of KaBOOM! and knew that in many more places, people could do it. They just needed a little bit of help.

How did I know this? People and communities were asking us for it directly. We were getting about 14,000 requests for technical assistance each year—e-mails, Web postings, and phone calls from people who didn't want to use the standard KaBOOM! model with a project manager and a corporate funder and the works. Instead, they were more or less self-sufficient, but they had questions on a few elements of the process.

And then it hit me: What if we could answer all those individual questions en masse over the Internet? We could get our information out in an efficient manner, to all those do-it-yourselfers across the country who were trying to build playgrounds and could benefit from our experience. Not only would this allow us to talk to more people, but we would provide a platform for those people to talk up the work they were doing in their own community—it would be a platform for the collective wisdom. Social networking programs would allow people to talk to each other as well as to trade ideas or inspiration and share all sorts of information—fund-raising, how to work with a landowner and work through liability issues, how to leverage optimal community engagement, what are the best playground designs, how to select an equipment manufacturer, etc. They could even suggest changes that we could implement at KaBOOM!. After all, the ultimate goal is ensuring every child has a great place to play within walking distance, regardless of whether KaBOOM! or someone else does the heavy lifting. We're not in this for the glory or the credit. We're in it for the cause.

In short, we could develop an advocacy role—fighting for play on a bigger stage—and build a movement, an ecosystem of individuals and other groups, all aligned toward the singular goal of more and better places for kids to play. The more success those entities have, the bigger the movement grows and the further and faster we all go, together.

Think about it in terms of financial resources. If you start with a hypothetical pool of money, say $75,000, we could use that to build one great playground with the standard KaBOOM! model, a lot of oversight from us, and a significant commitment of our employees' time. Or we could break that up into much smaller chunks of $1,000 each and use it to seed and support 75 individual playgrounds where local communities do almost all of the planning and work. Both situations have merit, but with this new approach, more playgrounds would get built.

We used to do everything "one to one." That was our project management model: one project manager leading one community to build one playground. When we started training people in large groups (either in person or through Webinars), the model became "one to many." One person or group of people from KaBOOM! teaching a lot of other people how to go back to their communities and build many play-grounds. We were sharing our expertise with a lot of people and groups at one time and giving them the tools to do the build without us.

But this model, the one that was developing in my mind, was "many to many." It's less about doing it the KaBOOM! way and more about the common experience and the different points of view and people sharing their experiences with each other. KaBOOM! would provide online tools and would foster people to talk to each other about play and playgrounds, sharing their expertise and motivating each other. In that scenario, we would be creating something that we started calling Mass Action. We would take the best of KaBOOM!, an offline orga-nization, and we would translate it to encourage online engagement and actions. Mass Action would inspire people to go from online to offline and back again. And it would be for the cause of play.

To be clear, a big part of our operation is still devoted to the stan-dard KaBOOM! builds—the roughly 200 projects a year that we lead using the model we've developed going back to our earliest days. We maintain control over that entire process, to make sure that the corpo-rations and communities we deal with have an optimal experience. These projects are what KaBOOM! is best known for.

But the rest of this new Mass Action strategy is a bit more radical. Essentially, it involves open-sourcing all of our information and expertise on playgrounds online, for free, to anyone who wants it. Everything we know about playgrounds—our secret sauce, all the institutional expertise we've built up over the years—is now on our Website. There are online planners complemented by online training, allowing us to reach far more individuals on their own terms. Many folks take the training at night or in the wee hours of the morning. We now annually train more than 9,000 people who are passionate about play, compared to fewer than 500 in the years when we conducted the in-person trainings—and it takes fewer resources. The numbers of participants is growing quickly. The planners walk people through every step of playground construction and give info on training programs, technical assistance, fund-raising ideas, tips on recruiting volunteers. If someone wants to know how much concrete a particular project will need, the answer's there. People can follow this to the letter, modify it, adapt it, tweak it for the specific demands of their neighborhood, apply the model to different community projects, you name it. Nothing's proprietary or off-limits, and we don't charge for any of it.

The Internet has enabled us to disseminate a lot of information easily and inexpensively, and allowed people to comment on that information and even improve on it. In a way, the Mass Action strategy is on the cutting edge of a larger trend in philanthropy (and society as a whole), in which nonprofits have started leveraging technology to increase the transparency of their operations.

Other nonprofits give their model away, specifically groups like Alcoholics Anonymous and Mothers Against Drunk Driving, both of which have a clear reason for trying to spread their expertise to anyone who needs it. We also drew inspiration from for-profit businesses like Meetup.com, which helps people meet online to organize real-world events and activities.

Actually WeddingChannel.com was a pretty big impetus in my interest in all of this as well. By 1999, Kate and I knew that we would get married but hadn't decided when or how. In November of that year, we were sitting in Kate's apartment after a fondue dinner, and we began talking about it—when, how many people, how would we decide who to include . . . and we could both feel the stress beginning to seep into the conversation. Kate said, "You know, I really don't think I want anything big or fancy, I know my attention will be pulled to the party and the guests' experience, and I really want to focus on our own experience and the commitment we're making." Both of our families are huge and are spread out. Figuring out a date and location, and creating something that would require people to spend money and travel, all felt overwhelming. Doing it quietly would be perfect.

We decided we would get married in 3 weeks' time in St. Michaels, Maryland, a small town on the state's Eastern Shore. (It's an hour and a half from DC, and neither of us had ever been there.) Kate wanted her parents to be there and her uncle (a priest) to officiate. That same night, we booked three rooms at an inn and called her parents to make sure they could make it and then called her uncle. We decided that we wouldn't tell anyone else other than those three people, so there wouldn't be pressure to extend the invitation list (though we both caved in and shared the news to a handful of people during the final days prior to the 17th of December, the date we had chosen).

Obviously, we didn't have much planning to do, but there were a few things like sending announcements, the wording for the announcement, getting a photographer, and other details. I was tooling around on the Internet looking for information on wedding planning and came across the WeddingChannel.com Website. It was a brilliant concept. Within a couple of hours of playing around with the features, I had the idea of creating something similar online for people who are planning a playground project. In a way, weddings and playground projects have a lot in common—both are 1-day experiences for large groups of people, both come after months of planning (in most cases), and both hinge in significant ways on making sure the details are correct. We soon began working on the idea and had the first version of a planner up on our site in 2001.

Around this time, innovative approaches were being developed by organizations like GlobalGiving, Kiva, and DonorsChoose.org. They have transformed individual philanthropy. They each let you choose exactly where your money goes through extremely user-friendly Websites.

GlobalGiving and Kiva have similar missions. GlobalGiving was founded by two former World Bank executives in 1997, and Kiva was founded in San Francisco in 2005 by a husband-and-wife team and scaled through a partnership with a former PayPal executive. Both organizations allow you to scan stories of individual entrepreneurs in developing countries and pledge money to the one you'd most like to support. GlobalGiving provides the monetary support in the form of a donation. At Kiva, the money goes out in the form of a loan, which is handled on the ground in individual countries by local nonprofits and agencies. Recipients have a great track record of repaying their loans, though many donors take the repaid sums and pledge them to another microenterprise on the site. In 2009 Kiva hit a major, impressive milestone—$100 million in total loans in just 4 years.

Similarly, DonorsChoose.org was founded in 2000 by a former high school social-studies teacher in the Bronx who grew disheartened by the school's chronic shortage of basic supplies. In response he created a Website where teachers can post funding requests for specific needs, such as a microscope, costumes for a show, a laptop, or a field trip to the local planetarium. Donors can sift through the posts by geography, age, type of student, or type of activity (sports, literacy, science, and the like) and support those that most personally resonate with them.

Each of these organizations has incorporated direct communication from the entrepreneur (in the case of GlobalGiving and Kiva) or classroom (in the case of DonorsChoose.org), which gets shared with donors about the impact of their loan or gift.

Sites like these represent a giant leap forward in philanthropic technology, but I think our Mass Action program goes a step beyond all of them. More than increasing the transparency between donors and the projects they support, we're trying to encourage people to take on projects themselves by self-organizing. We want them to learn how to build playgrounds on our site, then push back from the computer, go work with other people in the community to actually put one up, and come back to the site to tell other people around the country how they did it. Instead of simply facilitating transactions ("Click here to donate $50"), our site is aimed at facilitating *transformations*, both personal and civic.

In short, this isn't a zero-sum game that we're trying to win. The demand for more and better playgrounds is so great that there's enough work for everyone. Mass Action lets us go further, faster, by sharing what we know. The more that people use these tools to put up a playground in their own neighborhood or advocate with their local parks departments, politicians, and schools for better play opportunities, the better for everyone.

The transition to Mass Action as an overarching program presented a major cultural change for KaBOOM!. Prior to that, we were a very straightforward organization; everyone knew what everyone else was doing, and almost all of it was centered around building playgrounds in communities. The challenge we experienced in making the shift to a new model was less about the organizational chart, the creation of new departments, or the development of operating systems and new programs and more about the growth and impact to our culture and the mechanisms for communication and related perceptions. What were the decisions that needed representation of various teams around the table, and what were the ones that could be made without it? Once decisions were made in one team that affected others, how and when would it be communicated? How would we measure different and new outputs (immediate results that are fairly easy to measure) or outcomes (long-term, sustainable results), and how would the new measures compare against current program metrics—could they be comparable?

Mass Action also presented a challenge for us because its effects are harder to track. Because we have less control over the folks who are building playgrounds on their own, without our direct help (and that is the whole idea), it's hard for us to get them to check back in and let us know how things went. We're continually working to try to develop a reliable method for knowing how many playground projects we are inspiring. Our conservative estimates are that for every playground we build using our traditional model, we now influence 10 more through the online tools. In 2009 this meant we helped people around the country build 1,600 do-it-yourself (DIY) playgrounds, almost as many as we assembled ourselves in our first 14 years of operation.

▲ ■ ●

Which takes us back to Cynthia Gentry in Atlanta. Cynthia was one of the earliest and biggest users of our DIY resources. If we had a DIY

Hall of Fame, she would be one of the pioneer inductees. By the time she was ready to start building a playground to help memorialize the Cunard family, many of our resources were already available. "We had no idea what we were doing," she told me. "I'd never done anything like this before." So she used pretty much everything we had—the project planner, the list of vendors, the fund-raising ideas. Most of all, she liked the idea of a community-based model. After all, that's what was already happening: The community was coming together to help heal after a devastating tragedy.

She heeded our recommendation and set a 4-month timetable for the project and started fund-raising. The money flowed in, some in contributions as small as $5 and others through larger pledges and events. An art auction at a local gym generated more than $12,000. A restaurant benefit, in which 30 restaurants donated a portion of dinner sales for a night (along with the tips of many of the waitstaff), raised $20,000. When a local radio station took calls offering support and donations for the project, it raised $40,000 in a single morning. Cynthia even got a contribution from the rock band REM, which is originally from nearby Athens, Georgia. All told, she managed to raise $180,000 in cash donations.

Other community resources were coming in as well, adding another $100,000, give or take, in in-kind donations of goods and services. The Atlanta Community Tool Bank donated all the tools necessary for construction, the first time it had ever loaned its tools out for free. Local nurseries donated trees and plants for the landscaping. Twenty-five members of the local Cub Scout troop offered to camp out at the park to provide overnight security for the tools and materials that were on-site during construction.

The original plan, to refurbish a swing set, had grown to a much bigger project—a complete overhaul of the park with a budget of nearly $300,000. On a Saturday in mid-November, just 4 months after the accident, more than 400 volunteers came out to do the work. Not only did the old swing set get replaced, but a separate area was also leveled to create space for a new playground that older kids could use. The design included a fire-engine structure in memory of one of the Cunards' sons, Max, who loved fire trucks. CNN showed up to cover the event.

The upgrades didn't stop there. Over the next few months, the park was cleaned up, with new sod put in, along with a memorial garden and a bronze statue of Brad Cunard's wife, Lisa, and their two boys. That spring, the town held a grand opening of the park. More than 500 local residents came for the ceremony and stayed all day. Since then, says Cynthia, "It's become the heart of our neighborhood."

The effect wasn't just transactional, it was transformational. Cynthia got a lot of information from KaBOOM! to coordinate this project, but she has since contributed in major ways to our online community and forums as well. And she's become a resource and an expert for other community leaders.

▲ ■ ●

Another good DIY playground example comes from the suburbs of Boston. I'll let Wendy Minton, the woman who worked so hard on this project, tell the story in her own words. It underscores one of the key elements of our core philosophy: how people, after some initial hesitation, start to experience cascading steps of courage and leadership:

> We live in Peabody, Massachusetts. It's a pretty ethnic community. We have 6,000 families, and sometimes we don't always talk to each other as much as we should. In 2003 the Thomas Carroll elementary school in town was torn down and replaced by a beautiful new building. But it was missing one key thing: a playground. Our rec department said it wouldn't be safe to put the same equipment back up. We found out later that we probably could have reused it, if we'd taken certain steps to make sure it was safe. But we didn't know that at the time, and the builder sold the old equipment to another town for $2,500. At the new school, kids had no place to run around. There was a small area

with drainage pipes—just a little circle of nothing, not usable at all for kids.

We all knew we needed a new playground, but there was no funding. People thought, parents should do it, the school district should do it, the city should do it. This went around and around. A rough committee of parents came together, but it wasn't very organized or good with technology. A lot of the people didn't have e-mail addresses.

Thomas Carroll has about 600 students, and about half of them qualify for free or reduced lunch. About a third speak English as a second language. There's no other playground in the community, and many of the houses here are built extremely close together, with little or no yard. Some of the kids are being raised by grandparents because the parents work so much, and these families can't just jump into a car and drive to the playground in the next town.

At the same time, the school had scaled recess back to just 15 minutes a day. My son had started there by this point, and he came home one day and said that he wasn't allowed to run during those 15 minutes. He could walk fast, but that was it. I said, okay, enough.

I got onto the committee and did a Web search one day on "playground grants." We found KaBOOM!, and things started to happen. I went to a WE Play! [KaBOOM!'s Workshop Entirely on Play!] conference in Pittsburgh, where I learned a lot, and also attended a KaBOOM! build just to see how it's done. We applied for a grant from KaBOOM! and got $5,000. There were some steps involved, but they were all really necessary. I started in mid-2006, and one of the steps for the grant is that you have to pick a date for the build. I told everyone in my town that it was happening the following summer, August 2007. People said I was crazy, that it was never going to happen. But you have to set a date. That's key. Otherwise it just floats in the future.

I used everything I could get from KaBOOM!. Now it's all online, but when I did it, a lot of the information was in pamphlets and booklets. I work about 50 hours a week, so I had to do all my research nights and weekends. My daughter was about 2 then, and at her bedtime, I'd read the pamphlets to her. If you do them in a funny voice, she thinks it's entertaining. She doesn't know you're reading about planning committees.

Fund-raising—we sent letters to local churches and sent them home with all the kids in school. Because it's an ethnic neighborhood, we had to write the letters in six languages. We held an auction, "A Night on the Town for the Carroll School Playground," and we had five individuals and businesses step forward that night with checks totaling more than $30,000. Pure donations. Plus we raised another $23,000 from ticket sales and the auction itself. A walk-a-thon raised $6,000 and didn't cost us anything.

The biggest amount came from a grant through the Community Preservation Act, which is a hidden secret in the New England area. It's for open spaces, but there's a section in there for recreational projects. I had to do a ton of research, and there were all kinds of obstacles for it. We were told, don't waste your time. But I called everyone and met with everyone, all the way up to the governor's office. And finally the grant came through— we got $48,000, half from the city and half from the state.

In the beginning the project was going to cost about $40,000, and we ended up raising $126,000. So we didn't just build one playground, we built two. We brought in three of the biggest manufacturers to give us their ideas. We also got the kids involved in designing the playground—another KaBOOM! recommendation—by taking them to play dates at different locations around the county, sites that were built by different vendors, to see what they liked.

On the day of construction, about 200 volunteers showed up.

We handwrote letters to every contractor in Peabody, and almost all of them came—plus employees from local businesses, local college kids who wanted to do service projects, and tons of parents and grandparents of kids at the school.

Just like a wedding, the day arrives and you have to just roll with what you've got. No one knew all the hiccups that happened, and everyone felt they were part of something truly amazing. I wanted every child there to see their parents, teachers, grandparents, aunts, and uncles as their heroes for building these play structures.

Before school and after school, those playgrounds are like a zoo. There are so many kids on them, it's incredible. Our playground rep checked the site a year after it went up, and he said, "Oh my God, it's got five times the normal rate of use." That just shows me how much we needed it. Our family goes there at least four times a week. And people talk to each other—neighbors and parents, we see each other all the time now.

The whole experience was so meaningful to me that I even helped another school get a playground. My daughter was in a program at a different school, and their playground was condemned for safety reasons. Same thing—the school didn't have a place for kids to play. At the same time, we heard about a local minor-league baseball team, the North Shore Spirit, that was closing down. They were a few towns over, and their ballpark had a playground. They wanted to give that equipment away, so we contacted them, and we got it for nothing. They gave it to us for free!

Since then, I've talked to other groups working on similar projects. I help steer them through the process—how to get grants, how to raise funds. I have a big file of all the things I wrote up, which I send to people to give them ideas. I've helped people navigate the obstacles of the Community Preservation Act. And I've become a resource for the city and for my mayor.

Working with the school system and local government was exhausting, time-consuming, and often left us feeling beat up. We couldn't understand why it was so hard to do something that was so positive. But really, that all turned out to be a good thing. I don't think a city's just going to hand you the money, but even if they would, it's really better in the long run if you have to work for it. You'll learn more, and you'll make better relationships with the people around you.

It started with a playground, but it became so much more. Because of this playground, friendships came together for a common purpose and a sense of faith was restored, leaving us feeling that we could tackle anything.

Wendy's story exemplifies what we know happens as people go through the process of our model. When she started her project, people said she was crazy and that it would never happen. She persevered. Wendy identified assets within her own community. She not only raised the budgeted amount, but actually raised three times the money needed, enabling two playgrounds to be built. Following her own success, she has helped others to do the same. As Wendy said, the project left them "feeling that we could tackle anything." The community had realized their assets; their glass had gone from half-empty to half-full, and it was now overflowing.

▲ ■ ●

And then there's Wanda Cheeks, another all-star DIY playground builder who lives in Spartanburg, South Carolina. If anyone ever had a reason to give up on helping other people, it might be her. Wanda's mother had five kids, and she gave all five up for adoption. Growing up, Wanda and her siblings were raised by different families and never knew each other. Wanda was born in Spartanburg but taken in by an aunt in Atlanta. She came back to South Carolina a lot as a child, though, and gradually she got reconnected with her family. When Wanda was 12, she was brutally attacked in Spartanburg's Irwin Park, an incident that haunted her for years.

Almost 30 years after that attack, Wanda decided she wanted to do something positive for Irwin Park. As she puts it, "How do you turn bad things into good?" So she decided to build a playground there. She came to a few KaBOOM! trainings to learn how the process worked, and we gave her a challenge grant of $5,000, which Wanda quickly got matched by two local foundations. In all, she raised about $23,000. The city of Spartanburg donated another $10,000 in labor.

Construction took place in July 2006, with more than 200 people coming out to volunteer. The mayor was one of the first to arrive, at 6:30 that morning, joined soon after by other city officials and staffers from the local parks and rec department. TV and newspaper reporters showed up as well, along with some of her high school and college teachers.

Everything didn't go smoothly. Irwin Park was the first playground Wanda had overseen on her own. "It took us forever to build," she told me. "Fifteen hours. The triple slide—we didn't know you had to put that on first. We made multiple attempts. But in the end, it was awesome."

Through it all, Wanda's been a community activist in Spartanburg. She founded an organization, Southside Unity in the Community. "I don't like to call myself a director," she says. "We're all equal. We all love our community." The group holds neighborhood cleanups every 2 weeks, once a month in the winter, and Wanda works to get local kids involved in those efforts. "We're trying to give kids a sense of ownership," she says. Since Irwin Park, Wanda has volunteered on about six KaBOOM! projects. And she recently spearheaded construction for a second playground in Spartanburg, at a charter school she helped set up.

If anything, Wanda is an example of how KaBOOM! and our Mass Action strategy can serve as a platform for people, shining a spotlight on them and giving them third-party validation and credit for all the great things they're already doing. Wanda came to visit me recently, and she said that for a long time, people in Spartanburg viewed her as a hell-raiser—a vocal advocate who tried to do things that some people didn't like. But she said that with our support, she was able to achieve the same means in a different way. She's changed her approach and tactics slightly, to focus more on the positive elements of community service, and she's getting more results because of it. "I just want to share what we know and get other cities to do the same thing," she says.

▲ ▧ ●

An important component of our direct and indirect work is to be an advocate for play by impacting policy. There are a number of KaBOOM! programs that are intended to influence from both a grass-roots and a grass-tops manner. The Playful City USA program works to get cities and individuals across the country to start advocating for play. For the past few years, we've selected and profiled a growing number of communities taking exceptional steps in this direction and making specific commitments. These are big municipalities like New York City and small towns like Greenbelt, Maryland, and Credmoor, North Carolina (population 2,232). Wanda Cheeks got Spartanburg named three years in a row, and Wendy Minton, the mom in Peabody, is now working hard to get her town named as a Playful City USA Community. I wouldn't bet against her.

To make the list, these towns formally commit to improving the access to and quality of their play spaces. In return, they get local and national recognition, media coverage, and a shot at KaBOOM! grants that total more than $100,000. And most important, they become better places for kids. Of course, some cities go far beyond the basics.

In Greenbelt, Maryland, the city council agreed to cover 75 percent of the cost to fix up and maintain unsafe playgrounds inside home-owner associations, provided those communities opened their playgrounds to the public. In New York City, the local government partnered with the Trust for Public Land to build or renovate 221 playgrounds, with the goal of putting one within a 10-minute walk of every child in the city. Tucson, Arizona, opened 12 school playgrounds in the most play-deprived neighborhoods of the city after school hours, on weekends, and during the summer (many school playgrounds are closed to the public because of fear of lawsuits). San Francisco's city government forged a partnership with the Neighborhood Parks Council on a technology system called ParkScan, which lets people contact the appropriate city agency using their mobile phone or computer whenever they want to report a problem with one of the city parks.

Atlanta has been a Playful City for 4 years running, largely because of the efforts of Cynthia Gentry. After she finished the local playground to honor the Cunard family, she was so inspired that she went on to found a local organization, the Atlanta Taskforce on Play (ATOP), which serves as a central resource for the city. The group recently completed a survey of local playgrounds, to figure out their condition and which parts of town needed better access. "The whole west side of the city needs help," Cynthia says. She helped get a video made, which won a KaBOOM! contest (and the prize grant of $25,000), allowing her organization to hire a Website designer and a publicist to help promote some of its initiatives. And of course she still takes on projects that deliver the wow-factor. "I don't do small," she says.

A recent highlight? A tree house that's wheelchair accessible. Cynthia has long volunteered at a Georgia facility called Camp Twin Lakes, which hosts special-needs children. Kids with cancer or AIDS or learning disabilities, or those who have lost a sibling, get to come for a week and experience the outdoors with kids who are just like them. "The camp recently redid their playground," Cynthia said, "so I asked the director, 'What else do you need?' He said, 'I've always wanted a tree house for these kids, but you could never do it because of the wheelchairs.' Ding ding ding—bells went off for me."

She got campers to draw their dream playground (just like we do at

KaBOOM! on our Design Days) and then worked with one of the city's top architecture firms to convert those into actual designs. The whole package got presented to the camp's board of directors, and a woman stepped forward and said she'd fund it herself—the entire amount. Construction finished in the spring of 2009. The tree house is built into a cliff, so the kids can roll their chairs in, and suddenly they're in the trees. "It took us 2 years, but it's unbelievable," Cynthia told me.

▲ ■ ●

As hard as we work to create a movement for play throughout the United States, we've seen some international examples as well, like Mark White. In 2007 Mark came to a KaBOOM! training in New Orleans, where he was so inspired that he created his own nonprofit, Playgrounds of Peace, which now builds playgrounds overseas. Mark's first two playgrounds went up in Poland, the country where he and his wife adopted two children, and he's currently working on a similar project in Nepal. (Mark's known as "Mr. Playground" but also as *Pan Plac Zabaw*, the Polish equivalent, and *Shree Khelmaidan*, the Nepali version.)

In that same vein is a teenager named Alex Griffith. Alex was born in 1993 in Krasnoyarsk, a city in the Siberian region of Russia, and abandoned by his parents. They left him at Children's Hospital #20, suffering from a hernia and malnutrition. At 11 months old, Alex was adopted by American parents, who brought him from the hospital to his current home in Maryland.

He became a Boy Scout and earned the rank of Eagle Scout, just like my brother Pat and I did years ago. Achieving the honor of Eagle Scout requires a service project, and Alex wanted to give something back to the town where he was born. He decided on a playground at the site of the hospital. Children's Hospital #20 typically houses about 400 children—about 20 of them abandoned like Alex had been—and for years their play opportunities were limited to a single rusted swing and a sandbox full of mud.

The project took him about 2½ years. To fund the project, Alex raised about $60,000 through a variety of projects—selling candy door-to-door, writing letters to local schools and organizations, and even organizing a classic car and truck show. He designed all aspects of the playground himself. The components were in red and blue, which represented the colors of the US and Russian flags. He did some research and found that playgrounds in Russia often have carvings taken from the country's folklore, and he wanted his to match. So Alex tracked down a 20-foot Alaskan cedar log and found a chainsaw artist on the Internet to carve it into two totem poles, each weighing more than 400 pounds. One was cut into the shape of a bear (the unofficial symbol of Russia) and another in the shape of an eagle (the official symbol of the United States). They were shipped to Krasnoyarsk with the rest of the playground components.

Alex celebrated his 16th birthday during construction, when some Scouts and other volunteers, including his father, Dwight Griffith, put up the playground. Some children from the hospital saw what the commotion was about and came out to help. For the record, he didn't get help from KaBOOM! on this project, which makes his accomplishment— remember, he's a teenager—all the more impressive. So impressive, in fact, that Alex and his dad appeared on *Larry King Live* a few weeks after he got back, to talk about the project.

The two of them have come to some KaBOOM! builds, and they're committed to helping the cause of play in the future. Alex is on our Website, and he's a huge resource for anyone who wants to launch a similar project, overseas or in this country. We think his story will inspire people to wonder whether they can plan a playground project in their own hometown or fulfill any other dreams they might have. After all, he planned his from 6,000 miles away.

Me at the age of four. The picture was taken the day my family was being processed into Mooseheart Child City and School in 1975.

One of the few photos of my entire family (circa 1988). L–R, first row: the then-girlfriend of my brother Terry, Sherry (Hammond) Presson holding her son Parish, Shirley (Hammond) Woodard holding her niece Amber Hewitt, Robbi Hammond, Dawn (Hammond) Hewitt holding her son Nick, Kitty Hammond; second row: Terry Hammond, Darell, Pat Hammond, Mike Hewitt, my mother Lois Hammond.

I returned to Mooseheart on April 6, 2002, to build a playground and was joined by three of my sisters. L–R: Shirley (Hammond) Woodard, Darell, Dawn (Hammond) Hewitt, Sherry (Hammond) Presson

Bernice and Sid Drazin, the owners of Comet Deli and Liquor in the Adams Morgan neighborhood of DC. Sid died in 2005 and Bernice died in 2007.

On a trip to Rwanda in 2000, women show plans for the massive park they had hoped we would build on a remote parcel of land outside Kigali.

Celebrating a playground KaBOOM! built in Key West with the Ben & Jerry's Franchisees. L-R: Founders and namesakes for Ben & Jerry's Ice Cream, Jerry Greenfield and Ben Cohen with Kate Becker and me.

A pint of KaBerry KaBOOM!, the first Ben & Jerry's Ice Cream named for a nonprofit.

A KaBOOM! Playground Institute, one of our early trainings, was a great success. L–R: Helen Doria (a mentor and founding KaBOOM! Board member), Nancy Rosenzweig (former KaBOOM! Board Chair), Darell, Dawn Hutchison-Weiss (cofounder of KaBOOM!) and John Sarvey (City Year colleague from the Columbus CYZYGY conference and former KaBOOM Board member).

Darell and Bob Nardelli (left of author), then CEO of the Home Depot, ringing the bell at the New York Stock Exchange.

Jody Kretzman, cofounder of the Assets Based Community Development Institute at a KaBOOM! University of Play!

Former First Lady Hillary Clinton at a build honoring the 25th anniversary of the Children's Defense Fund in 1996, one of several the former First Lady has attended.

Vice President Al Gore, Tom Falk (looking down), current CEO of Kimberly Clark, and General Colin Powell at a KaBOOM! build in 1997 in Nicetown, PA, part of the President's Summit for America's Future.

Former First Lady Laura Bush cuts the ribbon at the end of the KaBOOM! playground build in Kiln, MS, the third of 141 playgrounds KaBOOM! has built in the post-Katrina/Rita Gulf.

Maria Shriver, a huge champion for KaBOOM! and playgrounds, at a Cesar Chavez legacy build funded by Shriver's California Volunteers. (*Photo by Ellen Kelson*)

First Lady Michelle Obama with KaBOOM! team members at a California Volunteers-funded KaBOOM! build in June 2009 in San Francisco. (*Photo by Dino Vournas*)

All KaBOOM! builds begin with children drawing their dream playground. This masterpiece is by an 11-year-old architect in the making.

Before: Drew Elementary School in New Orleans pre-build.

After: The site has been transformed for the kids of Drew Elementary.

Volunteers working together to construct a playground component.
(Many hands make the process fun!)

Ashley Brodie (smiling at center), the seven-year-old who was the honorary Project Manager for the
playground built at Livingston Manor in Washington, DC, in 1995.

Windsor Cove volunteers celebrate their work and their new playground
at the end of the day in Orlando, FL, in 2010.

The KaBOOM! playground build at Mooseheart Child City
and School, where I was raised.

Wray Hood, a determined grandmother and retired schoolteacher in San Antonio, TX, led her community in the building of one of our first playgrounds.

Completed playground in the Coliseum Oaks neighborhood of San Antonio, TX.

Our first Nature-Built playground was built (and planted) at Camp Erdman in Oahu, HI, thanks to the generosity of the Omidyar Network.

Darell and David Rockwell examine foam blocks in an early iteration of Imagination Playground in a Box (designed by Rockwell). (*Photo by Rockwell Group/Blandon Belushin*)

Students from KIPP DC, KaBOOM! employee Karen Duncan (far right), Susan Schaeffler, CEO of KIPP DC (left), and US Secretary of Education Arne Duncan look on as Redskins quarterback Donovan McNabb cuts the ribbon at KIPP DC Promise Academy.

Delighted kids find much to do using imagination and ingenuity at the destination park Imagination Playground at Burling Slip in New York City. (*Photo by Frank Oudeman*)

The Senior Team in a conference room in DC. The caricatures on the wall celebrate employees when they have reached their second anniversary at KaBOOM! L-R: Gerry Megas, CFO; Jim Hunn, VP Mass Action; Bruce Bowman, COO; and Kate Becker, VP of Programs. Missing from the photo is Susan Comfort, VP of Philanthropy.

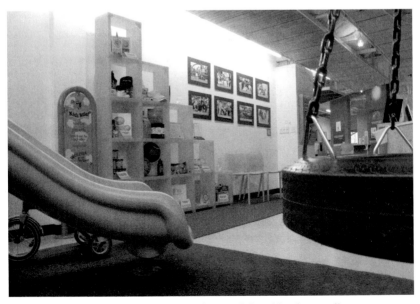

The KaBOOM! lobby in Washington, DC . . . it's a playground!

[13]

Imagination and Innovation

One hot day in July 2010, a few hundred people gathered at a site in Manhattan's South Street Seaport neighborhood for a ribbon-cutting ceremony at an Imagination Playground, a 12,000-square-foot site that includes almost no traditional equipment, things like swings or teeter-totters or monkey bars. Instead, it features interactive structures including two massive sandpits and fountains that shoot water up in unpredictable geysers for kids to dam up or sluice in different ways as it runs back down in shallow pools. The centerpiece of this play space is hundreds of jumbo-size foam blocks, which are the core of the Imagination Playground concept of bringing child-directed creativity and imagination into the playground.

Actually, calling them blocks is a bit oversimplified. Picture the wildest set of jumbo-size blocks you can imagine, like something out of Willy Wonka's imagination. They come in 23 shapes—some are rectangular, others are wheels, some look like gears, others are long U-shaped chutes like tiny aqueducts—and they can be lined up, stacked, ordered, and arranged in millions of different combinations. The largest block is about the size of a very long desk drawer, but because the pieces are made of foam, which is mostly air, they're very light. The heaviest block weighs about a pound.

One of the design principles of Imagination Playground is to couple a manipulable environment (such as sand and water) with the foam blocks to create a super engaging play experience. There's something called a bubble pump, the only one of its kind in the country, which puts out a mushroom-shaped dome of water. (One kid called it an "umbrella made of water.") In a forward-thinking twist, the entire Manhattan playground is manipulable and designed to be sculpted by kids—and despite the rich creations you will see rising out of the ground, you won't find any instructions written anywhere. Kids figure out how everything works by playing with it. The site, called Burling Slip, was a former commercial pier first built in 1835, so the design was customized to honor this heritage and includes some nautical elements like masts and pulleys and teak decking. In fact, the entire site looks a little like the deck of a ship, with a raised bow pointing west.

At the ribbon-cutting ceremony that July day, a bunch of local dignitaries had shown up to address the crowd, including New York City Mayor Michael Bloomberg and Parks Commissioner Adrian Benepe. But it was hot and the water was already running, and several dozen kids from a nearby summer camp program who'd come for the ceremony just couldn't help themselves. Even before the park was officially open, they started playing with the blocks, splashing around in the fountains, and trying to figure out how they worked. (To any kids reading this, here's a tip: There are five different settings, and some of the holes that shoot water can be plugged up, so the water pressure increases in the others. I highly recommend plugging all but one, creating the power of a fire hose!) A 5-year-old piled up some of the foam blocks in a tiny rolling cart and shuttled them from one side of the playground to the other, where he proceeded to pile them up and gleefully jump off them. His mother watched him and said, "We'll be here every day."

Imagination Playground was designed by David Rockwell, the renowned designer and architect. His Manhattan firm, Rockwell Group, has designed spaces including restaurants (Nobu, the famed sushi eatery in New York's TriBeCa neighborhood), hotels (several of the W chain), casinos (the Mohegan Sun), stadiums (Turner Field in

Atlanta and Heinz Field in Pittsburgh), theater sets (Cirque du Soleil, *The Rocky Horror Picture Show*, and *Hairspray*), single-event sets (the Kodak Theater Academy Award stage), and even cruise ships (Disney). And he's been increasingly involved in play spaces.

I first met David about a decade ago. At the time, he was just starting his family and was increasingly interested in playgrounds and their design. We stayed in touch, and I followed his achievements from afar. David has long lived in lower Manhattan, and he often gives back to the community. After the 9/11 attacks, he collaborated with a few other local architects to create a viewing stand for the wreckage of Ground Zero. And a few years ago, he looked around at the playgrounds around New York City and thought he could come up with something that would enhance children's play opportunities. He called Adrian Benepe out of the blue and offered his services pro bono.

A key part of the philosophy behind Imagination Playground is that kids will be more engaged if they can freely interact more with the stuff at a given playground. They'll play longer and harder if they can use their imagination to build things and then take those things down and start all over. So the site also includes things like milk crates that can be turned into carts for moving things around, and scaffolding structures with fabric so that kids can make forts. The park is supervised— lightly—by a member of the city's Parks and Recreation staff called a play associate. Play associates are modeled after the play worker concept of Great Britain. He or she creates the environment for the children to self-direct their play—they are, in essence, stage managers. They do this while unobtrusively observing the kids but not interfering unless it is a critical safety issue. One London play worker, Penny Wilson, coined the term *cloak of invisibility*, which describes this method of play facilitation where adults are both "present and not present at the same time." The goal is to let the kids make everything up on their own.

When you combine the jumbo foam blocks with milk crates and fabric, those components become a collection of "loose parts," and they're intended as a giant toy box. Children can pick and choose from the available resources to create and re-create as they play. The sandpit and running water make an environment that kids can manipulate, which only increases the possible combinations. It sounds simple—primarily it's blocks, sand, and water—but this taps into the oldest principle of play. The simplest toys are usually the best, and most of those complex, technologically "advanced" devices often aren't any more interesting to kids than the box they came in.

After all, most toys, no matter how cool they are, can only do the one thing they were designed for. More neutral objects, on the other hand, can be anything. A kid who's looking at a wrapping-paper tube doesn't think, "round cardboard cylinder that supports a roll of paper." Instead, the child goes into a conceptual world that's separate from the physical object. To the child, the tube stops being a tube and quickly becomes a telescope or a sword or a megaphone or a laser. That imaginative component alone has a critical purpose in development, but it also teaches kids to become more creative, which leads to better problem-solving skills. Bottom line—the more variations you can give kids in a given play setting, the more interesting it will be and the longer they'll want to stay. And blocks give kids pretty much unlimited variation.

The design for the Burling Slip playground is wildly ambitious and, because it's pretty expensive, probably one of a kind. (Construction costs exceeded $7 million, though only about $3 million of that was spent on the actual playground; the rest went to getting the site ready, a process that included rerouting a water main and a sewer line that ran underneath it.) David has an interest in creating similar parks in all five boroughs of New York City and ideally in other parts of the country; he is hoping to find the right partners and the right locations. Still, the three most critical and innovative aspects of the design—loose parts, a manipulable environment, and a play associate—could conceivably work just as well in other locations that can't support the full-blown version with an architect and major construction and a big budget.

When I heard about Burling Slip, I was initially intrigued and excited, as I always am when I hear about new, innovative play ideas in the works. I hoped that this project would see the light of day and not be a well-intended but unsuccessful stab at unconventional playgrounds, like some others that came earlier. I've seen plans for projects that either never got built or weren't well received by kids. For whatever reason, those projects never lived up to the aspirations of their designers. Burling Slip was different, and the more I learned about the project, the more I became its advocate.

As the largest single purchaser of playgrounds in the country, KaBOOM! wants to spur innovation in the field of play. We don't want to just build more playgrounds, we want to build better playgrounds so that kids will play longer, play harder, and want to come back and play more frequently. There's a lot of good stuff out there, and we constantly look at new ventures, potential partnerships, and big ideas. We feel like we need to keep changing and adapting, staying up with the latest developments in the industry, incorporating great ideas into our process, and seeing what kids think of them. We routinely work with playground manufacturers throughout the United States that have new concepts they want to try out. Not all are successful, but all are worth exploring.

In 2007 we started working with David Rockwell's firm to get the concept of the foam components at Burling Slip out into the world. We created a separate entity, called Imagination Playground LLC, which is a 50-50 partnership between Rockwell Group and KaBOOM!. Rockwell provides the design for the loose parts—which are mostly finished, though they're still being tweaked as we get more feedback from kids— and KaBOOM! provides the playground expertise and the relationships that we've established with communities and child-centered nonprofits across the country. All financial returns go back to the cause of play; no one profits from the venture.

The main commercial version of all this is something we call Imagination Playground in a Box. It's a set of 150 of the foam components plus a few other elements or "found parts" we wanted to include—such as fabric, balls, yoga mats, and long tubes known as noodles (those long skinny tubes that kids use in pools)—that can loosely connect one piece to another. It all comes in, yes, a box; in this case, a colorful, rugged rolling trunk similar to the crates that bands and theatrical companies use to transport their equipment.

The boxes can be rolled out to playgrounds (or used inside), locked each night with all the blocks and found parts back inside, and reopened the next day. And they can be deployed anywhere in the country: traditional settings like churches, community centers, and public parks but also unexpected places like airports and festivals. Ideally these are places with some kind of manipulable environment, like sand and water, and a play associate who can supervise the whole thing. (That last element is not hard—we can train people online for those responsibilities in about 2 hours. And an online forum provides ongoing and interactive support to play associates after they are trained.) Result? An instant playground. Just add kids!

I watched an unscripted test of the blocks back in 2008. The staff at the New York Hall of Science, a children's museum in Queens, had heard about the project and offered up their space so we could hold an informal focus group. We spread a few hundred blocks out on the floor in an open exhibit space, with no instruction manual, no guidance, no signs or hype. The kids would figure out what to do with them—or they wouldn't.

As soon as the kids saw the blocks, they picked them up. And as soon as they picked them up, they started playing with them. And they didn't stop. For 2 days straight, we saw kids make forts, stages, dollhouses, cars, skyscrapers (complete with skyways connecting them), and even a set of wobbly stairs.

The pieces—jumbo-size, soft, vibrant blue—just beg to be picked up and stacked and rearranged. The kids needed no help from parents, though in some cases the parents tried to get involved, almost *too* involved. We thought the blocks would be popular with kids up to maybe age 5, but kids as old as 12 and 13 were deeply engaged and actively playing.

In a few instances, they were having so much fun that their parents had to pull them away to go to a movie at the museum that they'd already purchased tickets to see. One kid came back to the blocks multiple times on Saturday, and his parents brought him back on Sunday—they said they'd never done that before. Children who didn't know each other, who started out playing separately, suddenly started playing together. The large size of some of the blocks encouraged that kind of collaboration.

I came away convinced that the idea was powerful, and that's when I became a believer. Kids loved it. Parents loved it and were surprised at how much their kids reacted to the concept and how much fun they had.

In 2009, we distributed these sets at a few locations around the country as a pilot, and the results were equally fantastic. A park in the Brownsville section of Brooklyn tried a set in 2008, with researchers from the City University of New York monitoring to see how kids interacted with the equipment. The park already had a traditional playground, but the study was designed to measure whether the addition of an Imagination Playground in a Box could increase the quality of play on the site or the time kids spent there.

Those researchers found that kids played together with the loose parts for longer periods (as long as 90 minutes), building structures from the pieces in groups of three to five children. The research also showed that kids preferred the new components to more traditional activities like basketball and that they spent the most time playing on a combination of traditional, fixed playground equipment and loose parts.

Significantly, the blocks helped reduce the number of behavioral incidents—fewer fights, less pushing and shoving—and it broke down cliques among children. Kids tended to cluster around the blocks, and the play grew more collaborative over time. If one group built a spaceship and another built a volcano nearby, the next step was that they would try to link the two. (Incidentally, this study took place during the 2008 Summer Olympics, and the kids, without any instruction or guidance, also built an Olympic obstacle course, complete with hurdles.)

New York's Parks and Recreation Department, a huge supporter of Imagination Playground, was so impressed with the early test that it expanded the pilot program in 2010 to 10 parks, where kids in the city's summer day-camp program played with Imagination Playground in a Box sets.

At the same time, a charter school and a YMCA in Miami were also running trials of the concept. Kids there tended to build boats with the blocks. The tests were so successful that the facility bought a box for its permanent collection, and two parents who happened to be there during the pilot lobbied their local school to buy one. Other early adopters were a kids' museum in Connecticut and a 24 Hour Fitness sports club in San Jose, California, where the staff now uses it to help kids get some activity while their parents are working out. Before that, the kids were playing video games.

It's a big leap forward in terms of intelligent playground design, and it lines up with our mission in so many ways. After all, KaBOOM! envisions a great place to play within walking distance of every child in America. The traditional post-and-platform playgrounds have taken us a long way toward that goal, but those have limits, particularly in terms of the space they require (at least 2,500 square feet) and cost ($75,000 and up).

By contrast, an Imagination Playground in a Box can go in spaces as small as 450 square feet, even indoors. It costs a fraction of what a complete fixed playground would cost. Right now the price is $20,000 for a set, but we hope to bring that down once we get enough orders to manufacture them in higher volumes. A lower price, of course, would increase the potential market.

In addition to better access, we think this design serves a key function in childhood development as well. To be clear, we don't see it as a replacement for fixed playground equipment. In a perfect world, it would serve as an addition to them. But there are a finite number of ways kids can experience these fixed structures. Imagination Playground, on the other hand, has no limits. Kids can use the blocks for anything they can dream up. They're in full control and can invent as much as they want, and they will never have the same experience twice. It's the freest kind of free play, entirely child-initiated and child-directed.

The early reviews of the design have been fantastic. The *New York Times* called the Brownsville pilot "a playground where imagination can run wild." The *Wall Street Journal* said it would lead to "more creative and collaborative play."

▲ ■ ●

As innovative as this all seems, it's actually not a new idea. The idea of child-directed, unstructured play with loose parts, instead of fixed components, goes back decades, and the original version is something called an adventure playground. The idea was formalized by a Danish landscape architect in the 1940s named Carl Theodor Sorensen, who noticed the way kids played in the bombed-out spaces of European cities left by World War II.

In adventure playgrounds, the equipment is more or less homemade, from whatever kids can find in their neighborhood and whatever happens to be on the site already. Over time it evolves to include structures, spontaneous games, sand, water, small projects that kids can build, and no preset rules or requirements. The sites are typically supervised by an adult, called a play worker (comparable to a play associate), who oversees things but doesn't get directly involved with specific games or rules and lets the kids make everything up on their own.

The concept made its way to the United States during the 1970s, and at one point there were more than a dozen adventure playgrounds around the country. Most didn't last. Many municipalities didn't like them, in part because of aesthetics (they looked pretty disheveled— Sorensen actually called them *skrammellegepladsen*, which means "rubbish playgrounds") and in part because the concept of a play worker was simply too strange.

There is also the safety element: Adventure playgrounds tend to involve things that can make most American parents quake in fear. Even today at some sites in Japan and Germany, kids as young as 7 or 8 are given hammers and nails to build structures out of lumber and crowbars to take them apart afterward. Surprisingly, a study of these facilities in Europe found that they have better safety records than standard playgrounds, even though the equipment doesn't conform to any industry specs or mandates.

Adventure playgrounds remain somewhat common in Europe and the United Kingdom, where "play worker" is an acknowledged profession that requires specialized training. But in the United States, only one of the original ones from the '70s remains, in Berkeley, California. We have learned of a couple that are opening from our online Playspace Finder (a tool that allows users to upload, find, and rate parks across the country), and we recently heard about one from someone's Play Day planner. I hope they will make a comeback in this country.

Imagination Playground is an attempt to incorporate the best elements of adventure playgrounds in a way that's replicable at different sites. However, no one would mistake the foam components in an Imagination Playground for "rubbish" or something homemade. Rockwell's designers put a tremendous amount of thought into every aspect of them—size, shape, number of elements, you name it. Technically, they're made from something called cross-linked polyethelene, a material used to support patients' limbs during surgery, which looks a little like the stuff in yoga blocks. It's completely nonabsorbent and resistant to microorganisms, heat, mold, mildew, and corrosion. Basically, it can take anything kids can throw at it.

As clever as the concept is, I think it avoids being too clever. The components are not perfect and preformed. Instead, they're a neutral set of tools. They invite children to do the real design work and show how inventive they can be. For example, people who see the pieces for the first time, especially adults, are surprised to find that they don't snap together. In the world of Legos and Transformers and other toys that fasten in very specific, preset ways, that strikes some people as odd, but it was a conscious decision. If the components had specific, prescribed connections, that would put a limit on the ways kids could use them, which would undermine the free-play element.

On the playground, this means that things don't always happen neatly. When kids form channels with multiple pieces and pour sand and water down them, it leaks down into the seams where two blocks are next to one another. For some reason, this seems to bother adults much more than it bothers kids, who understand that it's an imperfect experience—a lot like nature—and that's okay.

Same with color. People often ask why the components are all a single shade (royal blue), instead of the variety of bright primary colors that most toys come in. That was another conscious decision by the designers. They wanted to eliminate any kind of hierarchy among blocks and avoid situations in which a child might say that the red pieces were better than the yellow or that he didn't want to touch the green ones. And because these playgrounds are designed for both boys and girls, the color had to be gender-neutral, which effectively narrowed down the choices to blue and orange. Given that the blocks are primarily used outside, orange would have shown the dirt more.

Getting the Imagination Playground concept out into the world has been a new experience for both KaBOOM! and Rockwell Group. Neither of our organizations is in the business of manufacturing or selling products. It's safe to say that neither of us could have accomplished this on our own. It has been a true team effort, and all members of the Rockwell and KaBOOM! teams have exhibited true commitment and dedication to making Imagination Playground a reality. Even with our combined talents, it hasn't been easy, especially when it came to financing.

During the early stages, we put together a business plan and figured we'd need about $2.5 million to get the venture off the ground. We have some extremely talented people on our senior management team, including COO Bruce Bowman, who used to run operations at Ben & Jerry's among other organizations (and Bruce, along with his colleague and former KaBOOM! board chair Michael Sands, was also instrumental in making the KaBerry KaBOOM! ice-cream flavor a reality). Bruce has been leading this effort around Imagination Playground for KaBOOM!, and he's been critical to its success. His experiences in manufacturing, his talent for building something new, and his ability to carefully and meticulously move us forward have been invaluable. Bruce led the work related to material selection, supply-chain management, safety certification and testing, and development of the biodegradable blocks. And he really led the effort to create a business plan that was as good as I have seen. (I have been told the same by some venture capitalists who have read it.)

While the business plan is extremely strong, it unfortunately hasn't persuaded many of those investors to buy in, especially in the current economic downturn. In the business world, $2.5 million is not a lot of money, but I've been to more than 65 meetings with potential investors and haven't had much success. We have seen a lot of interest but no financial commitments at this point.

But that has not deterred us. Rockwell Group and KaBOOM! have funded the venture out of our own operating budgets, in an amount that exceeds six figures for both of us. But we believe in this concept, and we're committed to the venture. And we've seen a few signs that the idea is starting to gain traction. The John S. and James L. Knight Foundation made a commitment that helped us incorporate Imagination Playground in a Box into our more traditional "decks and post" model as part of the foundation's civic-engagement goals. This gave us the opportunity to build out our processes to incorporate this new playground and to work to see it placed at a variety of sites. We expect that the pilot will prime the pump in terms of spreading awareness of the Imagination Playground concept. Now, with Burling Slip open and hundreds of people a day able to experience the components firsthand, excitement is really starting to build for the concept.

▲ ■ ●

Another area of recent innovation for KaBOOM! is our environmental awareness. In the past few years, we've started working to reduce the impact to the environment of our construction projects, primarily by reducing waste and reusing whatever materials we can. We now coordinate with the planning committees in advance of a project to line up recycling plans for everything on-site during Build Day, even the cardboard in which the playground equipment is packaged. In some cases, other local nonprofits can use our extra materials—for example, leftover paint for the murals on a play site can go to an art-focused nonprofit nearby. For food and beverages, we've shifted away from single-use containers, which has a huge effect on reducing waste, and we recycle the packaging we do use. In years past, we used to fill (and sometimes overfill) a 40-cubic-yard Dumpster by the end of the Build Day. But since incorporating sustainable strategies during planning and construction, our projects have reduced waste by 67 percent.

The next step is playgrounds that themselves are greener—not just the installation process, but the equipment itself. In theory, the greenest playground imaginable is already out there—it's called the woods. But because of demographic changes, suburban sprawl, and a bunch of other reasons, fewer and fewer kids have direct access to nature.

This is something that Richard Louv has written about in his book, *Last Child in the Woods*. Louv is a journalist who focuses on family and community issues, and the premise of his book is that children gain in profound ways from contact with the natural world. In other words, kids *need* to be in nature. Yet increasingly, they're cut off from it. Maybe they see a few trees on their street. Or they go to soccer practice on a patch of mowed, fertilized, automatically watered grass.

What do kids get from time in the woods? Creativity. A sense of wonder. Solitude. An understanding of the physical properties of things, like dirt and water and leaves. As Louv puts it: "Nature is imperfectly perfect, filled with loose parts and possibilities, with mud and dust, nettles and sky, transcendent hands-on moments and skinned knees. What happens when all the parts of childhood are soldered down, when the young no longer have the time or space to play in their family's garden, cycle home in the dark with the stars and moon illuminating their route, walk down through the woods to the river, lie on their backs on hot July days in the long grass, or watch cockleburs, lit by morning sun, like bumblebees quivering on harp wires? What then?"

Some people might argue that manufactured playgrounds aren't as beneficial for kids as being in nature and that time spent on a swing isn't the same as time spent in a forest. Other critics of manufactured playgrounds say they've become too similar—that is, they all look and feel the same, in part because of liability issues and industry safety requirements.

I see their point, but I think there are enough components and variables that you can put together an excellent experience for kids. This shouldn't be an either-or discussion. Most people in the United States don't have access to a section of completely raw nature—many people don't even have access to a park (a recent CDC survey found that less than 20 percent of kids live within a half mile of one). Most of the communities where KaBOOM! helps build playgrounds are in cities, often low-income neighborhoods where children have little or no options whatsoever to play outdoors. Those kids shouldn't have to wait any longer while adults debate the perfect solution for them.

We also have a cultural challenge to deal with. In 2002 and 2003, KaBOOM! built 67 playgrounds at childcare centers in California through an initiative funded by the David and Lucile Packard Foundation. One of the frustrations we heard from executive directors of the facilities during that program was that they wanted to get the kids outside playing in sand and water and other natural elements, but parents still wanted to pick up clean kids at the end of the day. They had dealt with some situations in which furious parents somehow equated being dirty with not being well cared for. Shifting that perception is not an easy task.

At the same time, we've begun exploring the idea of playgrounds that incorporate more natural components. We recently undertook an unconventional project on the North Shore of Oahu called a Nature Built playground. Like all of our builds, we had it designed by experts— the local kids who would be using it. Instead of a bird's nest, they wanted a "human's nest," and they wanted a log that they could use to stage bug races. Unlike most other playgrounds, it was built almost entirely with natural products found on the island. (The landscape designer who worked with our team to incorporate the kids' ideas into a central vision was a former project manager at KaBOOM!.)

The site was at Camp Erdman, a 25-acre YMCA property that hosts about 10,000 kids a year, mostly through churches and other youth groups. It's remote, about 35 miles from Honolulu, and looks like the paradise you imagine when you think of Hawaii. (Camp Erdman has gained some fame recently as the place where parts of the TV series *Lost* were filmed.) The project was funded by the Omidyar Network, a philanthropic investment firm founded by Pierre and Pam Omidyar. Pierre is the cofounder of eBay, and his wife, Pam, grew up on Oahu. The Omidyar Network has pledged millions to KaBOOM!, enabling us to launch our many-to-many strategy. They wanted to fund an unconventional playground as well, and this allowed us to pilot the natural playground integration with Imagination Playground in a Box.

In the summer of 2009, 250 volunteers showed up to build a park that included a fort nestled into the landscape; an edible forest of local vegetation; a jumping course made of mangrove tree stumps that had been stripped of their bark and rooted 2 to 3 feet into the ground at varying distances, to increase the challenge for the kids; a maze of native Hawaiian plants; an outdoor classroom; and a boulder garden of climbable rocks. We built an ADA-accessible pathway to the playground, lined with recycled bottles buried in the ground, bottom up, as markers. The one prefabricated element on the entire site was a double-wide slide that we built into the landscape. But even that was earth-friendly—the slide was fashioned out of recycled milk bottles.

This was a big project for us and far more labor-intensive than the standard KaBOOM! builds, which are run according to a well-established system and process. In fact, it was more like our earliest projects, where the work was almost entirely custom. We designed and created on the site, and were forced to solve a lot of problems on the fly. The work took 4 days, instead of the usual 6 to 8 hours, but the extra effort was justified by the end result—kids who are healthier, more in tune with nature, and less likely to spend all day inside playing video games.

Being there for the build days made me reminisce over our early KaBOOM! projects. It also underscored the value of slow design: to build a park over years and add and change play elements as you see how kids are using the space. The park evolves in a way that encourages maximum use as kids come back and find changes and discover and rediscover play opportunities. An optimal play setting is one that allows increased confidence and the discovery of new challenges through repeat visits, not mastery in a single experience. These designs require a lot of space and a lot of maintenance, so we couldn't possibly convert all of our playgrounds to Nature Built designs. But we see some fun possibilities. We have hopes of building nature play areas alongside some of the traditional designs we've put up over the years. And we're trying to incorporate green elements wherever possible—planting gardens, doing landscaping, and planting shade trees and shrubs. The end result will be better playgrounds, healthier kids, and community-inspired gathering spaces.

▲ ■ ●

We've taken on some other initiatives over the years. We built a few ice rinks and a few athletic fields. All were great experiences, and all showed that we could apply our model—community-building with a mix of local and corporate volunteers who work on a done-in-a-day construction project—to structures beyond playgrounds.

As we pilot and experience, we learn a great deal. The first innovative play space we applied our model to was skate parks. The projects were successful—in fact, I get to frequently visit one in a Washington, DC, neighborhood and thoroughly enjoy watching the kids skate. We viewed these parks as a way to expand our community-building approach and, more significantly, as a way for us to reach kids who have aged out of traditional playgrounds.

At the time we built, the country had about 200 free skate parks. Everywhere else, kids were skateboarding on the streets; the number-one cause of injuries to these kids was collisions with vehicles. It's been said that if your town doesn't have a skate park, the town becomes a skate park. Around the time we embarked on the project, my father-in-law's business property was being damaged by skaters, and he was concerned there would be a serious injury. He led other businesses in his town to build a community skate park and do something good for the kids.

We recognized that there was a social component as well. Somehow skaters had gotten pegged as ragtag dropouts and stoners; they've gotten labeled with the stereotype that they're the "radical fringe." That's not accurate, and it's not the experience we had at all. The youth were courteous, they were kind, and they were extremely interested in not only improving their skills but also in helping other kids get better.

We had challenges with many stakeholders as we were establishing the program. If the safety elements of playgrounds can generate controversy, skate parks brought out even more vocal reactions in some communities. Concerns about liability and insurance can be major roadblocks, although they don't need to be—the rate of injuries that require emergency room visits are far higher for team sports like football, basketball, and baseball. (This is partly because kids who skateboard learn how to fall safely.) But that was a tough sell to uneasy municipalities.

There are two basic types of skate parks: concrete bowls (which look like empty swimming pools) and flat surfaces with prefabricated equipment in the form of ramps and rails. The former is not conducive to a volunteer build; the latter is. The KaBOOM! skate park program could really only offer ramps and rails to communities. Once we got the community at large partnered in the project, we discovered a new challenge. Working with this age group was a new experience for us. Many kids had very strong ideas about the skate park they wanted, and if large numbers wanted a concrete bowl, that presented a challenge when we got to Design Day. Financing became the other hurdle. We reached out to companies that sell skateboards and equipment, but they had little interest in sponsoring new parks. Many of them are small businesses, so they don't have substantial marketing budgets, and they were already known within the audience they wanted to reach.

We ultimately built about 25 skate parks, most with the sponsorship of American Eagle, and all of them were ramps and rails. They were fun projects. The process didn't require waiting for concrete to cure, as the posts on traditional playgrounds do, so the youth could start riding as soon as we were finished. It was extremely gratifying for volunteers to see their work immediately put to good use. Some of them would stay for hours after construction was over, just watching. Those parks are still used today. I've driven past them and seen kids out there, even in bad weather.

If we could get more interest to build larger numbers of skate parks, as in the American Eagle program, we could continue the program. But prospective funders have been few, and interest has been in one, two, or maybe five a year. In the end, although worthwhile, the skate program was costly in money, time, and energy. We would welcome an opportunity to build more skate parks, but the cost of keeping the staff trained to implement these projects was too great for us to do in a one-off model. I'm absolutely glad we tried. We learned some things about our operation, and we learned to pilot programs in a moderate way so that there is an opportunity to learn as we go before launching something full-blown. We also learned that we could get a ton of feedback online from certain audiences, and that's something we use across the organization today.

It seems reasonable that any organization that grows, evolves, and innovates, while getting better, will also have some failures (I prefer to call them challenges and learning opportunities). As the CEO, and certainly as the cofounder, I've frequently found myself in positions where, after weighing various options, I've decided to take a risk. While risk taking may inherently mean sometimes succeeding and sometimes not, I think the more critical issue is making certain we learn from the times we don't succeed. That's probably the best gift any failure can give you: an opportunity to learn what not to do and an opportunity to learn what to do differently.

Years after the skate park endeavor, when I was adamant about KaBOOM! taking on projects on the Gulf Coast in the aftermath of Hurricane Katrina, someone close to the organization cautioned that the venture would end up like our skate park program, taking a lot of time and resources. While it's true that the skate park program may have taken time and resources, we successfully built 25 skate parks, and they're all free and open to the public. Everything in life entails some amount of uncertainty, and I thought these initiatives were worth the risk.

[14]

The Blurry Line between
For-Profits and Nonprofits

There's a stereotype that holds that nonprofits are sleepy little entities, filled with well-meaning but somewhat ineffective people who want to save the world but can't manage to get much of anything done. Many believe that if you want to see real innovation, excellent management, effective goal-setting, and efficiency in achieving those goals, you should look to for-profits, not nonprofits.

As the cofounder and CEO of a national nonprofit that prides itself on high-quality work, excellent customer satisfaction (96 percent of our partners rate their experience with us as good to excellent), and innovative solutions, I challenge this stereotype of nonprofits. This just hasn't been my experience.

The principles of running a business, whether for-profit or nonprofit, are quite similar. I'm a fan of Jim Collins, a business writer, and in particular of his monograph, *Good to Great and the Social Sectors*. It's a kind of appendix to his bestseller, *Good to Great*, but tailored specifically for nonprofits. We give a copy to all new employees at KaBOOM! on their first day and revisit his concepts annually at our Play Academy (KaBOOM! staff retreats). Collins argues that success is not defined by the kind of business one does; rather, it hinges on whether the organization is merely good or great. I agree with Collins; an organization's performance really has very little to do with whether they are a for-profit or a nonprofit.

In fact, a bunch of innovative nonprofits are establishing businesses that sell products. One might think that the only difference between these organizations and for-profit businesses is that they devote all of their profits to social issues, but even that distinction is blurring. Consider organizations like Greyston Bakery, the much-celebrated institution north of New York City, which produces all the brownies and other baked goods that get stirred into Ben & Jerry's ice cream. (Julius Walls Jr., the former CEO of Greyston, serves on the board of directors at KaBOOM!.) Greyston produces amazing brownies, but that's really a secondary mission. It was set up specifically to provide work training and jobs to people who other companies consider unemployable. It takes in about $6.5 million in annual sales and operates as a for-profit entity, though it's owned by the Greyston Foundation, a nonprofit. Imagination Playground fits into this category as well, in that it's a for-profit venture that is not focused on profits, set up as a joint venture between a traditional nonprofit (us) and a for-profit design firm (Rockwell Group).

Like KaBOOM!, Greyston has a two-part mission: making good brownies and providing job training. For KaBOOM! it is about play and building communities. We don't think we need to choose between the missions because we think that each makes the other stronger.

TOMS Shoes is another example of an organization blurring the lines. It's a for-profit company animated by the kind of socially conscious mission traditionally associated with nonprofits. The model is simple—you buy one pair of shoes, and TOMS gives a second pair away to children in developing countries. So far, it has given away 150,000 pairs.

KaBOOM! is a nonprofit and we try to implement the best methods, regardless of where they come from. The result is a smorgasbord of ideas that come from the for-profit world, social organizations, and hybrid entities like Greyston; some we've come up with on our own. This philosophy is even reflected in the makeup of our staff, which includes a few people who once worked for or even ran major divisions at giant corporations along with people who similarly worked for or ran other nonprofits, or from national service (the Peace Corps, Ameri-Corps, etc.) and similar service organizations.

The combination must be working. Harvard Business School has done two case studies on KaBOOM!—one on our scaling strategy and launching the many-to-many approach, and the other on our performance dashboard that measures our impact and results. Perhaps the biggest manifestation of this for-profit/nonprofit hybrid philosophy comes in the way we fund our operations.

The traditional approach for addressing social causes is to ask entities that have money—foundations, wealthy individuals and families, or even the public at large—to donate. That approach works in many situations, and it has its challenges. During economic slowdowns, many of those grants and donations can dry up, which can mean a reduction in services. In more extreme cases, it puts the very survival of the nonprofit at risk. The Ponzi scheme run by Bernie Madoff led to the collapse of a few social entities that had relied on donations from Madoff's firm or from his investors.

Share Our Strength is a noteworthy example of an organization pursuing other avenues to foster social change. It was founded in 1984 by Billy Shore and his sister Debbie Shore (one of our early board members) to eradicate the problem of childhood hunger in America. Rather than applying for foundation grants or asking for individual donations, Billy's organization tapped into people's professional expertise and created events centered on that expertise.

For example, instead of asking chefs to donate money, Share Our Strength asked them to prepare meals for an event, which the public could buy tickets to attend. Authors dedicated dollars raised from designated book readings and sales of books to Share Our Strength. This allowed celebrated individuals to donate time and expertise, rather than money, which in turn made them feel more connected to the venture. And they were connecting to potential customers as well. In fact, Billy has always been extremely good at getting high-profile professionals for these events—some of the best chefs and writers in the country—which attracted a higher-income audience and directly linked those people to the work he was doing on hunger.

Throughout the history of Share Our Strength, Billy was also very conscious about not making donors feel guilty by showing the kind of tragic photos we've all seen used to illustrate hunger—starving mothers and babies with bellies distended due to malnutrition (what he calls the "fly-in-the-eye photographs"). He wanted to create a new paradigm for philanthropy, and he wanted people to feel good about the experience, not emotionally manipulated by grim images.

In the 25 years since its founding, Share Our Strength has raised more than $245 million and fed millions of meals to families and kids. Along the way, Billy also wrote a fantastic book, *Revolution of the Heart*, in which he argues that the traditional funding model for nonprofits needs to be overturned. He refers to it as the "Blanche Dubois syndrome," in that the organizations that operate this way find themselves relying on the kindness of strangers.

Rather than the old model of donations and grants, which he puts in the category of merely redistributing wealth, Billy argues that the best, most innovative organizations can actually *create* wealth. To do that, however, they have to think and operate like businesses. To be more blunt, they have to think about money and how they can generate a sufficient amount to cover their costs and fulfill their social aims on a larger and larger scale, without being at risk of having those funds cut off.

This can be a challenge. Without a rigorous, business-based approach for determining costs for a given service or experience, many nonprofits can't accurately match outlays to the donations and grants coming in. This may mean unintentionally underspending a grant, or it may mean operating at a loss, thinking it can be made up later by persuading donors to increase their pledges. Whatever the case, this management model is inefficient and unsustainable.

▲ ■ ●

I wish I could say that I strategically developed the primary funding model for KaBOOM! after a great deal of deep analysis and a lot of careful thinking about these issues. Instead, I think I was smart enough to spot a good idea when I saw it, and I was stubborn enough to stick with it. From our first playground in Livingston Manor, we've operated the core KaBOOM! program on a fee-for-service model. That means that we essentially get "hired"—typically by corporations—to perform a service. The organizations that have traditionally partnered with us pay the bulk of the cost of the new playground, our project management expenses, and our operating costs as well. These organizations are typically corporations and/or businesses that want to give back to their customers and stakeholders by doing good. It is the socially responsible thing to do. And frankly, there is a value exchange in the proposition. By giving back, each business is lifting up its reputation as well as its brand to its customers and employees.

Investing in KaBOOM! is investing in the cause of play while doing good work in a community. Our funding partners (corporations, etc.) can rely on us to coordinate a volunteer activity for their employees through a local organization that needs a playground. We actively manage the experience so that volunteers are effectively used, and we provide an opportunity for the organization to foster a bond with the local community. Meanwhile, we get the opportunity to work closely with the community to identify and activate their assets, strengthen their neighborhood, and build a great place for their kids to play. That's it—that's been our primary fund-raising model, and until recently it's worked well. The playgrounds create an immediate, tangible product—a place where children can play—that is ideally suited to the fee-for-service model.

When we launched our Mass Action strategy—enabling us to scale through programs with much larger, but more significant outcomes that would be accomplished through crowd-sourcing and online and offline action—we recognized the need to refocus our fund-raising approach. The fee-for-service model could no longer be relied upon for 90 percent of our funding. As we went about building the online tools, we also began the process of retooling our development approach and strategies. The funding model and the revenue streams we had been relying on would need to be diversified. This would mean exercising new muscles in order to strengthen our traditional fund-raising capabilities.

Throughout the transition of revenue diversification, our board chair Rick Kelson has been a great mentor to me and the management team. Rick is brilliant, seasoned, and has a depth of experience from the corporate world that's been invaluable to us. He retired from Alcoa Inc. in 2006 as chairman's counsel and had been executive vice president and chief financial officer for nearly a decade. But he also gets the grant making and social organization aspect of things, which in part derive from who he is as a person and in part from his experience as director of the Alcoa Foundation for more than a decade. He is a model leader and champion of our cause. We were very lucky to get Rick to join our board. He is the right person at the right time to be our chair, but he is also the right person at the right time to provide me with the sort of guidance that I personally need as a leader. Rick has effectively counseled us on balancing and diversifying our base, hedging against being overly concentrated in resources from one source. He has steered us toward being very thoughtful and strategic about protecting our brand and limiting or precluding exclusivity in our partnerships.

Expanding beyond the fee-for-service model and looking to broader streams of resources have made our financial health more sustainable and strategic. With multiple national partnerships, more foundations, and the benefit of individual and major gifts, we can earn more unrestricted dollars. These funds contribute to the support of the organization's overall mission and enable us to make the most of an unplanned opportunity while also providing some insurance.

The benefit of this diversification was demonstrated in 2005 when individuals who made donations to KaBOOM! through the Amazon .com competition unknowingly built the first permanent construction in the Gulf following Katrina. Similarly, we've made some of our greatest advancements, particularly with respect to Mass Action, through the support of foundations that are focused on longer term impacts and capacity building.

The fee-for-service approach is the same one used by almost all businesses that sell any kind of expertise, as opposed to a physical product. The most common examples are law firms and consulting companies. And, just like those firms, we use this system because we're serious about establishing exactly what each project really costs us in overhead. In our earliest projects, we would wing it a little bit, but those days are long gone.

Our employees break their working days down into 30-minute segments, and each segment gets allocated to a specific project or funder. It's akin to the billable hours at some for-profit companies. Project managers are even more precise, tracking their time in 15-minute increments. Those managers also get a budget for each project that is tightly managed. In other words, we watch the bottom line, ensuring that time and dollars are optimally managed. That kind of precision helps us to accurately budget and maximize the dollars spent in the community, and it allows us to manage programs to the outcomes we intend. I consider that a basic responsibility of any organization that operates with someone else's resources. It's a sign of respect to the funders who back us that we spend their money as effectively as possible.

This is the approach that has enabled KaBOOM! to grow. We reached $20 million in annual funding in 2006, about a decade after our debut. It's a milestone that very few nonprofits ever reach. About 90 percent of all nonprofits operate with budgets below $1 million, and a study by the *Chronicle of Philanthropy* found that only 24 of 2,100 nonprofits founded since 1970 reached $20 million by 2004. Why is there a record of slow growth? There isn't a straightforward source of capital for even the most compelling cause with the most brilliant plan. Generally the philanthropic community, especially foundations, tends to be extremely risk-averse. An untested idea does not typically have a chance of being funded, even if it has the potential to do a lot of good. In fact, this is one area in which there's still a fundamental split between nonprofits and for-profits.

Venture-capital (VC) firms help nurture the most innovative new for-profit companies, usually on the basis of a great idea and a strong management team. The VC firm provides the financial backing, giving managers the necessary resources to execute their idea. If those managers are not strong leaders, the VC firm often brings managerial and technical experience to the company as well.

VC firms tend not to look at the nonprofit sector because there is not the potential of a financial profit on their investment. Where it does exist, the return on investment is impact to society. Even the most promising, innovative start-ups are usually bootstrapped, self-financed with tiny grants and donations from family members. Like starting a for-profit, the founders and first few employees of a nonprofit usually have to live off their savings for a year or two, which significantly limits the universe of people capable of working in these organizations. Unlike for-profits, the founders of nonprofits don't have the hope of an unlimited income or an exit strategy.

An organization that makes it past the first few years and begins to have some success might get support from funders in small amounts, based on the record of having just proven itself. While the founder and management team devote a tremendous amount of time securing additional capital and lining up new partnerships, their energy and resources are probably really needed in-house, focused on executing their idea and strategy. But they get constrained by limited resources, and they're always scrambling to line up the next infusion of capital just to pay for the work they are already doing.

What VC firms have in abundance is a tolerance for taking risks. I wonder what social advances might be made if there were a similar culture of risk taking among the people and organizations that invest in promising nonprofits. Do funders simply invest in helping organizations with proven track records get bigger? Or do they invest in organizations that are getting the best results and allow them to be innovative? And when we measure results, are we looking at outputs or outcomes? These are big questions for the nonprofit and for-profit communities.

Fund-raising and development have to be critical parts of a non-profit leader's responsibility, but the primary focus should really be on executing and reaching the organization's goals. It is ironic that most of us in the nonprofit world were drawn in because of a passion about the mission, and we end up spending more time focusing on the money. Nonprofits would be far more effective if the people who ran them—including me—were given a lot of financial backing and a very short leash (which is the case with companies that rely on VC firms). We would be forced to prove we could really accomplish something with those resources, and if we didn't, we'd be gone—and frankly, I would readily accept that. In today's world, there are few models for investors who might be willing to accept a higher level of risk in exchange for greater social impact and gain down the road, as Omidyar Network did when it supported our Mass Action strategy.

▲ ■ ●

Our old office on M Street in Washington, DC, was less than ideal. You had to walk up two flights of stairs to reach it. There was one bathroom (a single-person bathroom) in the hallway shared by our staff plus the American Task Force for Lebanon staff. And the quarters were very tight for our numbers. That said, a rep from one of our corporate sponsors dropped by one day, and he was amazed to find out that the space actually had windows. The implication was that we should be operating out of a basement somewhere, with makeshift desks. After all, we were a young nonprofit, and lease payments can be expensive (especially for offices with windows). Those expectations about non-profits are unfortunate, but they're out there.

KaBOOM! is in a much larger space today, 15,000 square feet, with huge windows that run the length of one wall. To be honest, it feels a little like a tree house. We have a branch-level view of the dense foliage in nearby Rock Creek Park. I like that I can do a lot of bird watching while having serious conversations. We're extremely proud of the office, and we think it says a lot about who we are. If you walked in here one Sunday when no employees are around, you'd still be able to tell what kind of organization KaBOOM! is, just by looking around. All of the desks have toys on them. The walls are painted orange and purple, our trademark colors. One conference room that we call Sunny (because it faces out to the park, with sun streaming through the windows) has caricatures of employees covering the walls. We started the caricature tradition a few years ago. When Boomers hit their second anniversary, they get a framed caricature of themselves, and an exact replica of the drawing goes on Sunny's wall where they're immortalized.

In addition, we have some fun stuff in the lobby: a slide, a tire swing, a few dozen kickballs. There are a few chairs, but we also have "lily pads"—round plastic playground components about the size of a footstool that kids can climb onto and jump off. For a while we used those as an unofficial way to evaluate potential new hires as they waited in the lobby to be interviewed. Were they okay sitting on the lily pads? Did the pieces make them smile? Could they allow themselves to have a little fun in that nervous, pre-interview state?

In fact, our office design didn't cost more money (the fact that I feel compelled to tell you this is indicative of the challenge of a nonprofit). It was creative thinking as we planned the needed renovation, and we think the finished product is really a manifestation of our organizational culture. Any group of people that spends a lot of time together will develop its own group identity, for better or worse, but we think ours is special.

What's the fundamental purpose of this culture? I believe it's to make employees part of something special, something larger than themselves. From day one I wanted to establish this ethic and wanted to create a sense of esprit de corps. While the early elements of the culture were there, I often sabotaged them by pushing them too hard. I was trying to direct culture to happen. The organizational culture has evolved as I have evolved. Today we have a genuine and very rich culture. I no longer direct it to happen; rather, the workplace environment is fostered and nurtured by all of us, and the culture develops more naturally but with some intentionality.

We give employees at KaBOOM! a lot of responsibility. Project managers, for example, are sent around the country to meet with executives and neighborhood volunteers and kids and many other groups, to lead them in a great day of service. In that capacity, they represent KaBOOM!, and hundreds of people will base their judgment of us entirely on that experience. So it's absolutely crucial that the project managers hold up the best ideals of what we stand for.

This is true for a multiplicity of roles at KaBOOM!. Client service coordinators are essentially like program officers of a foundation. They are working to identify where the resources will be most successful for us and for the funding partner. The online team has developed and continues to innovate a very sophisticated online set of Web tools and community. The development team raises more than $20 million a year. It's the talented, hardworking individuals that make or break success for an organization. It seems appropriate to treat them well. One of my proudest achievements is our acknowledgment in 2010 by the *NonProfit Times* as one of the inaugural 50 Best Nonprofits to Work For.

We believe what matters most is how and what you do when no one's looking. Even if a project is the first build a particular project manager is leading, it is not the first build the organization is leading. Truthfully, KaBOOM! is bigger than any one employee. In fact, it's bigger than all of us put together. Our culture reinforces that.

As a result, we attract some of the most talented, passionate, high-performing people anywhere—not just within the nonprofit sector, but any sector. The KaBOOM! team works hard. They put their heads down and produce amazing results. They lift their heads up, and there's laughter and a sense of community unlike any other place I know. I have a lot of respect for my team. They are KaBOOM!, and we are a hard-driving, playful group of people that individually and collectively do consistent, professional, and extremely high-quality work in a very fun way while enlisting those around us to have fun with us.

We have a sophisticated hiring system. Having said that, once someone moves through the initial screenings and we know the talent is there, the basic hiring decisions at KaBOOM! come down to five key criteria—Can Do, Will Do, Team Fit, Damn Smart, and Damn Quick.

Can Do: *Can* the person do the job? Does the person have the ability and skills? Will Do: *Will* the person do what is necessary, when it is necessary? Team Fit: This is about our culture of serious fun; we are an eclectic group of people. We can all focus and put our heads down and achieve results, but we can also lift our heads up and have fun. Damn Smart: Does the person have the wisdom and intrinsic motivation? This is about the ability to know yourself when you do good and to push yourself to action. Damn Quick: Does the person have the mindset and drive to be able to work in a campaign type of environment? Work hard toward a very clear goal, get immediate feedback on whether that was successful, figure out what would need to be changed next time, document it, and move on.

Can Do, Will Do, Team Fit, Damn Smart, Damn Quick. When most people in an organization fit these criteria, it creates great synergies. It means you have great people to work and play with, and it means you will achieve amazing results.

Three of the five members of the senior leadership team came to KaBOOM! following highly successful careers in the for-profit sector. In addition to COO Bruce Bowman, our CFO, Gerry Megas, took several corporations public and had been CFO of US Foodservice. Gerry works hard on forecasting. He understands every variable of our business and is able to help plan and translate every nuance. That talent was particularly beneficial to us in 2009 and 2010, when we had some of our toughest and most challenging fiscal years. I always say that Gerry is the best CFO in the nonprofit sector, and the *Washington Business Journal* agreed with me: In 2009, the publication named him the best in DC (which has a very high concentration of nonprofits).

Jim Hunn, our vice president of Mass Action, came to us from Discovery Communications where he served as vice president of marketing. Jim's understanding of agencies and ability to speak the language of our partnering funders has been tremendous. He's refined our brand and communications, improving everything related to the look and feel of the organization, and he manages his team to some of the best results anywhere.

Susan Comfort is vice president of philanthropy and oversees the strategies and implementation of traditional fund-raising, including foundation and individual giving. Susan has a background steeped in the environment, having been with the Environmental Working Group and the Center for Environmental Citizenship. Her expertise has been critical in helping us exercise those new muscles and establish stronger support from sources that had largely gone untapped by KaBOOM!.

In many ways, the KaBOOM! culture comprises some elements of my personal philosophy of service, which goes all the way back to my upbringing at Mooseheart. This philosophy says that the things that matter in life are pushing yourself, transcending your limitations, and working hard to improve the lives of others, particularly children. It also means working with joy, which we think reflects the way that kids play.

This shows up in countless ways around our office, some of which are a direct, deliberate connection to the world of kids. Lots of offices put a coffeemaker in the kitchen for employees, but we keep peanut butter and jelly in there as well, along with cereal and milk. We also bring in lunch for the staff one day a month, so that no matter how busy everyone is—and we're always busy—we can stop and eat lunch together. Around Thanksgiving we have a potluck lunch. Everyone brings in a dish, we put a purple tablecloth out over the conference room table, and we share a meal—all staff-provided and staff-prepared.

Most nonprofits have some kind of black-tie affair each year to raise money and spread the word about their organization. Instead, we like to say that we have "purple-tee affairs," about 200 or so each year. That's how we refer to playground builds, where project managers wear T-shirts with our trademark purple and orange colors.

Culture is something that enhances our ability to accomplish things and something that we take active, conscientious steps to protect. It's an asset in the literal and financial sense of the word; it is an item on our emotional balance sheet. At the end of the day, happy employees perform better. They stay with us longer, and they're more willing to go the extra distance on the occasions when it's necessary. Honestly, we do what we do because we just want to do right by our employees, who define our organization.

These elements of culture are consistent with our mission—in fact, they're *part of* our mission. If our ultimate goal is to improve the lives of children, we need to walk the walk and see the world through their eyes sometimes. Amid all the hard work and busy days in the office, we need to make room for laughter, fun, and joy. In short, we need to make room to play.

▲ ■ ●

There's a potential risk in operating with a mix of for-profit and non-profit strategies. Critics sometimes say that KaBOOM! is overly focused on our fee-for-services model, which requires us to "sell" to big companies. Others say that we deal too closely with certain corporations. I think this goes back to the old way of thinking, which holds that nonprofits need to act like charities. I am not sure what that means anymore; there is a clear value exchange in how most nonprofits and businesses are working together today.

This reminds me of Dan Pallotta, a completely original thinker who tried to push the model of a social organization even further toward a for-profit structure: He launched a for-profit with a social mission, and he took significant heat for it. Dan's company, Pallotta TeamWorks, organized multiday bike rides and walks to raise money for certain diseases, primarily AIDS and breast cancer. Kate took part in a breast cancer walk back in 2002 and had a remarkable experience. Like KaBOOM!, Pallotta TeamWorks was set up with a fee-for-service financial model, and he was similarly obsessive about the details of execution. A fleet of 18-wheelers followed each ride or walk, and participants got showers, hot meals, and massages in camp at night. Dan's company even financed the events itself, so the charities it supported would not have to put up any money in advance.

During its regrettably short tenure, Pallotta TeamWorks was fantastically successful. No other organization raised as much money as it did in such a short time—$305 million for charity over 9 years. Of the 79 events the company ran, only one lost money. His organization was coming of age around the same time as KaBOOM!, and I remember being immediately impressed with the money he raised and the experience he consistently delivered to participants. I met Dan a few times back then. He's a dynamic individual, and his events were letter-perfect.

Dan's company generated very healthy profits. To be clear, he was running a for-profit company, and this created a lot of controversy. Some people thought every last dime should have been routed directly to the charities; otherwise, the company was profiteering. His company spent millions on sophisticated marketing campaigns, which critics said was unseemly and took further resources away from the causes he was trying to support.

Dan also had an approach to talent that was considered by many to be slightly radical: He recruited the best MBA grads he could find, and he paid them well. This is one area in which the line between nonprofits and for-profit companies is still largely intact. People from the corporate world rarely switch to social organizations—or they make that move exactly once, at the end of their careers, when they decide they can afford a lower salary and work for a social cause. A few

MBA programs have tracks in nonprofit management, but again, those grads typically start working at nonprofits and don't cross over. At some point the border will become a little more permeable, allowing talented managers to go back and forth easily, working at whatever organization in whatever sector presents the best fit. In fact, at some point, I fully expect that the head of a successful nonprofit will take over the top spot at a corporation.

But for Dan Pallotta, that transition didn't happen soon enough, and he was pilloried in the press. In response, Dan argued that you should judge his organization by the good it created, not by the way he went about creating that good. As he put it in his recent book, *Uncharitable,* which he wrote after the organization failed, "We allow people to make huge profits doing any number of things that will hurt the poor, but we want to crucify anyone who wants to make money helping them. Want to make a million selling violent video games to kids? Go for it. Want to make a million helping cure kids of cancer? You're labeled a parasite."

All the negative press turned into a drumbeat, and in the end, Dan was burned by that most simplistic measurement, the efficiency ratio. The ratio is intended to be a shorthand measurement of a nonprofit's effectiveness—it lists the percentage of total income that goes directly to the cause itself, with the rest covering overhead and other administrative costs including fund-raising. A number that's insufficiently high is thought to mean that a social organization is being wasteful.

Most people who really understand the nonprofit sector think efficiency ratios are overly reductive and don't measure what really counts. It's akin to judging a restaurant by how cheaply it pays its waitstaff and cooks, rather than by the quality of its food. Dan makes a number of pretty compelling arguments against efficiency ratios in his book. For one thing, he writes, they can be manipulated through aggressive accounting. A nonprofit can consider its advertising costs as "program-related" or count them as traditional overhead. If it opts for the first choice, it will show a higher efficiency ratio, even though it's spending the same amount of money toward the same goal.

The overly simplistic math behind these ratios also penalizes less popular causes. Why? Those organizations have to work much harder to find donors, thus incurring higher costs and making them seem less efficient. And if a group's incoming donations happen to fall—for example, during economic slowdowns—its efficiency ratios will go down as well, even though it hasn't changed the way it conducts itself. That scares away potential donors at the very time the nonprofit needs them most.

The costs of Pallotta TeamWorks events were more or less fixed (those 18-wheelers, the advance logistics of securing roads and campgrounds, etc.), and Pallotta would advance pay for securing them. The efficiency ratio for each event rose or fell depending on how many participants he signed up. When the negative focus on Pallotta began to play out in the media, there was a direct impact on his reputation, and walkers and riders were not signing up. He fell below certain key thresholds on the efficiency ratio, and several of the corporations that worked with Pallotta TeamWorks abruptly pulled out of their arrangements. The company ended up filing for bankruptcy.

Other entities are now running similar walks and bike rides for AIDS and breast cancer, but they're not seeing the same success, meaning less money is being raised to fight these diseases. Everybody loses.

I think a lot of the problems Dan came up against are grounded in the cultural history of the United States and in our complicated relationship to money. Personal wealth is generally thought to be a noble goal worth striving for; yet, at the same time, people feel that the rules of the free market should not apply to social organizations.

This thinking is old-fashioned, not productive, and just wrong. In a perfect world, organizations like Dan's would have a place at the table, along with nonprofits, other for-profits with a social mission, and anyone else trying to change things for the better.

▲ ■ ●

The most forward-thinking nonprofits are still trying to find the ideal balance, one that applies the best ideas from for-profits and nonprofits alike without jumping too far over the blurry line. At KaBOOM! we continue to look for that balance, but it's an active process, one that requires us to keep up with the latest innovations in the business world and apply those that can best mesh with our culture. Moreover, it requires that we take risks, because the well-being of thousands of children depends on us being very good at what we do. That includes getting others to do more so that we are achieving our mission sooner.

There is a play deficit in this country that is harming our children; we need the best ideas and the best people from across the spectrum—social organizations, corporations, even the public sector. Organizations working on this issue need every possible advantage if they're going to marshal their resources and execute at a high level toward the goal of a better, more playful future for children.

As Jim Collins wrote in *Good to Great and the Social Sectors*, the principles of execution are the same whether you're talking about corporate America or the nonprofit sector. It seems reasonable that a couple of great organizations partnering on an issue can execute programs that can do a tremendous amount of good.

[15]

What We're Up Against

Even those nonprofits that position themselves to do a tremendous amount of good still face serious challenges. For every worthy cause, there are people and forces out there that impede its progress. You might think that no one out there could possibly be against healthy children enjoying outdoor play, but you'd be surprised. In the spring of 2010, a condo association in Methuen, Massachusetts, fined a couple of families in the community $500 for letting their kids play in the common area of the complex. That's right—families were punished simply because their kids were playing outside, in the "non-designated" area. As one resident who didn't like the sound of kids having fun e-mailed, "I feel like we are living in the projects." Another took photos of the kids as they played Wiffleball so that their families could be identified and the condo association would know where to send the citations. That led to a lawsuit in which the federal Department of Housing and Urban Development got involved, telling the condo association that Wiffleball is not a crime.

In Douglas, Michigan, two women have been fighting since 2006 to close the playground at a preschool next door to their home. The women complained that noise from the playground was "deafening" and "unbearable." These are preschoolers, 3- and 4-year-olds, and the school had already compromised by limiting play time for the kids to just a half hour a day. But the women persisted. The playground was apparently such an annoyance to them that they shot video footage of the children playing and posted it on YouTube—they told reporters they were trying to document the noise. As if that wasn't enough, they allegedly parked a running scooter near the playground with the muffler pointing at the kids, so the fumes would force them back inside. And in the winter of 2010, these two women actually won. The city issued a cease-and-desist order to keep the school district from using the playground. The kids at this preschool have a playground sitting outdoors that they cannot use. I hope you find this as infuriating as I do.

These are extreme examples by people who, let's face it, might just be cranks. Unfortunately, the sentiment they express isn't new. Many of us think back nostalgically to when we played as kids—we had more freedom and more time for good old unstructured play than kids today—yet I'm willing to bet that every neighborhood probably had someone who yelled at the kids for running on their yard or trampling the flowers or maybe even just making noise. Let's call these folks play-haters. The difference today is that too often play-haters are taking legal action, and in many cases, like the one in Michigan, they're winning. In fact, these play-hater stories are only the most recent headline-grabbing examples of a larger and more pervasive trend in which play is dwindling in American society, and we're allowing it to happen. Every single one of us. The big question is why.

With all of the evidence about the benefits of play—neurological, physical, social, behavioral—how can we be allowing our kids to be playing less? The United States is facing a critical childhood obesity issue, our kids are doing worse in school, and we're seeing a decline in creativity. How are we allowing that to happen? Why are we not taking action and making decisions to ensure our kids have the time and place to play and, more importantly, to preserve their right to play? More to the point, are people in this country just nuts?

There's no question that we're living in a different time than people did a generation ago, and many of these changes reflect bigger shifts in society. For one thing, families have changed. Thirty or 40 years ago, more kids came from two-parent homes where one parent worked and the other stayed home, especially while the kids were young. That person was typically the mom, who would loosely supervise her kids and maybe the neighbors' kids as well. Everyone knew where the kids were and what they were doing, but there was less direct supervision. Those are ideal conditions for kids to play—on their own in a safe setting, without a lot of hovering grown-ups and no one blowing whistles at them. They were free to make up games in the basement or the backyard. Or they rode their bikes somewhere, with instructions to be home before dark. They were independent. And they learned to make their own fun without having to be entertained.

Today fewer and fewer families have one stay-at-home parent. Society requires that most households have two incomes to be able to make ends meet. With both parents at work, there are fewer eyes around the neighborhood, and the network of local support is slowly dissipating. As a consequence, there's a greater perceived risk—and sometimes a legitimate risk—of letting children play on their own. Parents fear that a child might get hurt or disappear. So kids increasingly spend time in structured, supervised activities like "playdates."

These days we are much more likely to buy and install our own playground in our own backyard, enabling us to keep a close and watchful eye on our kids. This is due in part to concerns of safety. But there is a serious lack of neighborhood parks in close proximity or good condition and in walking distance of our homes. We cannot overlook this as a contributing factor. We are losing the central gathering spaces in our neighborhoods.

Most older homes have a front porch, where people used to sit and talk with neighbors and could easily watch children play in front yards, stoops, sidewalks, and sometimes even the streets. Unfortunately, newer homes often do not include that feature. Children play in insular groups in backyards surrounded by privacy fences. We literally create physical barriers that prevent kids from coming together to play spontaneously.

Parents are inundated with hard choices every day about what is best for their child, what will make them smarter, what will position the child to get into the best schools, and what the parent should and should not do. Parents are being advised to get their kids involved in activities earlier to give them more of a competitive edge over their peers. The desire for the best education is creating more and more competition between kids at a younger and younger age as kids participate in team sports much earlier. The increase in this structured time is having a direct impact on the growing unstructured play deficit. All those hours of free play time that most adults today enjoyed when they were kids are long gone, replaced by soccer practice and music lessons.

Participation in things like soccer and flag football and Little League has doubled in the past few decades—estimates are that up to 90 percent of kids now take part in some version of those activities. Little League baseball was started back in the 1930s as a program for kids ages 9 to 12—which is probably the age when they need some coaching and help in specific skills—in addition to all the playing they were doing on their own. But today, kids as young as 4 play organized T-ball. And for most kids, that's it. That's their sole activity for the day, and they're driven to and from it. (One recent study found that kids today spend 1½ hours in the car each day.)

I am certainly not arguing against team sports, especially for older kids. I played a lot of sports when I was a kid. Football was my lifeline. And I learned invaluable lessons about life, sportsmanship, and teamwork that remain with me today. But there are benefits to all kinds of play, and I think organized sports should function as an *addition* to, and not a replacement for, so-called free play—which is the sort of play that I think is endangered and has critical value, especially for kids up to about 7.

Being a part of a team and learning and practicing and playing under the direction of a good coach has a lot of benefits: Kids get exercise, they learn to follow direction and be a team player, and discipline is instilled. Unstructured play provides opportunities for kids, too: They learn how to organize themselves, make up rules, change those rules, and resolve disputes. In short, without unstructured play kids don't get variety, and they don't get to use their imagination to invent and tinker.

When I was at Mooseheart, we were able to roam the entire campus during the time we weren't in school. There was a lake and a waterfall and a dam along with two playgrounds, lots of trees, and open fields for pickup games. I played for hours a day in the water, creating my own dam, moving rocks, and exploring. I ran wild with nature as my playground. There was sort of a communal bike system. Bikes that had been stolen and confiscated by the Aurora Police Department (Aurora is a neighboring town) got donated to Mooseheart. We weren't each given a bike, but they were around the campus and you just hopped on one and went tooling around. We made up games and challenged each other. While I can speak directly to the lessons I learned playing football and from my coach, I think what I learned and gained from the unstructured play helped shape the most fundamental aspects of who I am—my most basic character. I know that the unstructured play contributed to being more curious and more creative. It fostered the social skills I have today as well as a bent toward innovation and a desire to achieve and do better.

We have all heard of the so-called helicopter parents who hover over their kids and jump in to help whenever anything goes wrong. Undoubtedly, these parents believe they are helping in the short term, but they may be doing more long-term damage if they don't allow kids to go it alone sometimes. Children end up with an unhealthy reliance on adults, who direct every action of their lives, including resolving the sort of playground issues kids used to handle on their own. When those kids grow up, they can find themselves unable to deal with the world as independent adults. Incapable of evaluating risks, unwilling to push themselves physically, and lacking experience in dealing with social conflicts, they may find themselves, in a twist on that expression you see on T-shirts, *unable to play well with others.*

Stuart Brown, MD, founder of the Institute of Play, and coauthor of the book *Play*, has conducted more than 6,000 play histories, examining the play experiences of individuals over the course of their lifetimes. From his work we know that play has a direct impact on the adult the child becomes. Brown finds that play deprivation can lead to serious mental health challenges and that play contributes significantly to healthy social, cognitive, and emotional development. He concludes that curiosity and resiliency are two common traits among those who do have the opportunity to play as a child and as an adult.

▲ ■ ●

It's hard, in theory, to say that kids should spend less time in class or that we shouldn't measure what they're learning or evaluate their teachers. But realistically, a little less of that might help. Over the past 10 years, the No Child Left Behind Act has resulted in a ton of mandatory testing, which in turn requires drills and repetition, especially in math and reading. If the child does well, it is assumed that the child is learning and it is assumed that the teacher is teaching well. As a consequence, teachers I know are concerned with how much time they are spending "teaching to the tests"—that is, prepping students for standardized exams in math and reading. To maintain the 6 hours in a school day, something has to get cut to make room for those drills, and all too often, that's recess. How did it become recess vs. education? It should be recess plus education. The time to play and get some physical activity will improve the education our kids are getting.

The Surgeon General recommends 60 minutes of play every day. KaBOOM! applauds that recommendation: Kazoos are playing, confetti is falling, we are ecstatic! Thank you, Surgeon General! To this KaBOOM! adds: We recommend 60 minutes of *outdoor* play every day.

Of the 16,000 school districts in the country, more than 40 percent have shortened or eliminated recess, even though about half of a kid's opportunities for play come from recess during school days. After all, the thinking goes, it's hard to rank schools based on their playgrounds, and no one's getting into Harvard for playing a really good game of dodgeball (though Harvard would probably be a tad bit more fun if people could).

When I talk to kids and ask what their favorite subject at school is, the answer is inevitably recess or gym. And by the way, this is rigorous research I am conducting. The other day an employee came in with her 6-year-old son and 8-year-old daughter. She was in for a meeting and not actually supposed to be working that day. Her kids had books tucked under their arms, and their mom declared that they would be perfectly fine sitting and reading. Well, we have a playground in our lobby. The kids began playing, swinging on the tire swing and riding a tricycle around. I started a game of dodgeball with a KaBOOM! purple ball, throwing it (softly) at the 6-year-old; he was throwing it (not so softly) back at me. I decided to pursue my rigorous research, and I asked each of them to answer honestly, "Do you prefer play, or do you prefer reading?" The 6-year-old declared quickly, "PLAY!" The 8-year-old pondered the question, eyeing her library book on the floor . . . "PLAY!" she grinned! Yep. It's official—kids declare play as their preferred activity every time. (Okay, okay, I know my rigorous research is a bit tainted, and like I said earlier it really shouldn't be recess vs. education nor should it be play vs. reading; we all know the whole child needs both.) The thing is, we are not doing all we can to ensure children have everything they need to be whole.

Why are recess and gym the favorite parts of a kid's day? I love my work and what I do. I can tell you that when I'm not traveling and have the opportunity to be in my office, the favorite part of my day is walking down the hall and shooting the breeze with folks. I like laughing and talking and playing around. And after spending a half hour chatting with folks or eating lunch in the kitchen with a group of people and talking about things that aren't related to work, I go back to my desk and feel rejuvenated and more ready to tackle the work in front of me. Kids are the exact same way. We cut their recess and decrease the physical education time, and we wonder why they do worse in school and why they're becoming more obese.

Years ago, before Hurricane Katrina, I got a call from the superintendent of schools in New Orleans. She told me that the school board was about to eliminate recess in the schools there, against her recommendation. The board was able to take a step like that, largely without consequences, because only two people showed up at the public hearing to protest it. The previous week, the superintendent told me, when the school board was debating changes to the lunch menu, 600 people showed up.

How is it that the United States is not grasping what we're doing to our kids? I think 600 people should show up to speak out about the school lunches, and I think *1,200* people should show up to speak out on recess. At least with school lunches, you can choose to pack your kid's lunch if you don't like the menu. If the school cuts recess, there is no way for the kid to arbitrarily incorporate a needed break into their day. (Fortunately, a nonprofit called Playworks is working to improve the recess experience for both kids and school administrators. Playworks is scaling up to reach more school districts throughout the country, but it's still just one organization fighting this trend.)

Usually what replaces recess in the school day is more class time or test prep, but there's a growing stack of evidence that kids in these schools aren't getting any benefit from the added instruction. All that emphasis on standardized tests puts pressure on kids and takes away any opportunity they might have to run around a little and have fun. Or they get a ridiculously short period of time—15 minutes a day or less. In Rutland, Vermont, middle-school students used to have a 10-minute recess period, but that was taken away in early 2010, and kids there now get a combined session, for eating lunch and recess, of 22 minutes. Is that even enough time to digest your food? Do kids need unions advocating for them? At a minimum, there should be a mandatory amount of time to allow the children to run off some energy and rejuvenate their brains and bodies so they can keep learning. Kids who get to run around a little are actually better learners when they get back into the classroom. Kids just aren't wired to sit still for hours and hours at a desk.

We don't have to wonder what might happen from this heavy push of classroom learning onto younger and younger kids. Germany already tried it.

Germany more or less invented kindergarten. The word is a German term meaning "children's garden," and it was coined by Friedrich Froebel, the educator who developed the earliest version of kindergarten. Germany also invented playgrounds. Back in the 19th century, they were originally outdoor areas with gymnastics equipment.

In the 1970s Germany launched an academics-heavy initiative for kindergartners. To create that extra time, it cut recess. Soon after the program was implemented, educators in the country realized that the kids had more behavior problems, and they weren't learning well, either. The result? Germany scaled back the academic component of kindergarten in favor of letting kids be kids—and letting them play.

Finland routinely scores highest among developed countries in literacy rates and is among the top five for math and science. Yet the country puts an extremely heavy emphasis on play—kids there get a 15-minute session of free play after every 45-minute instruction session. The country's Minister of Social Affairs says, "The core of learning is not in the information being predigested from the outside, but in the interaction between a child and the environment."

Kids in this country might be under a little too much pressure and suffering from the lack of healthy opportunities to play during their day: In 2002, 11 million prescriptions for antidepressants were written for kids. More than 5 million children are on some kind of stimulant, like Ritalin. Recently, we've seen the new phenomenon of "kindergarten rage," like the 6-year-old who was arrested, with handcuffs, for a kicking, screaming tantrum. Connecticut expelled more than 900 kindergartners in 2002 for behavioral problems, twice as many as in 2000. On a broader level, a lack of play can also lead to increased levels of stress and anxiety, shorter attention spans, and higher rates of depression later on in adolescents and teenagers. Some studies have shown that a chronic lack of play may be linked to attention-deficit/hyperactivity disorder (ADHD) in kids.

There are also big-time health risks associated with the lack of play, like obesity. A 2003-2004 survey found that about one in six kids between the ages of 2 and 5 is technically overweight. For kids between 6 and 11, the numbers are slightly worse—one in five are overweight. Those rates are up about threefold from the 1970s. That excess weight can lead to all kinds of health complications for kids, like diabetes and heart problems. It also dramatically increases the odds that they'll be overweight or obese as adults, when the health complications can get more severe (everything from high blood pressure to certain types of cancer). Health-care and lost-productivity costs are expected to soar over the coming decades, and obesity is increasingly becoming the dominant health-care crisis in the country. This is a problem of staggering proportions.

▲ ■ ●

Unfortunately, politicians haven't been able to help much, either. Consider the debate about health-care reform in 2009, when Senator Mike Enzi fought for months to get an amendment added to the bill to ensure that none of the money slated to fix the health-care system would be spent on "sidewalks, playgrounds, or jungle gyms." He argued that he wanted the money restricted solely to medical-policy issues and not spread into the less quantitative realm of "wellness."

I couldn't believe it. As childhood obesity rates continue to rise to epidemic levels, with all the attendant health complications for those kids and future costs to treat them as adults, there is something seriously wrong with the discourse when politicians are fighting against funding spaces where kids can play or even walk.

And yet I know that Congress understands the importance of recess. If you're curious about the congressional recess schedule for 2010, you can see it at thecapitol.net/FAQ/cong_schedule.html. To be clear, I do not for one moment begrudge recess for our senators and representatives. The breaks are important, extremely important. Our kids need them, too.

The United States is one of the last countries in the world to not ratify the UN's Convention on the Rights of the Child, which was created by the UN in 1989. It declares that people younger than 18 years old must be protected from exploitation, violence, neglect, and discrimination. It overturned the common-law approach previously applied in many countries, which stated that children had the legal status of property, owned by their parents. Since its creation, the Convention has become the most widely adopted human-rights treaty in the world. Nearly 200 countries have signed and ratified it, virtually every nation in the world—except for the United States. There are child-protection laws on the books in this country, of course, but our failure to get behind the treaty is hugely symbolic and casts us in a negative light. Most other countries endorsed it way back in 1990. Even so-called rogue states like Afghanistan, Bulgaria, Iran, Cuba, Romania, and Yemen have ratified it.

For a long time, the two holdout nations were the United States and Somalia, but even Somalia recently announced it would ratify the Convention, leaving America alone. We signed the treaty back in 1995, but Congress hasn't ratified it, in part because of pressure from social conservatives, who fear imposing international standards on domestic policy. President Obama said during his campaign that our failure to ratify the treaty was an "embarrassment," and he promised to do so if elected. It hasn't yet happened.

▲ ■ ●

On top of all these issues, the play deficit is exacerbated by the ever-present fear of legal liability. Believe it or not, this phenomenon is not as new as it might seem. As early as 1915, a family sued a school board in Tacoma, Washington, over injuries their son suffered at a school playground. After they won, the school board was forced to pay damages and later removed some of its playground equipment; other school districts around the state quickly followed suit.

In recent years, lawsuits have gotten out of control, to the point where some families sue—or threaten to, which is almost as bad—for what basically amount to routine accidents. I'm not suggesting that there are never legitimate reasons to call a lawyer. If a playground is unsafe because of bad maintenance or unauthorized modifications or some other reason, that's a problem. Yet those are the rare cases.

In fact, the bigger problem is the people in our society who want to be paid whenever something, *anything*, goes wrong. There's a fundamental difference between an accident (meaning a freakish, outside-the-norm incident) and an injury that could have and should have been prevented. Somehow we've lost the ability to tell them apart. We've become a society that needs to lay blame.

As a result, towns across the country have taken some stunning steps. After settling 189 legal claims over 5 years for playground accidents, the school district in Broward County, Florida, banned running. Running. Plano, Texas, got rid of swings. Hundreds of districts have gotten rid of tag and dodgeball. Schools in Pinellas County, Florida, cut all recess and scaled back free-play time for first-graders to a single 25-minute session *each week*. (Only on Fridays, kids.) Multiple localities—Warren County, New Jersey; Flagstaff, Arizona; a middle school and high school in St. Cloud, Minnesota—have eliminated sledding, in some cases going so far as to install fences across popular hills. Sacramento, California, schools ruled out all games that involve "bodily contact," including kids pushing each other on swings. A Chicago suburb requires a permit before kids can use the ball fields, meaning no spontaneous pickup games.

In some cases, a lawsuit leads to all equipment being removed from a playground—the scorched-earth policy of legal self-protection. A school district in Albany, New York, was sued by the family of a girl who broke her leg and collarbone in 2000 when she fell off a slide at a playground. The girl, who was 10 when the accident happened, fell because she was pushed by her sister. But the family sued over safety surfacing, and while the case wound its way through the courts, the school district ripped up the playground. That's a decade of kids who had no place to play because one girl got hurt.

The result of all this is that kids are possibly safer in the short term, in the same way that you'd be safer if you never left your house. But even if you put Bubble Wrap around kids and bundled them into helmets and elbow pads and steel-toed high-tops, they'd come out worse in the end. They'd reach adulthood unable to evaluate risk, and they'd be terrified of the world. They would have missed their chance to experience the small hurts (bruises, scraped knees, stitches) that prepare them for the big ones they will undoubtedly experience as adults. The fact is that kids generally want to push the limits a little, just to see what happens. They *want* to take risks.

Dr. Stuart Brown's research demonstrates the impact of too much rigor and not enough play. Underlying the seminal research he lays out in his essential book *Play* is this important truth: We must ensure that our kids are allowed the irreplaceable freedom for unstructured play so that they have the opportunities for learning and development that freedom affords.

Philip K. Howard, a lawyer who has written multiple books on the subject of our litigious society, writes eloquently about how our efforts to mitigate risk through legal action have impacted this freedom: "America has a public health crisis but doesn't know how to make the legal choices needed to let children take the risks of growing up. We don't know how to say that sometimes things go wrong. This is an odd phenomenon, as if the adults fell on their heads and developed a kind of amnesia about how life works. The victim of an accident appears, demanding satisfaction, and we shrink back in legal fear."

This legal stuff impacts play outside of the headlines in more sneaky ways as well. Because of the risk of legal action, some of the playgrounds that do go up these days are *too* safe. Components are lower to the ground, they're covered with guardrails, and in some cases they're banned entirely in place of something that's easier for kids to master. Many municipal parks and school districts have gotten rid of all seesaws and any platforms more than 7 feet high. Texas got rid of fireman's poles (and Texas has pretty strict rules on civil lawsuits). It's as if these places were building playgrounds for the adults and their interest in mitigating any challenge or risk whatsoever, when we should be building playgrounds with the intent to provide an environment of play, fun, and risk. We should be building playgrounds *for* kids! Unfortunately, the threat of legal action makes many municipalities reticent to push standards and embrace innovation.

Playground safety standards are reassessed on an ongoing basis, and the evolving nature of the guidelines and regulations require constant vigilance of anyone involved in playgrounds. Even the most vigilant of us are sometimes challenged to stay ahead of the knowledge so we are making the best decisions for our kids.

Here's a high-profile example: President Obama installed a playground on the White House lawn for his daughters, complete with a safety surface made of recycled tires that is an approved material for playgrounds. But a few months after that, the EPA reconsidered its endorsement of that surface, pending a study of potential health effects. If it had changed its decision, the First Playground would technically have been out of compliance. Would that make the Obamas vulnerable to a lawsuit by the family of one of their daughters' friends? Probably. Is that okay? I don't think it's okay. It's not okay in the backyard of the White House, and I don't think it's okay in your backyard.

Naturally, ours is not the only country facing problems like this. Europe is generally much better about accepting the inevitable risks of daily life, but England and Australia are almost as bad as the United States. A British school employee sued a 13-year-old boy who ran into her while playing tag. In a bit of sanity, the case was thrown out.

Philip Howard recommends that the US legal system make some institutional changes to eliminate cases like these. And he advocates creating "risk commissions" that can establish reasonable levels of risk for different activities. Those steps would help, but a broader solution—and one that's probably more of a pipe dream right now—is for Americans to understand that there's value in risk. There's no way to remove all danger from playgrounds, and even if you could, the end result would be so dull and tame that kids would probably walk past it to play on their own in the grass nearby. And they'd likely play something dangerous, like tackle football, dodgeball, tumbling, jumping . . .

▲ ■ ●

In the past year or so, I've seen some modest but growing resistance to the fear-of-risk trend, which is heartening. Books like *Free-Range Kids* (by Lenore Skenazy), which advocates letting kids take risks again, have gotten a good reception from some parents who are relieved to learn that they don't have to treat childhood activity as a dire physical threat.

There's also an organization called Playborhood, a nonprofit run by a veteran of several software and tech start-ups who grew frustrated about how kids today don't play together the way most grownups did when we were young. The concept of Playborhood is pretty simple: to return play to kids' lives, in part by connecting parents in neighborhoods and online at the Website playborhood.com. The best place to play, according to that organization? The front yard!

In fact, the play deficit may seem complicated and overwhelming, but the solution really isn't. The only thing kids need is opportunity. That means a play space nearby—a playground, a ball field, a skating rink, even just a patch of grass—and unstructured time. Play requires no instruction, little or no money, no uniforms or electronic screens or software, no batteries, no chargers, no software upgrades. It doesn't even require adult supervision. Just access and time, nothing more. Mix those two together, and stand back—kids will figure out the rest.

[16]

When Better Is Expected, Good Is Not Enough

One day a few years ago, I got a call from the president of Ripon College. Other than paying off my student loan, I'd had nothing to do with the school since leaving after my sophomore year nearly 15 years earlier—no donations, no reunions. So this came as a complete surprise.

He wanted to know if I would be able to join the graduating class of 2008 to receive an honorary degree. It turned out that Tony Deifell and Wayne Meisel, two longtime friends, knew that the fact that I'd never gotten a degree was one of my biggest regrets. They had some influence and connections at Ripon, and unbeknownst to me, they went on a 2-year campaign to get the school to recognize what I'd accomplished since I'd dropped out.

I told the president I'd be honored to come back, and when the time came, Mrs. Edelman will be pleased to know, I even packed a suit for the occasion.

It was my long-delayed graduation party, and we blew it out. Kate and I rented a big house on Green Lake, the same lake where Dale Valentine, the owner of the rivet factory, had his vacation home and where college friends and I had taken his pontoon boat out for beer-soaked cruises on fall afternoons when we were students. We invited Dawn Hutchison, the cofounder of KaBOOM!, who came for the weekend with her family. Kim Rudd was there, my old mentor from the Chicago Park District who later became head of marketing for KaBOOM! (and still serves on our board). My sister, Dawn, and her entire family made it. My mom joined the celebration as well, making it particularly special. And because this graduation day fell on Mother's Day, we combined a Mother's Day celebration into the festivities.

We put everyone up and rented a pontoon boat so we could take the party onto the water. Just as when we'd returned to Mooseheart more than a decade after my graduation to build a playground there, I felt like this was a kind of homecoming and a chance to show people where I'd come from.

At a breakfast panel discussion, I found out that I wasn't just receiving a bachelor's degree—it would be a doctorate. At Ripon, the board decides who will receive honorary degrees, but the faculty votes on what kind of degree it will be. I had no idea until that morning, and it made the accomplishment that much more special. I am Dr. Hammond. And please, call me doctor. My mom was bursting at the seams. Kate jokes that her grandmother always wanted her to marry a doctor, and now it was finally—sort of—true.

The morning was rainy, so the ceremony was held inside, at Wyman Gymnasium. On top of my suit, I wore the doctoral hood, complete with satin trim in the Ripon colors, red and white. Each of the honorary graduates was given a few minutes to speak to the senior class and their families, and I prepared the way I always prepare to speak in public. Whether it's to funders or employees or at a conference, I always use the same system: I bring a blank sheet of paper, folded in half so it will fit inside my jacket pocket, and in the minutes leading up to my talk, I pull out my purple felt-tip pen and jot down some ideas.

I was one of several speakers, and I'd already talked that morning at the breakfast for seniors and their parents. I felt the way I imagine a lot of the graduating seniors that day did. My family was having a party as soon as this was over, and I was ready to loosen my tie and unwind. So my speech that day might have been one of the shortest in the history of graduations. It consisted of a Boomerism: "When better is expected, good is not enough." I repeated that twice, then I looked out at the assembled mass of graduates, bright young students about to start their professional lives, and said, "Only you will know the difference." Then I sat down.

This expression came from an experience we had with a project manager years earlier. She'd been a longtime employee and had built 25 or so playgrounds for communities around the country. When she returned from one trip, I asked her how it had gone, and she said, "It wasn't my best, but they all seemed to like it."

I was bothered by what she said and how she said it. In fact, I thought that was exactly the wrong answer, in that it implied we had somehow pulled one over on the funder and community. We gave them second-best, and because they didn't know the difference, they thought it was great. This is something I've tried to impart to people at KaBOOM! and tried to express that day to those Ripon graduates. There are a lot of times in life when you will be the only person who knows the difference between your best effort and your actual effort on a given day. If there's a big gap between the two—even if no one else realizes—then you failed.

▲ ■ ●

I'm proud of the degree, which I think is a reflection not of me but of KaBOOM! as a whole. It's the accomplishments of the entire organization that are noteworthy, not my contribution (but remember, call me Dr. Hammond!). So far KaBOOM! has raised about $200 million and built more than 2,000 playgrounds. We've sustained $20 million a year in revenue for 6 years running and become the single-largest purchaser of playground equipment in the country. And we've helped to transform a lot of communities across all 50 states, Puerto Rico, Mexico, and Canada.

When the organization started back in 1996, less than 1 percent of playgrounds were constructed using the community-building model, in which residents do the bulk of the work. Two companies, Learning Structures and Leathers and Associates, deserve credit for coming up with that approach, but they applied it more or less exclusively to middle-class or wealthier communities, those with obvious economic and social resources.

Our contribution at KaBOOM! was to help spread that idea by taking it to communities in need. As a result, more than 40 percent of all playgrounds being built today use local volunteers to plan and build the finished product. Those aren't all KaBOOM! projects, of course, but I'm happy about the trend, and I think the competition that we've created is a good thing. It means we've got to keep working to stay ahead.

As fantastic as this all sounds, I don't believe for a minute that it's enough. All our work, all those play spaces have helped alleviate the problem, but they haven't made it go away. The best efforts of KaBOOM! and dozens of other child-centered nonprofits are not enough to fill the large and growing gap between what's currently out there for kids and what's needed. We're all primarily mitigating damages, rather than creating sufficient quantities of permanent, positive change.

In fact, the play deficit is reaching crisis proportions, and there are disaster-level conditions in every city in America right now— economic devastation and a lack of clean, fun, safe public places for kids to play. The crushing poverty in some of these places is almost environmental. It becomes part of the background noise. And while millions of people go about their daily lives, another generation of children gets swallowed up.

Play deficit—the slow but seemingly relentless disappearance of that phase in kids' lives—is an emergency. And as such, it requires an emergency-level response. We all (including myself, including KaBOOM!) get distracted and caught up in the smaller battles we fight each day, instead of combining our efforts for the larger war. That has to change.

The fight for play is a tricky one; there's no enemy out there. Also, unlike the fights against cancer or AIDS—in which activists are usually inspired by very personal connections—with play, as with poverty, the problem is almost atmospheric. It's like climate change: People don't often see how it directly impacts their day-to-day lives—at least, not yet—and for many people, it's all too easy to go along thinking that kids who don't play will be fine.

To solve the play deficit, what's needed is not simply a collection of individual efforts but a coordinated approach: mass-level collaboration. No single individual or organization can do enough on its own. Instead, the best way to generate change is for a coalition of people with various types of expertise and insights to come together and persuade more individuals and communities to move from interest to action and to move from individual efforts to coordinated community approaches that can be sustained over the long haul.

In other words, this is a big tent, and although we all might have certain philosophical differences, we need to speak with a more unified voice. We need to remember the larger goal that we're fighting for. The best historical precedent for the kind of movement we're envisioning is probably the civil rights movement, in that there wasn't a single organization or entity that took on the issue of systemic racism in the United States. Instead, dozens of groups and thousands of individuals and events steadily applied pressure from many directions, and they ultimately led to historic change.

This kind of collaboration can be a challenge for nonprofits that sometimes simply don't trust each other enough to work together. We say that we trust each other, but the reality is that we compete—for employees, for media attention, for funding dollars. Social organizations tend to grow in silos, and as a result we seldom join forces to create real, lasting change. You sometimes hear about squabbles in which one group of researchers or specialists will take on another and say that they're not taking the right approach or that they need to be doing more of this or less of that.

Bickering and focusing on what makes us different won't lead to real progress. Part of the reason that Imagination Playground has gotten as far as it has is that there is an inherent trust in our partnership with Rockwell Group, the architectural firm that designed the blocks and created the Burling Slip playground in lower Manhattan. We rely on them for their tremendous knowledge about design; they rely on us for our expertise in community-building and child-centered service. Collaborations like this require a tremendous amount of time and communication and effort. But the end result is worth it.

▲ ■ ●

The insistence on federal funding for further scientific studies misses the point. You can never know too much, but from a policy perspective, we've already established, clearly and convincingly, that play is important for kids and absolutely crucial to their development. Research is important, but to be honest, we're not doing enough based on the research that's already out there.

At a time of crisis for our children, the choice should not come down to funding research or funding more and better play environments. We have to take action for our kids now. Research takes a very long time, years in some cases, and right now we don't have the luxury of time. I'm impatient—we need to create an immediate impact. We cannot sacrifice the children of today for the children of tomorrow. Let's act on the body of research we have in hand while continuing new research.

Governments need to become more involved as well. This means that the curriculum standards developed by the federal Department of Education and individual states should require recess in school. Cutting back on some of the standardized tests—especially for the youngest kids, below grades three or four—would help as well. And on the local government level, what's needed has less to do with policy and more to do with infrastructure. In fact, it's pretty simple. More playgrounds. More play spaces. Better parks. More innovative designs.

▲ ■ ●

Parents play a critical role in this movement. Most parents want to do what's best for their children. That motivation is a powerful force. And for generations, this motivation has caused parents to spend a lot of money on products that have come to market. This has become even more prevalent in the past decade, with a large number of toys and products that are marketed specifically to promote learning.

In her book, *Buy, Buy Baby,* journalist Susan Gregory Thomas suggests that many of these pitches are built on a pair of flawed notions, specifically that (a) every minute of a child's day needs to be filled with learning activities, and (b) the right exposure to the right balance of consumer products, primarily technological gizmos, can make kids smarter. It's true that many of these products have value and many are fun. But I worry that parents might be spending dollars on activities and toys because of a promised outcome that doesn't happen.

Some kids have every minute of their week accounted for, as they are being shuttled from one supervised, scheduled activity to the next: violin lessons, dance, soccer, school plays. Even unsupervised play has been subsumed by scheduling or playdates. The concept of scheduling parents to gather so the kids could gather for unstructured playtime initially struck me as odd. But it's clear that parents are doing it because they are trying to ensure their kids get some playtime, and it is an opportunity for the adults to connect. I think the key is not to invest too much in one single solution—it is the variety and balance of opportunities to play somewhat independently from adults that gives the greatest benefit.

If the goal is to turn out healthy, well-adjusted kids, it's time to concede that there are some good old approaches that might just work better than some of the newer innovations. For thousands of years, kids have managed to grow up and take their rightful role in society, not because they consumed the correct packaged goods and the appropriate electronic games but because they were involved in community and because they got the time for lots and lots of play. Kids don't need blinking lights. They need free time—unstructured, unscripted, without any goals or objectives or lessons—accompanied by a few basic things that can inspire their curiosity. When they're young, sand and a plastic bucket (along with just a bit of adult supervision) are enough. These kids will turn out healthier in the long run, not only physically but also emotionally. In addition, as a few recent studies have shown, they'll actually turn out smarter.

And if parents can see that they'll have the greatest impact on their own kids if they are able to focus on the community at large—wanting to do what's best for *everyone's* kids—the neighborhood will be stronger as well. In other words, we need more activism. This applies not only to parents but to all of us who care about kids—we all need to step up.

Here are just a few ideas:

Identify play deserts Map your local state of play and pinpoint play deserts. Canvass your community for playspaces. Take and upload photos. Describe the playspace and rate it. Get others to become fans.

Form a playground watch Put parents at ease and encourage more playground use by gathering a group of volunteers to rotate shifts on a playground watch. Not only does this ensure that a responsible adult is always at the playground, but it also protects against vandalism and crime. And don't forget to add the playground to our Playspace Finder so you can easily organize the community around the park.

Use your writing skills and your voice to advocate for play Write about play, and use social media to get the word out to a national audience and to rally locally. Letters to the editor and op-eds in your local paper are a great way to start a public conversation about how to improve the state of play in your community. Whether you're concerned about the lack of recess in local schools, childhood obesity, or closed or ill-maintained playgrounds and parks, writing is a powerful tool to rally your community.

Convene local support around the cause of play There are many local departments, committees, organizations, and individuals who can help you advocate for play. These include your Parks and

Recreation Department, PTA, PTO, school board, city council, schoolteachers, school principal, YMCA, Boys and Girls Clubs, and hometown mayor. Write e-mails, make phone calls, and attend meetings.

Form a play committee Take your outreach one step further by inviting individuals from these various entities to join a play committee and take concrete actions for play. You can form a committee at your child's school, in your neighborhood, or on a citywide level to advocate for more time, space, and resources for play.

Organize a play street Work with your neighborhood and your city to close the street on a regular basis (maybe once a week like Jackson Heights in Queens, New York) and open it up for play!

Take on the KaBOOM! Park-a-Day Summer Challenge Challenge your kids to find as many local playgrounds as possible this summer, and spend a day at a different park. You might even want to get other families to join the fun and create passports for the Park-a-Day challenge, earning stickers for each one that you visit. While you are at the park, take photos and upload the park to the KaBOOM! Playspace Finder!

Hold a Play Day Use our online planner to organize a Play Day, a chance to gather your neighbors, teach children new outdoor games, improve your local park or playground, and be part of an annual national Play Day campaign. Playmaker Pat Rumbaugh has taken it a step further and tours the idea of a traveling Play Day around to different parks all year-round.

Spruce up your playground A playground needs care and attention to thrive—an ill-maintained park becomes vulnerable to vandalism and crime. Organize a playground cleanup and consider other done-in-a-day improvement projects, such as planting flowers, painting a mural, or building a bench.

Build a playground Don't have a playground in your neighborhood or school? Build one yourself! Use our online project planner, which will take you through every part of the play space building process, from idea to fund-raising to ongoing maintenance. The planner gives you all the tools you need to follow our unique done-in-a-day, community-led build model.

Turn your front lawn into a neighborhood play space Open up your yard to the neighbors, throw together some loose and found parts, and let the kids have a ball! Be playful. Be creative. Have fun wherever you are.

Whatever you do, make sure to let us know what you are up to through kaboom.org so others can get in on the fun and learn from you. The important thing to take away from this is, just do something for play and do it today!

What's at stake? The future. The right combination of activism and passion, sustained across a movement, won't just help kids—it'll help the community. I know. I've seen it firsthand. I have experienced it firsthand. I have personally benefited as a child who was on the receiving end of the passion and activism of others.

KaBOOM! has done a lot over its 15-year history, but we haven't done enough, and we can't do it alone. To solve the play deficit, everyone has a role to play—from playground equipment manufacturers to academics to the dozens of other youth-oriented nonprofits to teachers and parents. We all need to become more active and more integrated. We need to coordinate with and recruit others. And we need to lobby local municipalities, along with government agencies at the state and federal level, to give play the prominence, attention, and funding it deserves.

And if you ever get tired or think the effort isn't worth it, I have a surefire way to reenergize yourself. Go outside and play! Grab a kid and have a snowball fight, or jump wildly into a huge pile of leaves, or get a good ol' game of dodgeball going. Use your imagination and build a fort from makeshift supplies (like cardboard boxes) that are on hand, go to a local playground and swing as high as you can, or pick up a basketball and shoot some hoops. And if you don't have a kid to grab, just do it without a kid! Remember how the experiences you had as a child shaped you. Stay focused on what's at stake. And then get back to work . . . or back to play. Better yet, get back to both.

Anatomy of a Build

How does it work on the ground? Here's a basic primer on what goes on behind the scenes—the anatomy of a playground.

Six Months Out:
We Line Up the Funding Partner

Playgrounds cost money, and without funding partners who believe in our cause and support the communities, we would never be able to do what we do. On occasion we'll work with trade groups, academic organizations, families, and other institutions, but most typically this role is filled by corporations.

Some of the biggest and best-known companies in the world–and in many cases, their respective foundations–have funded KaBOOM! projects, including Target, Fannie Mae, Dr Pepper Snapple Group, Nestlé, Chrysler, Stride Rite, Motorola, SAP, Discover, Kraft Foods, KOOL-AID, MetLife, Foresters, Walt Disney Company, National Basketball Association, JetBlue Airways, and dozens of others. And while we're proud of that list, we're even prouder of our retention rate—about two-thirds of our corporate funders come back to build another playground in subsequent years.

These companies commit to covering roughly 90 percent of the cost of a playground, along with planning the project and showing up on the day of construction with about 100 volunteers. In rare instances they'll be extremely precise in their requests, down to a specific date and ZIP code where they want the project. That ties our hands a bit, in terms of finding a community where they can put that money and muscle to best use. But a bigger challenge comes from the companies that want to work with us at the last minute.

I once got a call from CNA, the insurance giant based in Chicago. The company wanted us to build a playground just 6 weeks from then, and I said I didn't think we could do something we would be proud of on that kind of short timeline. But I met with then CEO Dennis Chookaszian, who asked what it would take for us to work with them. "If I commit a million dollars to your cause, assuming you pull this off satisfactorily, would you do it?" he said. I didn't have to think too hard—we could help build a lot of playgrounds with that money.

We made the project happen, and it turned out to be a great success. Though it was a tremendous amount of work, a key part of the organizational ethos at KaBOOM! is that we try very hard to never, ever disappoint.

At the end-of-day party to celebrate the new playground we'd all built together, Dennis told his employees about the million-dollar promise he'd made to KaBOOM!, then doubled it on the spot to $2 million, enough to build nearly 40 playgrounds.

That said, those situations are extremely uncommon. On rare occasions, we'll sign on with funding partners as close as 4 months to a construction date, but any less time than that and we feel as if we can't do our best community-building. Our work becomes more of a transaction, and we lose the transformational quality we strive for. Yes, the playground goes up, but creating community ownership becomes extremely difficult and less likely.

Four Months Out:
We Line Up the Community Partner

Once we have a funder, a rough date, and a geographic area, the next step is to find a specific community that can take on the project. Sometimes this means Boys and Girls Clubs, community centers, charter schools, or YMCAs and YWCAs, along with low-income housing organizations. We've also worked with summer camps, battered women's shelters, and drug treatment centers, where kids who are visiting their parents need a place to play. Our goal is to put 80 percent of our playgrounds in low-income communities, which we define as places where 70 percent or more of children qualify for the federal government's free or reduced-cost lunch program.

On rare occasions we'll work with a local parks department or public school, but those projects are rare because parks departments typically have a bureaucratic process by which they build playgrounds at multiple sites around town. Doing a single project with KaBOOM! and allowing volunteers to build the playground can be challenging for them, because they tend to think of us merely as a vendor. After all, they do this kind of work all the time (unlike a Boys and Girls Club, for instance, which builds a playground once every 15 years or so). This usually means that when we do work with parks, there is a push-pull that can be difficult and take a lot more time and energy.

Park and rec departments exist to manage parks and provide recreation for the public. It's hard for us to justify spending our time and energy to build a playground in a park when that should be their priority. We believe we should be serving other nonprofits that serve kids, and parks departments should be providing good recreation and play environments.

That said, we know that dollars can be tight for parks, and sometimes the need pushes us to dive in. When this happens, it helps to have committed leadership in that municipality who can embrace our model. In one instance, we found a special park district in East St. Louis, Illinois, a fairly low-income area. The good news was that it had 11 parks for its roughly 30,000 residents; the bad news was that many of those parks had fallen into disrepair. The park director, Irma Golliday, grew up in East St. Louis in the 1950s, and she took field trips to some of those parks as a Girl Scout. When she took over the district in 2005, she was surprised to find that some of the same playground equipment was still in place from more than 50 years earlier—and it hadn't been new then.

To spruce up the sites without any money, Irma resorted to buying cans of spray paint and painting the pieces herself. But those were purely aesthetic changes. "The equipment was totally out of compliance," Irma says. "It wasn't safe," let alone fun. When we heard about Irma and the parks she oversees, we knew East St. Louis would make an ideal recipient—it had a strong need for a playground and a strong community of people with longtime ties to the area.

The KaBOOM! Outreach team works hard to find appropriate prospective community partners for the done-in-a-day definable project on a definable timeline. Once we find a potential community partner, we assess whether they can do everything necessary to make the playground project happen. Specifically, we look at things like the number of kids served and the impact the playground will have on the community.

Additionally, these partners will be doing a lot of work, so they have got to be philosophically open to our process. They have to round up parents and community members who will commit to being on the planning committee. Through the planning committee, the partner recruits volunteers, raising a financial contribution and getting water and food donated—meaning breakfast and lunch for about 200 volunteers—along with entertainment (typically a disc jockey; everyone works better with music), and lots and lots of tools. They agree contractually to insure and maintain the playground for its life. The community partner gets a wonderful opportunity, but it comes with a lot of responsibility.

In order to make these projects come to fruition, having VIPs involved can help bring visibility and credibility. Three First Ladies have attended our builds over the years. In addition to the several that Hillary Clinton attended, Laura Bush came to our third Gulf Coast build after Hurricane Katrina, in Kiln, Mississippi, and Michelle Obama worked at one in San Francisco in conjunction with her campaign of service. I noticed something in common among the three, very different First Ladies: When it came to play and children, all of them instinctively understood our cause. They each support service, and they expressed genuine appreciation for the impact of the day spent building a playground and for the model of civic engagement. It was also clear that the service day itself wasn't the beginning and the end of their interest in KaBOOM!. Rather, in my conversations with them, they were all clearly interested in the play deficit and its important role in the development of healthy children.

We've had other VIPs at KaBOOM! builds over the years. Joseph Simmons—a.k.a. Rev Run, from Run DMC, who is a big fan of ours—and his wife, Justine, have come to projects across the country along with their children and friends. We also have relationships with all four pro sports leagues. NBA All-Star Antawn Jamison loves KaBOOM!. He funds projects himself, shows up early, works all day, and stays long after the cameras stop rolling. He's there for the cause, not the credit.

Dwight Howard from the NBA's Orlando Magic and Dustin Brown from the NHL's LA Kings both support us in huge ways—and are just two examples of professional athletes who have joined our cause. We've worked with NBA Cares and with a number of NFL teams—the Minnesota Vikings have done four builds in a partnership with the Toro Company. Every player on the team shows up and works, along with the coaches. We have built playgrounds with major-league baseball teams, most recently the Tampa Bay Rays. We're fortunate that so many celebrities believe in the cause of play enough to give their time and energy.

We've hosted many, many CEOs from some of the most successful corporations in the country, including Bob Iger of Disney, David Stern of the NBA, Irene Rosenfeld of Kraft Foods, George Mohacsi of Foresters, and Bob Nardelli, formerly of The Home Depot and Chrysler. Bob, by the way, attended more than two dozen builds. He always impressed my team by being the first to arrive on-site and the last to leave. He worked hard all day and got around to meet employees while putting real sweat into the physical work.

Potentially less fun than helping to secure VIPs for the Build Day are the host of seemingly mundane things that community partners are responsible for, like portable toilets and sunblock and a first-aid kit and a hundred other details. The planning phase also includes critical construction elements like getting soil samples from the site analyzed to make sure there aren't unsafe levels of lead or arsenic in the dirt. Communities must get a utility check done for the location of underground water, gas, or electrical lines. They have to get any old play equipment removed and in some cases have the site graded so that it's level.

It can seem a little daunting, especially for a neighborhood that has never taken on a project like this before. But we're there to help at each step along the way and to teach local residents what Jody Kretzmann and the Asset-Based Community Development Institute taught me a long time ago—that every neighborhood has assets it can organize around a common goal.

For food we suggest they organize a potluck or reach out to local supermarkets, restaurants, fast-food chains, bakeries, coffee shops, and catering companies. For tools, we tell them to try tool banks, local contractors, churches, and schools and also to ask volunteers to bring their own. We recommend trying local fire departments and ambulance services for safety patrol. All of this is meant to help the community establish relationships with these places and institutions, so that the social capital of the neighborhood gets fortified and the community is in a stronger position to solicit donations, ask for support, and be strategic about how to track down resources. All of this enables the planning committee and the community partner to be able to take on future projects beyond the playground.

At the project in East St. Louis, for example, Irma Golliday served on the planning committee and volunteered to round up tools. She talked to the two townships adjacent to the park and got their maintenance crews to donate tools for the day. (Irma also talked the crews themselves into volunteering during construction.) She called local contractors, who promised her the augers she needed, and a highway commissioner committed a truckload of wheelbarrows. She even got the Southern Illinois Health Care Foundation to send its mobile health unit during the Build Day as a first-aid center, including the van and three nurses.

Most people find that a lot of local businesses and other organizations actually *like* to give things away, especially for a neighborhood project like a playground. It's a good way to spread the word about their business, connect with the community, and bring in new customers.

All of this planning is a crucial part of the process, and it underscores exactly what we're trying to accomplish with these projects: convening people around a common cause, getting them to take steps to improve their neighborhood, and giving them achievable wins throughout the process. This is where those wins start to happen.

Imagine a single mom who's working multiple jobs and strapped for both time and money. Suddenly, she finds herself going to the local supermarket to ask the manager to donate hamburgers and hot dogs for 200 volunteers. Maybe the first store says no, maybe the second one does, too. But eventually one says yes. And what a lift it is when that happens. She excitedly reports back to the planning committee, and she is celebrated for this huge success. Her confidence increases.

And then she goes to another place and gets water donated. And yet another place offers coffee, doughnuts, and fruit. These are the kinds of small victories that lead to cascading steps of courage and leadership. And they lead to relationships with local merchants that can help the community coordinate future projects for years afterward.

▲ ■ ●

Many corporations are willing to write a check for the entire cost of the playground—after all, they're already paying for 90 percent of it. But we ask the local community to raise the remaining 10 percent, about $8,500, to ensure they feel a sense of ownership over the project, both before and after it's built. Ideally, these are grassroots efforts.

Though it's harder to get $1 each from 100 people than to get $100 from a single person, it's ultimately better to do it this way because the goal is to get more people to be invested with the project.

In one town, organizers decided to hold a "flamingo hop." They put a few giant neon pink flamingos in the yards of people in the neighborhood, who then paid $15 to have them moved to another yard, and then another yard, and so on. The town raised nearly $2,000 this way. Another community in a more rural area staged a "truck touch." They persuaded local authorities and residents to bring out interesting trucks (like a FedEx truck, a fire truck, a dump truck, a Hummer, etc.). Then they charged a flat rate for people to come in and see all the vehicles in one place. This idea was especially great because who loves trucks more than kids? The community charged $5, and more than 800 parents and kids showed up, raising about $4,000 in a single day.

A favorite of mine was the event held at Dallas Elementary School in the tiny town of Dallas, Georgia. The school set a goal of raising $8,000, and if the students achieved that goal, they would not only get a new playground but also win the privilege of duct-taping their principal to a school bus. Seriously. Thanks to a penny drive, snack sales, and other small events, the students exceeded their target—raising $8,252—and all 640 kids got to put a piece of duct tape on their principal, attaching him to the front grill of a school bus like a Christmas wreath. (A county sheriff was there to make sure everything was safe.) Once the principal was firmly in place, the bus actually started up and drove a short way down the street, past a crowd of screaming kids. They loved it.

(One element that most community partners do not have to worry about is additional liability insurance. A lot of people are surprised to learn that playgrounds don't require specific upgrades in coverage. Any child-centered nonprofit with so much as a sidewalk in front of the building should already have the kind of policy that would cover a playground, and their premiums should not go up when one gets added. If you serve children, the insurance company assumes that they'll need to be outside playing.)

▲ ■ ●

The choice of a community partner is probably the most significant decision we face in planning these projects. Occasionally, a corporation wants to build in a neighborhood where there isn't a great need for a playground or someplace where the process can't be leveraged to create a community that's ready, willing, and able to take on future projects. That's a challenge for us, but we try to communicate that the community partner has to be philosophically aligned to the entire community-build process. Not all of them are, and matching the wrong partner can turn the whole process into an uphill struggle. At the same time, the right community partner—one that really senses a need, one willing to do whatever's necessary to fill that need, and, ideally, one with a few passionate leaders who can rally their community around the cause—can make these projects magical.

In the spring of 2007, for example, a NASCAR race was scheduled to take place in Concord, North Carolina. As part of the events leading up to that race, a playground project would be planned someplace nearby, ideally a few days beforehand. Tony Stewart, one of the more successful drivers in NASCAR's history, has appeared at a number of KaBOOM! projects, along with members of his pit crew and Joe Gibbs Racing, and he worked with us on this occasion.

We thought we could put something good together—it was only a question of finding the right recipient. So we started researching child-centered nonprofits in the region, looking for someone who could really use a new playground. Within a few days, we found a fantastic local nonprofit called the Cabarrus Victims Assistance Network (or CVAN, as it's commonly known). CVAN is an emergency shelter where battered women and their kids can go to escape abusive husbands and boyfriends. In its nearly 30 years in existence, it has directly helped more than 4,000 women, along with launching education programs to reduce domestic violence and giving victims the legal help they need to navigate the court process.

In the early 1990s, CVAN had put up a small wooden structure in the backyard of the first residential house, and by the time KaBOOM! contacted the organization in 2007, the equipment was overdue to be replaced. Even the best components only last about 15 years, and wood versions don't make it that long. "We used to joke that you needed a tetanus shot to climb on it," said Mary Margaret Flynn, the founder and executive director of CVAN.

On a Friday afternoon in the spring of 2007, after researching child-serving entities in the area, one of our Boomers phoned Mary Margaret, who had never heard of KaBOOM!. "A playground?" she said. "Yes, we can definitely use one." Because of the work CVAN does, sheltering women and children from abusive partners, it asked for some security requirements. The organization doesn't give out its street address, for example, and it doesn't have a Website. That meant that we would have to control how the volunteers got that information.

Some of the women who had stayed at CVAN in the past were still living in the area, so they would be able to come back and volunteer during the Build Day along with local residents. We would also get a little star power—not one but two complete NASCAR teams agreed to come to the site during construction: Tony Stewart, who at the time was driving for Joe Gibbs Racing, and Brian Vickers, who drives for Red Bull Racing. In Charlotte during NASCAR season, those people count as royalty. Things were coming together.

Three Months Out: Design Day

Once we've lined up the funding partner and community partner, a project manager from KaBOOM! gets assigned to oversee the whole venture. We have about 18 project managers on staff, and they're our front-line troops. They also happen to be a fantastic group of people—young and incredibly passionate. It's a tough job. Project managers spend 6 months a year on the road, often traveling with little advance notice, and they have to be able to deal with extremely different types of people—executives of a Fortune 500 company, a 22-year-old single mom who might not have finished high school, an 8-year-old kid who's been dreaming of a playground on this spot for years, not to mention construction contractors and the playground installers who might have a preestablished system of doing things that doesn't always match up to the way we ask them to work.

Project managers also must be able to keep tabs on four or five projects at a time, in various stages of planning, so they have to be detail-oriented and extremely good at managing their time. They also have to solve problems on the fly, smile when things might not be going well, and inspire a group of several hundred volunteers, all while lugging around a 75-pound toolbox. We can train people in some of these skills (and project managers receive a tremendous amount of technical training once they start at KaBOOM!), but many others are innate. The trick is identifying them during the interview process, which is intensive and includes firsthand experience at a build.

A few months before the construction day, all the major players—the project manager along with representatives from the funding partner and the community partner—meet in person at the site of the new playground for an event we call Design Day. As we have done from the very beginning, we ask kids in the community to help design it. After all, they're the real experts in play and will be using the playground most. We start by asking the kids to close their eyes and to imagine their dream playground. "Consider all the playgrounds you've ever played on, and even some you've never seen. Dream about the most fun playground you can possibly imagine. Think about the colors, the activities, think what is around it and what you can do on it." Then we tell them to open their eyes, and we give them some paper and crayons and ask them to draw it.

The things that kids put on these drawings are almost always pretty imaginative. Their designs often include water slides or swimming pools, especially in the South, though sometimes the kids ask them to be filled with alligators. Other kids want secret tunnels, obstacle courses, and castles. A girl once requested a funnel-cake machine. One boy asked for a helicopter that shoots chocolate sauce (which really should be part of a playground someday).

Occasionally kids will ask for a TV or a Nintendo Play Station to be included, which just underscores how much they need the outdoor, non-electronic kind of gaming. Even sadder, once in a while you get a kid who's never seen a playground, who finds the Design Day a little intimidating because he's never been on swings or a slide. One of the children at a Design Day in the Gulf Coast after Hurricane Katrina literally asked, "What's a playground?" As grim as these situations seem, they also give us a sense that we're in the right place, a community with a dire need for a great place where kids can play.

After the kids present their drawings, the project manager talks to the adults. The project manager lays out the timeline for the project and helps them settle on a design that incorporates the kids' choices— how many slides, which colors, where the swings will go, and so on. (And by the way, KaBOOM! playgrounds tend to be in bright, vibrant colors that adults might consider unconventional choices, because the kids pick them. We wouldn't have it any other way.) Leaders get designated at this meeting for the various committees—like food, volunteers, construction, and safety, among others—and they will spend the next 3 months lining up those resources. The community volunteers also discuss and decide on any play enhancement and side projects they might want. These are projects that are made from scratch, as opposed to the prefabricated playground equipment, and will further enhance the site and the experience of both the kids and the adults who will be using the site. They include things like benches, sandboxes, shade structures, and picnic tables, sometimes with game boards for checkers and chess built in. We paint murals and asphalt games, landscape and plant trees, and sometimes coordinate with horticultural nonprofit groups to enhance the greenery around the site if the time of year in which we are building is appropriate for planting.

The point is to create a place where the people in the neighborhood can congregate rather than just drop off their kids and stand around the perimeter to watch. We want the playgrounds to become gathering places, similar to town squares, and we want the site to undergo such a dramatic transformation that it makes people look around the neighborhood and say, *Wow, now what else can we improve the way we improved this?* As one elementary school principal in Minneapolis said with pride as he looked around at the finished product after a recent build, "We wanted it to feel more like a park than a playground." I couldn't agree more.

▲ ■ ●

It is important that playgrounds be inclusive for all kids. Inclusivity speaks to kids with many different special needs. Public playgrounds have to comply with the Americans with Disabilities Act (ADA) of 1990, which requires, among other things, that at least one-third of the components must be accessible to a child confined to a wheelchair. KaBOOM! playgrounds incorporate elements that offer access to kids who are wheelchair-bound or to the adults playing with them who also require easier accessibility.

Sometimes we build what's called a "fully accessible" playground, which means that it's completely ramped, so that a child in a wheelchair can access all areas. A more recent trend is the idea of parallel play, in which two children—one in a wheelchair and one not—can be playing together on the same piece of equipment but with different access points.

In addition to the ADA, which is a federal law, a few government agencies weigh in on playground safety, publishing incredibly detailed guidelines for how playground equipment needs to be designed, manufactured, and installed. These are technically recommendations and not laws, but California and 13 other states have made them mandatory.

The various requirements can be tough to keep track of, but equipment companies in the industry have organized themselves into a trade group called the International Playground Equipment Manufacturers Association (IPEMA). The association not only ensures that all the equipment that its members manufacturer complies with all requirements, but it also has that equipment tested by a third-party lab. If that equipment bears the seal of IPEMA, that means it was all manufactured according to current industry standards and is thus safe.

Kids are challenging themselves on a playground and taking risks as they explore and learn, and they will inevitably fall. When I was growing up, playgrounds were usually built over asphalt or grass. That resulted in a lot of injuries whenever kids fell—sometimes skinned knees, sometimes more serious stuff. According to the Consumer Product Safety Commission, about 80 percent of all injuries on playgrounds resulting in a visit to an emergency room happen because of falls from a piece of equipment to the ground. To reduce those injuries, all sites today must include some form of cushioning underneath the equipment. Some playgrounds have a surface made of rubber tiles, or, in the more high-tech version, made of a compound that's poured in place and then sets as it cools. It's squishy and pleasant to walk on, and it's also tremendously expensive—about $40,000 for a typical playground. That would blow through more than half the budget for the projects we typically take on (though in some cases, due to environmental conditions or local standards, it's mandatory).

As an alternative, we most commonly use something called engineered wood fiber, which is basically a kind of mulch. The pieces are processed so they're all about the same size, and as they settle under the feet of children, they knit together, forming an almost woven mesh surface that provides the necessary cushioning.

This fiber has a lot of advantages—it's environmentally friendly and has been ADA approved (tested to ensure a child can roll a wheelchair over it), and it's less expensive than most other surfacing options. It runs about one-tenth the cost of rubberized surfacing, just $4,000 for a typical site. The material settles over time, so it needs to be topped off or replaced every few years, but because it's inexpensive, that's not a big hurdle for most communities. Another nice thing about wood fiber is that it's what we call volunteer-friendly. That is, it's a big, labor-intensive job. The fiber gets delivered via dump trucks and forms a giant mountain or two, and on the day of construction, we get volunteers to haul it all from those mountains over to the playground site. That task doesn't require any special expertise, but it takes teamwork to make it happen, so it gives volunteers a good project to team up on and accomplish during the Build Day. One hundred and fifty cubic yards can occupy a lot of volunteers for a long time.

Two Days Out: Site Prep

There's a famous Dolly Parton quote about how much time and expense she puts in to getting ready before venturing out into the public: "It costs a lot of money to look this cheap." The KaBOOM! equivalent is that it takes a lot of hard work to make things look easy. I don't mean to suggest that the playgrounds we build are in any way "cheap," but rather that when we have 200 volunteers showing up for a very busy 6-hour period, we need to do a tremendous amount of preparation and staging to make sure everything is ready for them to jump right in. Prep Days are when that all happens. They're when we finally start to get our hands dirty and where things get a bit technical.

First off, we need holes on the site—a lot of them. About 98 percent of playgrounds built today use what's called a post-and-platform design. You dig a bunch of holes, put in tall posts that provide vertical support, and then bolt horizontal platforms and other components to those posts. The holes are dug on Prep Day, and when the playground is erected on Build Day, the posts are concreted into the holes. A typical design will require 20 or 30 posts, so it takes time to dig the necessary holes and make sure they're positioned correctly.

In our early years, the project managers and local volunteers used to dig the holes by hand using posthole diggers, those long, hinged tools that look like giant chopsticks. Nowadays the community usually finds a local contractor to donate those services, drilling them using landscaping equipment and a hydraulic auger. While we're digging, we also have to ensure that we won't hit any utility lines or other pipes, a lesson we've learned the hard way.

In the office we have a photo of two project managers standing in front of what looks like the Old Faithful geyser. They were digging on a playground site in Tucson and hit a water main. It was a massive rupture—the water pressure dipped for blocks around in every direction. Because of that incident, plus one or two others and many close calls over the years, we now ensure that the community partner contacts all utilities before the Prep Day to come to the site and mark any lines running below ground.

In one extreme example from years ago when I was more involved in the day-to-day work of the project management team, one of our project managers arrived at a site in Tennessee and found that under a few inches of dirt there was almost solid bedrock. The Design Day had been overseen by another Boomer, and for various reasons the new person hadn't been on the site until that day, 5 days before construction was to start (something that would never happen today). The playground manufacturer had sent a few installers—as they do at all projects, even today—who said that they had already broken a few auger bits trying to drill holes in the bedrock and that there was no way the playground was going to happen. "My first thought," remembers Georgia Gillette, the project manager that day, "was that there's no way I'm telling Darell. I have to solve this problem on my own."

The installers said that one possible fix was to bring in dirt from somewhere else to cover the bedrock. So Georgia sent the other Boomer helping her with the project to the nearest pay phone (this was before cell phones) to find a Yellow Pages directory and start calling dirt companies, which they quickly found were listed not under D but under E, for Excavation Contractors. But dirt was expensive, and these projects have a fixed budget that we can't exceed.

As Georgia was arguing with the installers, she saw two dump trucks go by, filled with . . . dirt. "I thought, wait a minute, where are they going?" she says. It turned out there was a construction site down the street. She rushed down and talked to the foreman—in fact, they happened to have some excess dirt they were getting rid of, so she negotiated for a few truckloads. "I actually did them a favor," Georgia says. In a mad rush, the installers built a retaining wall, drilled all the necessary holes into the new dirt, and two days later the build took place, exactly on schedule.

I love this story, because it shows what we look for in project managers. There will inevitably be glitches in these projects—some small and some large—and the managers need to be resourceful and adapt to the situation to solve whatever problems come up, especially those that don't show up in any manual we can give them. And for the record, Georgia did call me to explain what happened once everything had been resolved. We want our project managers to have the wherewithal to fix their own problems, but we want to know what's going on as well.

This story also shows how we're constantly learning from these situations and improving our process. After the build was over, we examined how this had happened and put new systems in place to prevent it from happening again. From that project on, Design Days *always* included an in-person visit and photos of the site.

Build Day!

This is when magic happens, when all the hard work over the past few months results in a 6-hour blur of activity—what one participant called organized chaos—and a shiny new playground. Build Day is the only part of a KaBOOM! event that most volunteers will see, not all the hundreds of hours of advance work and planning that happened to make that day possible, but merely the day itself. So we feel we're only as good as this experience, and we go to great lengths to make sure that every single build is a positive one for every person who shows up.

The volunteers sign in, eat breakfast, and get broken into random teams. At 8:30, we have a kickoff ceremony and then everyone gets to work. One team is on "decks and posts," helping to erect the foundation of the playground. Other teams start to assemble the playground components or haul mulch or mix concrete or paint (we like to include hopscotch squares, maps, and murals) or work on landscaping, and on and on.

The overall feel is more like a barn raising than anything else. Years ago Jeff Swartz, the CEO of outdoor clothing maker Timberland, came to a playground project that his company had funded, and he described a Build Day as "watching disbelief disappear and the impossible become possible." For the next 6 to 8 hours, the site looks like an ant colony. On YouTube there are a couple of time-lapse videos of KaBOOM! projects going up. I've been at several hundred of these projects, but I still find the videos fun to watch.

"I had never seen so many people in one park working together," says Irma Golliday of the East St. Louis project. "From the little kids to the adults, even the seniors. We did a project in one of the flowerbeds, and they [the seniors] helped out with that." In addition to the main playground, side projects at her build included tree benches, planters, a stage for outdoor classes from the local school, and arbors. If you look at the roster of volunteers from that day, you'll see the Golliday name a lot. "My husband was there, our son, nieces and nephews, a grand-daughter," Irma says. "One of my nephews works at the alternative high school. He brought his whole class to help."

The biggest unknown on Build Days is probably the weather, which can vary widely, depending on where the community is and what time of year we're working. Lightning is the most typical of the few weather conditions that can stop construction. If that happens, we'll evacuate the site for safety reasons and get everyone inside to wait it out. But for anything less than that, we keep working.

We've built in minus-30 degrees Fahrenheit, in Saskatoon, Sas-katchewan. (It was an ice rink, one of a couple that we've worked on over the years. The volunteers in Saskatoon were used to temperatures like that and had no problems—the KaBOOM! staffers were puffed out in extra layers and looked like Michelin men.)

We've built in extreme heat, sites where the temperature never dropped below 100. Once we built in pouring rain at a new school in Georgia, on a field that hadn't yet been sodded. The red, mucky clay was so thick it literally sucked people's shoes off their feet. The pile of mulch was a good distance from the playground site, and because tarps full of wet mulch are too heavy to carry and wheelbarrows were getting bogged down in the clay, the volunteers had to carry it using buckets. They still finished only 45 minutes late.

We even built in the wake of a tornado. We were building six projects in one day with Fannie Mae in New Orleans after Hurricane Katrina. A tornado blew through in the early morning on the day of construction, ripping out trees and damaging homes (again). It also knocked out all electricity for several blocks at one of the build sites. But the volunteers showed up that morning nonetheless, and a generator was generously loaned to us for the day by a longtime KaBOOM! supporter so the build could still happen.

▲ ■ ●

At the CVAN build in North Carolina, the weather was perfect, and our biggest challenge was simply managing all the volunteers. We had 275 people show up, partly because of the local enthusiasm for the project, but also because we had two NASCAR drivers and teams on the site.

This was complicated by the fact that we were building in a residential area with limited space. To accommodate everyone, we had to set up food tents in the backyards of adjacent homes that are owned by CVAN. We also had to get the engineered-wood fiber (a.k.a. mulch) delivered to a driveway across the street from the main CVAN shelter, instead of much closer to the playground site, the way we usually do. As Mary Margaret puts it, "The pile was so big it blocked out the house behind it." But, as with other challenges, we tried to turn this into a fun challenge and a form of entertainment. The NASCAR pit crews from the Home Depot and Red Bull teams raced each other to see who could deliver mulch the fastest.

Because of heroic efforts like those, most of the work at the CVAN site was done by mid-afternoon, and it was time to cut the ribbon. The project manager congratulated everyone on a great job, and we got some closing remarks from Mary Margaret Flynn and executives from Joe Gibbs Racing along with a few other notables. We always take group photos of all the volunteers in front of the new site, which is unrecognizable from the vacant field that had been there just hours before. We always know that the volunteers there made a few new friends and learned how to do something they never knew before, skills that they would be able to apply on future projects.

One thing we can't do at the end of Build Day is let any children onto the playground just yet. The concrete holding the posts in place is still wet and needs a few days to properly set. You'd think that would be a minor disappointment to some people, and it might be, especially for kids who've been waiting for this playground for months. But to most volunteers, that's not really the case. As one of our earliest project managers puts it, "The day really isn't just about the playground. It's not about the monkey bars. It's about sweating alongside someone you didn't know until today, solving problems together and figuring stuff out. And then at the end of the day, it's such a huge sense of accomplishment that it really doesn't matter if the kids can't play on it yet."

I think the kids understand that, too. Most of them are simply amazed that so many people—strangers!—would come together and build something for them, and, like the adults, they realize that something bigger is going on. Of course, once the playground opens, we get flooded with pictures of them using it, along with thank-you notes. And we hear from volunteers who drive by the playground weeks and months and years later, to watch the kids play and point out the components they worked on. As I mentioned, these playgrounds last for 15 years when they're properly maintained, so the kids using it during its first few weeks and months will probably be in college by the time it needs to be replaced. For that kind of timeline, everyone understands the need to wait just a few more days.

▲ ■ ●

After the KaBOOM! build, Mary Margaret reported a few positive developments at CVAN. It's the kind of thing we love to see, where relationships first forged during the project result in further positive changes to a community after the playground is in place. For starters, Tony Stewart and Brian Vickers donated a combined $10,000 of their own money to the organization, and Joe Gibbs Racing later named the organization as the sole beneficiary of its Fall Fanfest, meaning another $25,000 donation later that year.

In addition, a great feel-good story happened a few months after the build. Because of security issues, all shelter residents at CVAN need to sign out whenever they leave, so the staff knows where they'll be. One Friday evening, a mother and her twin toddler girls who had recently arrived signed out and said they were going to the park. Mary Margaret and another staffer watched them head to the new playground behind the house.

When they came back in, Mary Margaret asked the woman, "Never made it to the park, huh?" The woman didn't understand, until Mary Margaret explained that the playground wasn't a park, it was part of CVAN itself, and that the woman didn't need to sign out—she could take her girls there anytime she wanted, just by walking out the door. The woman replied, "You mean the park is ours? It's here just for us?" When Mary Margaret said yes, that it had been built by volunteers and past residents specifically for children coming to the shelter with their moms, the woman started crying.

As Mary Margaret of CVAN puts it, "These are people in crisis, leaving everything behind, and they're scared to death. But they come here, and the playground is a great place, not only for the kids to play but also for the moms. They go out there and see that their kids are playing, and it's a bit closer to normal for them. The process involved a lot of hard work, but there's a difference between hard work and things that are hard to do."

Boomerisms

Boomerisms are a set of expressions that guide the work of Boomers (KaBOOM! employees). These were things that I'd say again and again, in meetings or during individual conversations with employees that have become pillars of the KaBOOM! culture. The Boomerisms don't describe what we do; rather they describe how we do what we do to collectively achieve exponential impact. They reflect where we've come from and how high we aim.

The process is as important as the product. A result will always be stronger and better if the journey of getting there is significant and if it is in and of itself an accomplishment. It is not just what we do, but how we do it.

No regrets. Focus all your energy and brainpower on doing the best possible job you can do, especially when your work impacts others. Operating at peak performance means never having to wish for a "do over."

Be a better us, not a worse them. Deflect negativity. Positive energy draws people to your cause and fuels innovation, collaboration, and productivity.

Under promise and over deliver. Promise what you know you can deliver and then work like heck to exceed the expectation.

When better is expected, good is not enough. There are a lot of times in life when you will be the only person who knows the difference between your actual effort and your best potential effort on a given day. Consistently give your best and minimize the gap between the two.

Name names and give credit where credit is due. Recognize and appreciate those who have contributed to the process, the product and the success.

You can do routine tasks without doing them routinely. There may be established best practices for a specific situation. Customizing a process keeps it fresh and personal. You can continuously bring joy, creativity, and fun into an experience without recreating the wheel.

Good ideas bad execution. Don't let failure to follow through or fully execute undermine your good ideas. Don't let a lack of discipline to fully execute undermine good ideas.

It only takes a single spark to start a fire. It takes oxygen, fuel and a spark to ignite a flame. It is a skill to be the spark and a greater skill to identify and gather the needed oxygen and fuel so that your spark can catch fire.

Practice doesn't make perfect; perfect practice makes perfect. The idea is that you don't need more practice, you need *better* practice, and you need to train to exceed expectations over and over again. It's not your all-time best performance that matters, it's how you perform consistently, day in and day out.

Losing is what happens when you don't perform up to your ability. Getting beat is when someone performs better than you. You may not win even if you give your full effort, but performing at less than your full ability is failure. Getting beat is not failure, if you give it your best.

Persuade by using rationale and facts, motivate by telling stories. Facts motivate the mind and stories motivate the heart. Put them together and you unleash a powerful combination that has greater potential to inspire action than either by themselves.

Acknowledgments

As the saying goes, it takes a village to raise a child. There is a village of people around this country who spend their lives working for the betterment of our children. Many of these people and organizations are associated with KaBOOM!.

Thank you for the work you do every day and for the energy and time you continually give whether you are a teacher, a childcare worker, a caretaker, a parent or grandparent, an aunt or an uncle, a researcher, an advocate, a friend, or a volunteer. It matters not what your fulltime work is, if you are someone who cares about and takes action for the kids in your life, in your community, or in your village, than I thank you. And if you are someone who values the importance of play in the well-being of the whole child, I especially want to share my deepest gratitude because there just are not enough of us yet. I acknowledge you for the work you have done, the work you are currently doing and for the work you have yet to undertake.

To those whose stories are told in the book and those who are not, I'd like to acknowledge you for working to build spaces for kids to play every day, thank you for your effort. Keep on doing what you do. And we will keep working to be a resource and to support you in what you do.

KaBOOM! is what it is today due to the 241 Boomers over the last 15 years who have contributed their skills and energy to the important cause and mission of this organization. In their honor, all Boomers past and present are listed in the following pages. You come first and foremost, always.

KaBOOM! could not achieve its mission without the generous

support of our funding partners; in the interest of giving credit where credit is due, we have acknowledged all major funders as well.

I am certainly a product of a village of people who made me who I am today. I owe many thanks to the Moose members who allowed me to "enter to learn and leave to serve." I hope I make you proud.

I would like to give special appreciation and acknowledgement to my Mom, Lois Hammond. Thank you for recognizing that the best thing you could do for us was probably the hardest for you. I also want to call out my sister Dawn and my brother Pat for being there for me. Thank you also to Mark Penzkover, a classmate of my sister Kitty's and longtime role model, friend, and mentor.

Bill Airey believed in me and saw something in me I didn't yet see in myself when I was just a young upstart. Bill and Jean Airey opened their home and their hearts to a bunch of 18-year-old kids who had very limited options after graduating high school.

The Urban Studies Program was a transformative experience, and the leadership and role model I found in Jody Kretzman ignited the spark of concern for social justice in me. Jody has played an integral part in my life and in the shaping of KaBOOM!. I also have Jody to thank for leading me to two other very important people in my life: Kim Evans Rudd and Helen Doria at the Chicago Park District, thank you for taking me under your collective wings, bringing so much joy to your day-to-day work and those around you, and for leaving an indelible mark on me.

Andy Carroll, my good friend, gave me the encouragement to write this book and introduced me to his agent, which was the first big step in making it a reality. I have long admired all the good work he has done and the incredible books he has authored and edited.

This book was ten years in the making and when it came time to move it forward, Miriam Altshuler's insight, direction, and counsel has been invaluable. Thank you for getting us into many incredible publishing houses and helping us to partner with the right one.

Shannon Welch took a chance on us and expertly edited the book. Stephanie Knapp, Aly Mostel, and the Rodale team have been a critical part of this larger village of folks who have made this project possible and made it better than it would have been.

As with so much of my life, relationships have played a key role in the evolution of this book. Julie Schlosser introduced us to Jeff Garigliano who helped me write the book. Jeff conducted hours of interviews with me and dozens of people to write the book. Jeff understood my passion for the importance of play and he worked hard to capture my story.

Jim Hunn led the marketing and publicity efforts and was a key part of the team, and he did everything from overseeing contract negotiations to sharing insights. Many thanks to the online team at KaBOOM! who built out the website and the social marketing plan for the book and the philanthropy team who worked to plan and organize the private events around the country—Kerala Taylor, Mike Cooper, Laurence Hooper, Alison Risso, Anna Morozovsky, Erin Hamilton, Sejal Shah, and Susan Comfort.

Sebastian Junger, Andy Carroll, and Miriam Altshuler led us to Cathy Saypol and Johanna Ramos Boyer—the talented duo who ensured that we were not missing any opportunities and capitalized on all possibilities for the book.

A number of people contributed to the editing process. Thank you first and foremost to Rick Kelson and Ellen Kelson who read every draft in detail, shared important and relevant feedback, and gave their time and energy. They have been invaluable supporters throughout this process.

Thank you to the many other reviewers, editors, and contributors: Bill and Jean Airey, Stephanie Barksdale, Ginny Reynolds, Carrie Leovy, Jim Hunn, Sarah Pinsky, Roopal Saran, Carrie Ellis, Alison Risso, Bridget Hankin, Miriam Altshuler, Paul Carttar and Team Carttar, Kim Rudd, Lori Johnston, Nancy Rosenzweig, Georgia Gillette, Tom Mitchell, Danielle Marshall, Kerryn Kent, Kerala Taylor, Bruce Bowman, Judy Lem, Leslie Crutchfield, Melanie Barnes, and Dawn Hewitt.

Many, many people shared photos and other important documentation. Special thank you to: Bob Zaininger, Bill Airey, Melanie Barnes, Ian Fisk, Ted Adams, Carrie Leovy, Tom Mitchell, Georgia Gillette, Kim Rudd, Dawn Hutchison-Weiss, and Mary Ann Hutchison all of whom uncovered and shared many photographs and relevant documents from our years together.

Dawn Hutchison-Weiss's energy and enthusiasm is enormous. She was a co-architect of this organization that has achieved so much for such an important cause. Thanks also to Bob and Mary Ann Hutchison who were a tremendous support to our work in those very early days and whose support has been unwavering over the years.

Jonathan Roseman was, a good, good friend to Kate and me. We miss him a great deal. We wish you were here, buddy.

I owe so much to Sid and Bernice Drazin who became de facto parents. Their love, support, and confidence meant the world to me during a time when I had audacious dreams, and they gave me the courage to believe I could do anything. I wish everyone could have people like the Drazins in their lives.

Kathy Huston keeps me organized, makes my life better, and improves the quality of everything. She is the backbone of my office and has a joy-filled, consistent, and caring approach to all that she does every day.

Finally, I'd like to give special thanks to my wife, partner, and best friend, Kate Becker. I have much to thank her for. There is no doubt that this book would not have ever come to be without her direct involvement, support, and energy. She worked hand in hand with me on every aspect of the book. Every step of the way, she made the book better as she has made me better. The trajectory of KaBOOM! can be tracked against her time here. She is a true example of an advocate who works for the cause and not the credit. I thank her for being my work partner, but I am especially grateful that she is my life partner.

Onward and upward!

Boomers, Board Members, and Major Funders

Boomers, Past and Present

Nicholas Ackerson • Richelle Adams • Ted Adams • Bishara Addison • Anita Shekar Akerkar • Kenny Marv Altenburg • Scott Anderson • Adam Arata • Erin T. Baker • Melanie K. Barnes • Mary Barr • Ivan Baumwell • Kate M. Becker • Emily Belyea • David Bender • Brooke Bennett • Amanda Bernard • Unique Bexley • Jerrilyn Black • Tabitha Blackwell • Jennifer Blenkle • Lisa Block • Angela Blount • Tenisha Bourne • Carol Bowar • Bruce Bowman • Michelle Boyd • Ann Councill Brown • Mary Lou Bruno • Janie Burkett • Joyce Byrd-Bilski • Paul Caccamo • Alejandro V. Cardemil • Tiffiney Carney • Dan Casey • John Chamberlain • Carolyn Check • Mike Coleman • Brian Collier • Susan Comfort • Jorge Contreras • Jason Cooper • Michael Cooper • Sidney Cooper • Bobby Cooper • Alanna Copenhaver • Jennie Connor Councill • Brian Crowley • Mickey Daguiso • Meredith Darche • Janette Davis • Jen De Melo • Hope Deifell • Samantha DeNafo • Sandhya Deshetty • Laura DeWitt • Amy Dickinson • Nora Donaldson • Brooke DuBose • Stacey Duckett • Ben Duda • Jane Duket • Karen Duncan • Mike Dunn • Maria Durana • Susan Elliot • Candace Elliott • Carrie L. Ellis • Aaron Evans • Rhonda Faison-Straud • Jenna Farley • Wayne Farmer • Allison Farrington • Christine Feller • Trevor Ferkler • Justin Fitzgerald • Jane Flake • David Flanigan • Mory Fontanez • Ariel Fortune • Jeannette Fournier • Ben Frasier • Meghan E. Fugate • Carrie Valentine Fuller • B. Campbell Fuller • Evelyn Furia • Brian Gaines • Aubrey Garcia • Jennifer Garner • Heather Garrett • Georgia Gillette • Joellyn Gilmore • Jennifer Golden • Javier Gomez • Laura Goodman • Sarah Gores • Kelly Ortner Grant • Betsy Haibel • Lowell Hall • Erin Hamilton • Michael Hammerstrom • Darell Hammond • Whitney Hampton • Bridget Daly Hankin • Cassie Haslett • Beth Hayes • Damien Heath • Desiree Hill • Mark Himmelsbach • Leslie Hinton • Tia Hodges • Kara Hoffman • Laurence Hooper • Farrell Howe • Emily Hummel • Jim Hunn • Kathy Huston • Peyton Hutchins • Dawn Hutchison-Weiss • Christine Jackson • Tiffany Jacob • Shira Jacobson • Sara Jaffe • Thor A. Jensen • Ginny Muir Johnson • Scott Jones • Chad R. Jones • Leah Judge • Matt Kaftor • Amy Kaufman • Mary "Meg" Keaney • Kerryn Kent • Tiffany Lane King • Adam Klarfeld • Lexi Klein • Jennifer Klein • Kelly Kohut • Lana Kovnot • MJ Kurs-Lasky • Kyle Lafferty • Fabio LaMola • Elliot Laster • Nicole M. Lazo • Hanh Le • Amy Lee • Judy Lem • Carrie Leovy • Noah Z. Levy • Chrissy Lewis • Mila Liachenko • Erica Liberman • Mark Lindquist • Julia Lohela • April Lomax • Suzie Lovercheck • Matt Lucas • Nicole C. Lucas • Kathryn Lusk • Lindsay Luthe • Annie Lynsen • Kate Lysaught • Rie Ma • Lian Mah • Heather J. Maldonado • J. Annie Malone • Christine Elsea Mandojana • Kate Manolakos • Courtney Marsh • Caleb Marshall • Danielle Marshall • Laura Martini • Michael Mazza • Lisa Davidson McDaniel • Megan Taormino McFarland • Drew McGowan • Sarah Thurston

McGuire • Nancy McLaughlin • Meredith L. McLean • Nate McMichael • Jodie Medeiros • Gerry Megas • Sarah Megad • Matt Megas • Kristen L. Mehr • Aliya Merali • Derek Messier • Aron Michalski • Stevan Miller • Tom Mitchell • Heidi Mitchell • Jennifer Modell • Gina Montefusco • Kate Morgan • Rabiah Morning-Parker • Anna Morozovsky • Kaushik Mukerjee • Ellen Murphy • Evan P. Mynatt • Margaret Napoline • Cynthia Nell • Stephanie V. Nelson • Amy O'Donnell Noland • Michelle Offutt • Becky Ostendorff • Zoe Paglee • Lisa A. Palmer • Katrina Parker • Lexi Paza • Jessica Perlmutter • Jennifer Peplowski Perritte • Sarah Rose Pinsky • Donald Pitcock • Greg Pogue • Keely Porter • Nathan Postell • Evan Procknow • Natalie Proffit • Margie H. Quina • Brianna Reeb • Dennis J. Reynolds • Brad Rezza • Holly Richardson • Alison Risso • Pam Rockland • Dustin Rogers • Christopher Romero • Maritza Rosario • Nate Rosenthal • Nancy Rothgerber • Kimberley Evans Rudd • Anel Ruiz • Nicole Saini • Kristina Saleh • Izzy Santa • Roopal Mehta Saran • Juliet Sarau • Amy Sarosdy • Scott Saxman • Liz Cotter Schlax • Brittany Short • Ascala Tsegaye Sisk • Ericka Bolinger Sisolak • Kevin Skolnik • Adam Sloey • Armentia Snyder • Susan Spence • Adwoa Spencer • Stacey Steidler • Ellen Stiefvater • Natalie Sukienik • Allison Goter Sumners • James E. Tatum • Mary M. Taylor • Kerala Taylor • Allison Q. Taylor • Kelli Thomas • Melissa Thompson • Lakisha Thompson • Ashley Thompson • Amy Thorn • Danielle Timmerman • Mathew Todaro • Gayle C. Todd • Laura Toscano • Bruce Townsend • Lauren Townsend • Danielle Trezek • Joeffrey Trimmingham • Hilda Vega • Mike Vietti • Eddie Villacorta • Chavon Waddy • Patrice Wakeley • Terry Walker • Zakia Washington-Nurse • Liz Weatherly • Becky Webb-Morser • Ann Gaudard Weeby • Sarah Welsh • Heather Eden West • Amy Whittaker • Shannon Wilk • Tim Williamson • Kiva R. Wilson • Melissa Winchester • Bing Wu • Sarah Yellin • Riche Zamor Jr. • Frank Zhu • Lauren Ziegler • Helen M. Zimmerman

KaBOOM! Board Members, Past and Present

Suzanne Hollis Apple • Michele R. Atkins • Mark L. Bodden • Bruce Bowman • Michael Brown • Tony Bucci • Paul L. Carttar • Peter D'Amelio • Michael Deich • Tony Deifell • Rich Delvaney • Rob DeMartini • Kim Dixon • Helen Doria • Jonah Edelman • Peter Farnsworth • Timothy M. Fesenmyer • Jonathan Greenblatt • Ken Grouf • Robert Hackett • Andy Harrs • Brian Heidelberger • Gayle Holcomb • Dawn Hutchison-Weiss • Martin L. Johnson • Rick Kelson • Jonathan Kozol • Carl C. Liebert III • Delores B. Lindsey • Wendy Masi • Carolyn Williams Meza • William D. Novelli • Erin Patton • Rey Ramsey • Nancy Rosenzweig • Kimberley Evans Rudd • Pam Selby Salkovitz • Michael Sands • John Sarvey • Brad Shaw • George Sherman • Debbie Shore • Andy Stefanovich • Paula Van Ness • Julius Walls Jr. • David Wofford • Chris Wolz • Christopher Zorich

Major Funders, 1995-2010

1st and 10 Foundation • 24 Hour Fitness • AARP • Acuity Brands • Akin Gump Law Firm • Allergan • Alpha Epsilon Pi Fraternity and United Jewish Communities • Aly, Stacey, and Bruce Bloom • American Academy of Dermatology • American Academy of Orthopaedic Surgeons • American Eagle Outfitters Foundation • AmeriCares • Ameriquest Mortgage/AMC Mortgage Services, Inc. • Amgen Foundation • Amway/Alticor, Inc. • Antawn Jamison • Arena Football League and Arena Football League Player's Association • Armstrong World Industries, Inc. • Ashoka • Atlanta Falcons • Avon Products, Inc. • Baltimore Ravens • Bank of America •

Barksdale Management Corporation • BASF • Becker Funeral Homes • BellSouth • Ben & Jerry's • Bexar County 4H Youth Development • Big 8 Food Stores • Black Entertainment Television • Blue Cross and Blue Shield Association • Blue Cross and Blue Shield of Illinois • Blue Cross and Blue Shield of North Carolina • Bradley Turner Foundation • British Airways/ Patterson Communications • Build-A-Bear Workshop, Inc. • Burt's Bees • Bush Clinton Katrina Fund • Business Strengthening America—Charlotte • CA (formerly Computer Associates International, Inc.) • Cable Cares • Cadbury Schweppes/America's Beverages • Cafritz Foundation • California 4H Foundation • California Community Foundation • California Governor Arnold Schwarzenegger and First Lady Maria Shriver's Conference on Women • CaliforniaVolunteers • Capital One • CarMax Foundation • Case Foundation • Cass Darien School District #63 • CHF International • Chicago—Cook County 4H Foundation • Chicago Housing Authority • Chicago Park District • Chicago Tribune Foundation • Children's Defense Fund • Chrysler • City of Cupertino and Rotary of Cupertino • City of Grand Rapids • Clarian Health and Bob Sanders Chasing Dreams Foundation • Cleveland Browns Foundation • CNA Foundation • CNN Fit Nation • Comcast Corporation • Corporate Executive Board • CoStar Realty Information, Inc. • Dell • Deloitte & Touche LLP • Delta Health Alliance • Discover Financial Services • Discovery Health • DJR Foundation • Doug Finley • Dr Pepper Snapple Group • Dustin and Nicole Brown • Eli Lilly and Company • Energizer • Epstein, Becker & Green • F.I.S.H. Foundation, Inc. • Fairytale Brownies • Fannie Mae • Fibar Systems Inc. • First Steps to School Readiness of South Carolina • First Tennessee • First Union Corporation • Foresters • Foundation for the Mid South • Fourth Generation Fund • Fred C. Rummel Foundation • Freddie Mac Foundation • Friedman, Billings, Ramsey • Friends and Family of Daniel Soloma • Friends of Danneel, Inc. and the City of New Orleans • General Mills • GeoGlobal Partners • Georgia 4H Foundation • Georgia Pacific Professional • Glenwood School for Boys and Girls • GMAC Mortgage • Habitat for Humanity International • Hatfield Family Fund • Hillary Rodham Clinton • Holder Construction Company • Huggies • Hunt Alternatives Fund • IBM • Illinois Attorney General's Office • Illinois Departmenr of Human Services • Indianapolis Colts, National Starch Food Innovation and Lucas Oil • ING Direct • ING Direct Kids Foundation • Iqbal Foundation • Irwin Industrial Tool Company • Jamba Juice • JCGC Foundation: A Donor Advised Fund of Waterstone • JetBlue Airways • Jewel/Osco • Jewish Children's Bureau • Jewish Federation of New Orleans and UJC • John Nuveen & Company • Johnson & Johnson • Johnson Levels and Tools • JPMorgan Chase • Junior League of Birmingham • Junior League of Des Moines • Junior League of Macon • Junior League of Pittsburgh • Kaiser Permanente • Kankakee Valley Park District • Kansas City Chiefs • Kansas City Orthopaedic Institute • Ken Grouf and Family • Kimberly-Clark • KOOL-AID • Kraft Foods Foundation • Kresge Foundation • Kudzu • Leave a Legacy of Play Fund • LIVE with Regis and Kelly/ABC Domestic Television • Los Angeles Kings • Madieu Williams Foundation • Maria Shriver, First Lady of California & VONS • Marriott International • Maryland 4H Foundation and Maryland Cooperative Extension-Baltimore City • MedImmune • MetLife Foundation • Minnesota Orthopaedic Society • Mississippi Hurricane Recovery Fund • Mississippi Orthopaedic Society • Morgan Stanley Foundation • Motorola • Mr. Webb Sowden • Mutual of Omaha Foundation • Nardelli Family Charitable Fund • National Association of School Psychologists Children's Fund, Inc. • National Business Aviation Association • National Heritage Academies • National Society of Collegiate Scholars • NBA Cares • NeighborWorks America • Nestlé USA • New York State Society of Orthopaedic Surgeons • Newell Rubbermaid

• NFL PLAY 60 • Nike/Reuse-A-Shoe Program • Northrop Grumman • Northside Development • Northwestern Mutual • NYMEX Foundation • Odwalla/Fresh Samantha • Omnicom • Opus Northwest and Opus Foundation and Opus South Corporation • Oregon Association of Orthopedists • Orlando Magic • Orthopedic Association of Kankakee • Orthopedic Hospital of Oklahoma • P&G Gillette • Pacific Dental Services • Peace for The Children Foundation of Donald and Lisa Pliner • PECO An Excelon Company • Pennsylvania League of Cities and Municipalities • PepsiCo • Piper Jaffray & Co. • PlayCore • Playworld Systems, Inc. • PNC • Post HOPE Foundation • Primordial/Zoob • Project Rebuild Plaquemines • Prudential Foundation • qubo Channel, an ION Media Network • Radio Flyer • Randall Weisenburger and family • Redwood City School District • Reedy Industries, Inc. • Retired Peace Corps Volunteers • Roche • Rock Bottom Restaurants, Inc. • Rotary Club of Stennis Space Center • RREEF Funds • Ryobi • Salesforce Foundation • San Francisco Housing • San Francisco Neighborhood Parks • San Francisco's Promise • San Jose Redevelopment Agency • SAP America • Singing for Change Foundation • SIRIUS XM Radio • Six Flags • Skadden, Arps, Slate, Meagher & Flom LLP • Smart Start Georgia • South Carolina Orthopaedic Association • Sprint Foundation • St. Louis Rams • Staples, Inc. • Starbucks Foundation • State Farm Bayou Classic • Students of American University • Subway Restaurants • SUPERVALU • Surgical Care Affiliates • Tampa Bay Rays • Target Corporation • Texon • The Andy Foundation • The Ben Gordon New Life Foundation at The Giving Back Fund • The Boston Consulting Group • The Cahn Family • The Cheesecake Factory • The Chrysler Foundation • The Cohen Family • The David and Lucile Packard Foundation • The Goldhirsh Foundation • The Grable Foundation • The Harris Corporation • The Home Depot • The Home Depot Canada Foundation • The Home Depot Foundation • The Horace W. Goldsmith Foundation • The J. Willard and Alice S. Marriott Foundation • The John Buck Company • The John S. and James L. Knight Foundation • The Junior League of New Orleans ~ Women Building Better Communities • The Klein Family • The Kline Family • The Madison Square Garden Cheering for Children Foundation • The National Academies • The National Society of Collegiate Scholars • The Omidyar Network • The Prout Family • The Rapides Foundation • The River School • The Spivak Family • The Stanley Works • The Stop & Shop Family Foundation • The Stride Rite Corporation • The Toro Company and the Minnesota Vikings • The W.K. Kellogg Foundation • The Walt Disney Company • The Washington Post Company • Thrivent Financial for Lutherans • Timberland • Tucson Medical Center • Tucson Orthopedic Institute • U.S. Cellular • Underwriters Laboratories • Unilever • United Cerebral Palsy • United Jewish Communities • UnitedHealthcare • Universal Forest Products • USAA Charitable Trust Foundation • Village of Sun River Terrace • W.C. Bradley Co. • Wachovia Corporation • Walgreens • Warner Music Group • Washington Capitols and So Kids Can • Washington Mutual • Washington Redskins • Wasserman Foundation • William Blair & Company • Winston & Strawn, LLP • Wisk/Unilever, Inc. • Yahoo! Employees Foundation • Youth Service California • ZS Associates

END NOTES

Chapter 9

Angier, Natalie. 'The Purpose of Playful Frolics.' *New York Times*, Oct. 20, 1992.

Barros, Romina, et al. 'School Recess and Group Classroom Behavior,' *Pediatrics* 123 (2009): 431–436.

Begley, Sharon. 'Your Child's Brain.' *Newsweek*, February 19, 1996.

Brown, Stuart. *Play: How It Shapes the Brain, Opens the Imagination, and Invigorates the Soul.* New York: Penguin, 2009.

Burghardt, Gordon. *The Genesis of Animal Play.* Cambridge, MA: MIT Press, 2005.

Eisen, George. *Children at Play in the Holocaust: Games Among the Shadows.* Amherst, MA: University of Massachusetts Press, 1990.

Elkind, David. 'The Power of Play.' New York: Da Capo Press, 2007.

Marantz Henig, Robin. 'Taking Play Seriously.' *New York Times Magazine*, February 17, 2008.

Miller, Edward and Almon, Joan. *Crisis in the Kindergarten: Why Children Need to Play in School.* College Park, MD: Alliance for Childhood, 2009.

Orenstein, Peggy. 'Kindergarten Cram,' *The New York Times Magazine*, May 3, 2009.

Pelligrini, Anthony D. et al. 'Play in Evolution and Development.' *Developmental Review* 27 (2007): 261–276.

Stanford Prevention Research Center. *Building 'Generation Play': Address the Crisis of Inactivity Among America's Children.* Stanford: Stanford University School of Medicine, 2007.

Tsao, Ling-Ling. 'How Much Do We Know about the Purpose of Play in Childhood Development?' *Childhood Education*, 78 (2002).

Wenner, Melinda. 'The Serious Need for Play.' *Scientific American*, February/March 2009.

Chapter 16

Alvarez, Lizette. 'Educators Flocking to Finland, Land of Literate Children.' *New York Times*, April 9, 2004.

American Association for the Child's Right to Play, 2004.

Curtis, Henry Stoddard. *The Play Movement and Its Significance.* Washington, D.C.: McGrath Publishing Company and the National Recreation Association.

Howard, Philip K. "Life Without Lawyers: Liberating Americans from Too Much Law," Norton, 2009.

Miller, Edward and Almon, Joan. *Crisis in the Kindergarten: Why Children Need to Play in School.* College Park, MD: Alliance for Childhood, 2009.

Skenazy, Lenore. 'Free-Range Kids.' Jossey/Bass, 2009.

Stanford Prevention Research Center. *Building 'Generation Play': Address the Crisis of Inactivity Among America's Children.* Stanford: Stanford University School of Medicine, 2007.

Thomson, Michael. 'The Impact of the Loss of Free, Undirected Play in Childhood (And What Camps Can Do About It.' *Camping Magazine*, May/June 2009.

INDEX

An asterisk (★) indicates that photos are shown in the insert pages.